1948 and 1968 – Dramatic Milestones in Czech and Slovak History

This volume has been published to coincide with the anniversaries of two significant milestones in Czech and Slovak history – the establishment of communist rule in 1948 and the Prague Spring of 1968 – and in anticipation of the 20th anniversary of the 1989 'Velvet Revolution'. Given the ultimate failure of the communist system, these events and their legacy for Czech and Slovak society and politics merit continued study, particularly given the wealth of new data made available when state and Party archives were finally opened in the 1990s.

The essays in this volume, by witnesses, historians and social scientists working in the Czech Republic and Slovakia, the USA, Australia and Europe offer a reappraisal of those turbulent events. They present new and original research, based on information from archives which were not opened until after 1990 and which is not yet available to audiences who do not speak Czech or Slovak. This volume will, therefore, be of interest to both specialists and general readers who are curious to learn more about these events.

This book was published as a special issue of *Europe-Asia Studies*.

Laura Cashman is a Lecturer in Politics and International Relations at Canterbury Christ Church University, UK.

Routledge Europe-Asia Studies Series

A series edited by Terry Cox
University of Glasgow

The **Routledge Europe-Asia Studies Series** focuses on the history and current political, social and economic affairs of the countries of the former 'communist bloc' of the Soviet Union, Eastern Europe and Asia. As well as providing contemporary analyses it explores the economic, political and social transformation of these countries and the changing character of their relationships with the rest of Europe and Asia.

Challenging Communism in Eastern Europe
1956 and its Legacy
Edited by Terry Cox

Globalisation, Freedom and the Media after Communism
The Past as Future
Edited by Birgit Beumers, Stephen Hutchings and Natalia Rulyova

Power and Policy in Putin's Russia
Edited by Richard Sakwa

1948 and 1968 – Dramatic Milestones in Czech and Slovak History
Edited by Laura Cashman

1948 and 1968 – Dramatic Milestones in Czech and Slovak History

Edited by Laura Cashman

Routledge
Taylor & Francis Group
LONDON AND NEW YORK

University of Glasgow

First published 2010 by Routledge
2 Park Square, Milton Park, Abingdon, Oxon, OX14 4RN
52 Vanderbilt Avenue, New York, NY 10017

Routledge is an imprint of the Taylor & Francis Group, an informa business

First issued in paperback 2013

Typeset in Times by Value Chain, India

British Library Cataloguing in Publication Data
A catalogue record for this book is available from the British Library

ISBN13: 978-0-415-49990-3 (hbk)
ISBN13: 978-0-415-84571-7 (pbk)

Contents

List of Contributors

STEFAN AUER is a Senior Lecturer in History and Politics at La Trobe University in Melbourne and Deputy Director of the Innovative Universities European Union Centre. His book, *Liberal Nationalism in Central Europe* (Routledge, 2004) won the prize for Best Book in European Studies (2005) with the University Association for Contemporary European Studies (UACES). He has published articles in *Critical Horizons, East European Politics and Societies, Nationalism and Ethnic Politics, Osteuropa* and elsewhere.

MAUD BRACKE is a Lecturer in Modern European History at the University of Glasgow. Her most recent book *Which Socialism, Whose Détente? West European Communism and the Czechoslovak Crisis of 1968* (CEU Press) was published in 2007. She has published articles in *European Contemporary History, Journal of European Integration History* and *Soundings* and she has contributed chapters to a number of edited volumes.

SCOTT BROWN is a PhD candidate in the Department of History at the University of Washington. His dissertation, 'Socialism with a Slovak Face: The Slovak Question in the 1960s', funded by a Fulbright–Hays Doctoral Dissertation Research Abroad Fellowship, examines the re-emergence of the Slovak question as a political issue and the role of a reactivated Slovak nationalism in the 1960s and upheaval of 1968. He has published an article in *East European Politics and Societies* and presented his research at academic conferences and forums in Urbana-Champaign, Illinois, Bratislava, Pittsburgh, Glasgow and Philadelphia.

LAURA CASHMAN is a Lecturer in Politics and International Relations at Canterbury Christ Church University, UK. She obtained her doctorate from the University of Glasgow in 2007. Her doctoral thesis focused on Romani integration policies in the Czech Republic and her subsequent research continues to examine Czech politics and society and the integration of Romani communities in the EU. She has published articles in the *Journal of Contemporary European Research* and *Studies in Ethnicity and Nationalism* and a chapter in the edited volume, *Trans-National Issues, Local Concerns: Insights from Russia, Central and Eastern Europe and the UK* (University Press of America, 2008).

MARY HEIMANN is a Senior Lecturer in the Department of History at the University of Strathclyde, who has published widely in the field of English Catholic history and the history of modern Christian thought. Her next book, a revisionist history of the Czechoslovak state, is to be published by Yale University Press.

JURAJ MARUŠIAK is a Senior Research Fellow at the Institute of Political Science, Slovak Academy of Sciences. His book *Slovenská literatúra a moc v druhej polovici 50.rokov* (*Slovak Literature and Political Power in the 1950s*), was published by Prius in 2001. He has contributed many chapters to edited volumes and between 1999 and 2004 he edited *Global Report Slovakia*, published by the Institute of the Public Affairs, Bratislava.

MARTIN MYANT is a Professor at the University of the West of Scotland Business School, Paisley, UK. His has researched and published for many years on economic and political developments in East-Central Europe, concentrating on the Czech Republic, Slovakia and Poland. Recent publications include: *The Rise and Fall of Czech Capitalism: Economic Development in the Czech Republic since 1989* (Edward Elgar, 2003), *Varieties of Capitalism in Post-Communist Countries* (Palgrave, 2007) edited jointly with David Lane, and *Reinventing Poland: Economic and Political Transformation and Evolving National Identity* (Routledge, 2008) jointly edited with Terry Cox.

RIIKKA NISONEN-TRNKA is a Doctoral Researcher in the Department of History and Philosophy at the University of Tampere in Finland. Her thesis 'Scientific Relations between Czechoslovakia and the West in the Cold War Context' examines cooperation of natural scientists in the Cold War period. She is currently working in the Aleksanteri Institute at the University of Helsinki on the project 'Knowledge Through the Iron Curtain' financed by the Finnish Academy.

LIBORA OATES-INDRUCHOVÁ is an Assistant Professor in the Department of Sociology at Masaryk University, Brno and Marie Curie Fellow at the Collegium Budapest/Institute for Advanced Study. Her research has focused on the theory of discourse and its application to Czech culture by means of gender analysis. Her next book will focus on Czech social sciences and humanities during the Normalisation period (1968–1989). She recently edited *Ženská literární tradice a hledání identit: antologie angloamerické feministické literární teorie* (*Women's Literary Tradition and the Search for Identities: An Anthology of Anglo–American Feminist Literary Theory*) which was published by Slon in 2007.

VILÉM PREČAN is a Czech historian and the co-editor of *Seven Prague Days* (*The Czech Black Book*) the famous eyewitness account of the 1968 invasion. He was the first director of the Institute of Contemporary History of the Academy of Sciences of the Czech Republic, which he established in 1990. Since 1999 he has been the Chairman of the Board of the Czechoslovak Documentation Centre, a non-governmental institution for research into the history of the anti-totalitarian resistance in Czechoslovakia and abroad during the communist era. He has published many books and compiled anthologies of documents from the communist period including *Prague–Washington–Prague. Reports from the United States Embassy in Czechoslovakia, November–December 1989* (Václav Havel Library, 2004) and *Charta 77: dokumenty 1977–1989* with Blanka Císařovská (USD AV, 2007).

CHARLES SABATOS is an Assistant Professor in the English Language and Literature department at Yeditepe University, Istanbul, Turkey. He received his PhD in Comparative Literature from the University of Michigan. His main fields of research are Central European and

American literature, especially modern and contemporary fiction. He has published articles in such journals as *Comparative Literature Studies* and *Slovo*, as well as literary translations from Slovak and Czech.

Remembering 1948 and 1968: Reflections on Two Pivotal Years in Czech and Slovak History

LAURA CASHMAN

IN THE HISTORY OF ANY COUNTRY PARTICULAR YEARS tend to stand out as major turning points or critical junctures. The chain of events that took place in a particular year is seen as having profound consequences for subsequent trends in the state's economic, social, political and cultural development. In the case of the former Czechoslovakia, 1948 and 1968 were two such years. Indeed, until the spell was broken by the momentous events of 1989, it seemed that, as Stefan Auer suggests in his contribution to this collection, there was something magical about the number 'eight' in the key dates of Czechoslovak history. As the following list of dates suggests, the number eight has featured in many milestone years of Czechoslovak, and particularly Czech, cultural and political history: 1348, Foundation of Charles University, Prague; 1618, Second Defenestration of Prague and the beginning of the Thirty Years War; 1848, Year of European Revolutions; 1918, Foundation of the independent state of Czechoslovakia; 1938, Munich Agreement cedes Sudeten territories to Nazi Germany and paves the way for German occupation of the state; 1948, communists gain full political control of Czechoslovakia; 1968, Prague Spring and Warsaw Pact invasion.

It is apparent from the many anniversary conferences and events that were held during 2008 that the events of two particular years, 1948 and 1968, still have strong resonance in the politics, the popular imagination and the academic history of the Czech Republic and Slovakia, as well as in East Central Europe more widely. These were two of the most significant dates in Czech and Slovak history: 1948, the year Stalinist communists took power in Czechoslovakia, and 1968 the year of the doomed attempt of Slovaks and Czechs to develop their own 'Socialism with a Human Face'.

1948 and 1968 in the context of Czechoslovak history

The twentieth-century history of the state of Czechoslovakia had its origins in the aftermath of World War I. Czechoslovakia was a multinational state with Czechs as the largest national group but not large enough to form an overall majority. Slovaks and Germans constituted the other main national groups (there were more Germans than Slovaks in the state), and there were also smaller Hungarian, Ruthenian (or

Ukrainian), Polish, Jewish and Romani minorities. The state was made up of fragments of the Austro–Hungarian Empire and as a result there were significant regional differences between the highly industrialised Bohemian, Moravian and Silesian regions and the rural, less developed Slovak and Ruthenian regions. However, these challenges were not insurmountable and in the 1920s the Czechoslovak economy recovered to become as strong as that of many Western states.

The 1920s are often regarded as the golden era of Czechoslovak history. Tomáš G. Masaryk, the country's first president and 'father of the nation', was widely respected internationally and when compared with its neighbours Czechoslovakia was also regarded as a very successful liberal democracy. However, it might be fairer to refer to it as a golden era for Czechs, as other national minorities became increasingly dissatisfied with how they were being governed. The state was ruled by coalitions of democratically elected parties and unlike in many other countries in the region, the Communist Party of Czechoslovakia (*Komunistická strana Československa*, KSČ) was allowed to function as a normal political party. It had a core base of support among the working classes in the Czech industrial cities.

The first shock to the political system was the Great Depression of the 1930s; unemployment rose dramatically and the industrial bases were weakened. The German minority in the Sudetenland was most severely affected given the high levels of industrialisation in those areas. The rise of Nazi power in Germany also affected Czechoslovak politics. The antipathy ethnic Germans had felt for the Czechoslovak state since its foundation was intensified by the economic crisis and many voters moved away from the ethnic German political parties who cooperated with the Czechoslovak state to the more chauvinist nationalist Sudeten German Party. This was the backdrop to perhaps the greatest trauma of twentieth century Czechoslovak history—the Munich betrayal of 1938. With increasingly vociferous demands from the Sudeten German Party for national autonomy and threats from Hitler that any infringement of the rights of Sudeten Germans would have drastic consequences, the Czechoslovak state looked to the West for support. However, Czechoslovakia fell victim to the now infamous policy of appeasement. The Munich Agreement signed on 30 September 1938 by Germany, France, Italy and Great Britain, gave Germany permission to annex the Sudetenland. Czechoslovak representatives were not invited to the conference. We now know that the 'peace for our time' which Chamberlain had hoped this agreement would guarantee was not to be. The consequences of this agreement in 1938 were to have far reaching repercussions for Czechoslovak politics and society.

Following the war six political parties [four Czech parties—the Communists, the National Socialists (*Československá strana národně socialistická*), the People's Party (*Československá strana lidová*) and the Social Democrats (*Československá sociálni demokracie*)—and two Slovak parties—the Democratic Party (*Demokratická strana*) and the Communists (*Komunistická strana Slovenska*, KSS)] formed the 'National Front' (*Národní fronta*) to rule Czechoslovakia. Their policy programme was based on three shared principles: close alliance with the Soviet Union, nationalisation of industry and the expulsion of as much of the ethnic German minority as possible. In the 1946 national elections, the KSČ emerged as the largest party of the National Front and its leader, Klement Gottwald, was appointed prime minister under the presidency of Edvard Beneš. As president, Beneš had to be independent of party politics but he had been a member of the National Socialist Party and this was where his sympathies remained. The KSČ enjoyed a number of advantages which explained its popularity among voters. While the Party had always enjoyed some support among core working-class voters, it benefited from the positive feelings towards the Soviet Union at the end of the war. Although the Western allies could have liberated Czechoslovakia a few days earlier, it was the Red Army which arrived as liberators at the end of World War II. This, combined with the perceived failures of capitalism during the Depression and the bitter feelings towards the West following the perceived abandonment of Czechoslovakia in 1938, only served to strengthen popular support for the Party. Thus, it is often argued that the events of 1938 paved the way for the imposition of communism in Czechoslovakia.

At the beginning of the year 1948 the democratically elected KSČ still shared power with other democratically elected parties in the National Front coalition. However, tensions within the coalition, which had been building since 1947, came to a head on 20 February 1948 when ministers from three coalition parties—the National Socialist Party, the People's Party and the Slovak Democratic Party—submitted their resignations to President Beneš. Following a tense few days culminating in general strikes and mass protests in support of the Communist Party, Beneš accepted the ministers' resignations and approved the new cabinet proposed by Prime Minister Klement Gottwald on 25 February. The new National Front coalition was made up of members of the KSČ, KSČ sympathisers from the other National Front parties and one independent, Jan Masaryk, Minister for Foreign Affairs and son of Tomáš G. Masaryk. The 'Victorious February' celebrated while the KSČ was in power has since become known as the 'February Coup'. However, recent historiography would also challenge that label, given the mass appeal of the KSČ and the fact that the KSČ leadership appeared to take tactical advantage of events rather than instigate them. As demonstrated in the essay by Martin Myant in this collection, there are still many open questions surrounding the events of 1948 which deserve scholarly attention.

Following the events of February, the KSČ rapidly consolidated its position and used all the state powers at its disposal to implement Soviet-style (Stalinist) socialism. The nationalisation of industry, already underway, was accelerated and agriculture was rapidly collectivised. Five-year plans were introduced to manage economic activity and all spheres of social and cultural life came under the control of the Party apparatus. The secret police (*Státní bezpečnost*, StB) watched and recorded everything. Initially the Party and the reforms enjoyed public support. Students, in particular, were enthusiastic about modernising the state and following the successful model of the Soviet Union. However, it did not take long for the dark side of Stalinism to appear. Political opponents and potential opponents were arrested and then, in the early 1950s, purges within the Party claimed even high ranking Party officials including Rudolf Slanský, the General Secretary of the Party and Vladimír Clementis, Minister for Foreign Affairs. The trials also had a significant anti-Semitic element: of the 14 people on trial with Slanský, 12 (including Slanský) were Jewish (Skilling 1976, p. 26).

Following Stalin's death in 1953, and Khrushchev's subsequent rise to power in the Soviet Union, other states in the region began to address the worst excesses of

Stalinism. However, while Khrushchev's 'secret speech' at the Twentieth Congress of the Communist Party of the Soviet Union (CPSU) on 24 February 1956 led to public protests in Poland and revolution in Hungary, the Czechoslovak regime kept tight control and did not introduce any reforms. Gottwald died in 1953, but the man who replaced him as leader, Antonín Novotný, was also implicated in the show trials and purges and so denouncing Stalinism would have meant denouncing his own actions. There was also less public pressure for reform than in Hungary and Poland in the 1950s, as the economy was still performing relatively well.

Only in the early 1960s did problems with the centrally planned economic system become fully apparent in Czechoslovakia. This coincided with Khrushchev's second attack on Stalinism at the Twenty-Second Congress of the CPSU in October 1961. As Heimann discusses in her essay, it was under increasing pressure from both Moscow and from Party members at home that Novotný reluctantly allowed the reform process to begin. While it was apparent that economic reforms were urgently required—Czech export sales were falling as a direct result of their poor quality and at home there were shortages of consumer goods—it was less clear whether this would require political reform too. Ota Šik, the leader of the economic reform process, insisted that the economy could not function in an authoritarian system. As these debates continued within the Party, restrictions on social and cultural life were gradually eased. More citizens had opportunities to travel and study abroad and film-makers and writers enjoyed much more freedom: Miloš Forman could direct *The Fireman's Ball* and Milan Kundera could publish *The Joke*, mocking the Party and criticising Stalinism.

The Prague Spring is usually dated from January 1968, when Antonín Novotný was replaced by Alexander Dubček as First Secretary of the KSČ. This is generally presented as a triumph for the reformist wing of the Party. Dubček acknowledged the need to speed up the de-Stalinisation process begun under Novotný's leadership. The Party's *Action Programme*, which was launched in April, increased freedoms of speech and of the press and introduced economic reforms to improve the quality and availability of consumer goods. The programme was still based on the principles of socialism, with emphasis on the leading role of the KSČ, but the combination of economic and political reforms was supposed to lead to a new, more democratic kind of socialism—'Socialism with a Human Face'. The abolition of censorship allowed opposition voices to be heard and alternative political clubs to be formed, but their demands quickly became more radical, culminating in the 'Two Thousand Words' Manifesto published by Ludvík Vaculík on 27 June, which criticised the reluctance of conservative elements in the KSČ to support reform and speculated about the danger of a Soviet invasion.

Although the appearance of this manifesto could have been interpreted as a sign that the reforms were spinning out of control, something the leaders of other states in the Warsaw Pact greatly feared, Dubček was confident that the majority of society supported the Party and its leading role in the reform process. During bilateral talks between the Soviet Union and Czechoslovakia in July at Čierna nad Tisou, near the Slovak–USSR border, Dubček defended the reforms while pledging continued commitment to both the Warsaw Pact and Comecon. However, these assurances were not enough for the other members of the Warsaw Pact. Just before midnight on 20 August 1968, on the grounds that they were defending a fraternal socialist state from the threat of internal counter-revolution, the armies of five Warsaw Pact states—Bulgaria, East Germany, Hungary, Poland and the Soviet Union—invaded Czechoslovakia (Figures 1–3). As the rest of the world watched, Dubček called on the Czechoslovak population not to resist the soldiers. Although there was no armed resistance to the arrival of tanks and ground troops, Czechs and Slovaks challenged the occupying forces in other ways. Strikes were called, petitions were signed, posters and graffiti begged the occupiers to return home and mass protests on the streets obstructed the paths of tanks. Images from the time show how the invading soldiers looked even more confused about what was happening than the people of Czechoslovakia (Figures 4–6). Despite the lack of armed resistance, in the first week of the invasion more than 70 people were killed and hundreds more were injured.

On the morning of 21 August, Dubček and other members of the leadership were taken to Moscow for negotiations. By then it was clear that, given the levels of public support they enjoyed, the leadership could not simply be removed. Instead, the reformers were put under pressure to sign the Moscow Protocol, which they did on 26 August. The protocol effectively rolled back the freedoms introduced in the spring: alternative political groups were banned, censorship was reimposed and central economic planning was given priority once again. Some of the reformers, including Ota Šik and Jiří Hájek, lost their positions, but Dubček remained as General Secretary of the KSČ and Ludvík Svoboda remained president, at least for the time being. The

FIGURE 1. Wenceslas Square, Prague. Photograph Courtesy of the Institute of Contemporary History, Academy of Sciences, Czech Republic

FIGURE 2. SOLDIERS AT THE ASTRONOMICAL CLOCK IN PRAGUE. PHOTOGRAPH COURTESY OF VILÉM PREČAN

Moscow Protocol marked the beginning of the end of the Prague Spring. What followed was the gradual erosion of freedoms so that by the following August 1969, Czechoslovak society was well on its way to being 'Normalised', or put another way, to being turned back into what the Soviet leadership regarded as a 'normal' socialist society. Dubček was replaced as First Secretary of the Party by Gustáv Husák, another Slovak, in 1969. Although Husák was part of the reform wing of the Party in the 1960s, and a close ally of Dubček, his name will forever be associated with the harsh Normalisation regime of the 1970s and 1980s.

The events of 1968 marked both the highs and lows of the Czechoslovak de-Stalinisation process but everything of importance did not happen in that fateful year.

FIGURE 3. SOLDIER AIMING AT CROWDS IN BRATISLAVA. PHOTOGRAPH BY LADISLAV BIELIK, COPYRIGHT PERMISSION PETER BIELIK

Mary Heimann shows in this collection how the de-Stalinisation process began, albeit slowly, under Novotný, and Vilém Prečan argues in his contribution that it was only finally crushed in August 1969. From the early 1960s, film makers and writers made the most of the easing of Party control over their work and Riikka Nisonen-Trnka's contribution demonstrates how scientists had begun to take advantage of better relations with the West long before the spring of 1968. Nonetheless, it was the complete abolition of censorship in April 1968 and Dubček's promise to introduce 'Socialism with a Human Face' that captured the world's attention. The brutal manner in which this 'Spring' was cut short, by the invasion of Warsaw Pact troops in August 1968 and the subsequent suppression of all political dissent in the Normalisation period, only added to the status of the Spring. However, as some of the contributors to this collection show, legends which have grown up around the events are mostly mythical. Mary Heimann challenges the iconic status of Alexander Dubček as a self-sacrificing champion of democracy, showing how his actions may have been motivated by a personal desire for power rather than anything more heroic. Equally, Maud Bracke highlights the discrepancies between how the French Left viewed events in Czechoslovakia during the reform process and after the August invasion. A process that had been dismissed as embarrassing or insignificant was subsequently appropriated as a model of democratic socialism for the Eurocommunist movement in the 1970s.

Perhaps the most significant consequence of the Prague Spring for Czechoslovak history was not the brief taste of freedom enjoyed by citizens but rather the federalisation of the state and the limited devolution of power to Slovakia. As argued by Scott Brown, the cracks in the foundations of this multinational state, which were partially papered over in 1968, foreshadowed the final separation of the state 25 years later. Ever since the foundation of the state of Czechoslovakia in 1918, Slovaks had

FIGURE 4. Signposts Blacked Out in Brno. Photograph Courtesy of the Moravian Museum

complained that they were treated at best as junior partners and at worst, that they were 'ruled' by the Czechs. In the communist period the clearest examples of the imbalance or asymmetry between the Czech- and Slovak-speaking parts of the country were the key institutions of power. Whereas Slovaks had their own institutions of self-rule and their own Communist Party, the *Komunistická strana Slovenska* (KSS), for Czechs the nationwide institutions of the Czechoslovak National Assembly and the Czechoslovak Communist Party doubled up as Czech institutions. As Brown demonstrates in his essay, Slovaks disliked this arrangement because it meant that Czech national organs were in fact legally superior to their Slovak counterparts. Slovak grievances were increased with the introduction of the 1960 Constitution, which revoked some of the powers previously enjoyed by Slovak national institutions but the simmering discontent could not be publicly voiced until the political climate relaxed in the late 1960s. The Slovak proposal to create Czech and Slovak national institutions which would be subordinate to Czechoslovak bodies was discussed but, perhaps logically, Czechs were less interested in the idea than Slovaks. While the proposals were debated over the summer of 1968, the Warsaw Pact invasion and subsequent clamp down on political freedoms did not end the federalisation process. The Constitutional Law of Federation was passed on 28 October 1968 and led to the

FIGURE 5. LIBEREC. PHOTOGRAPH COURTESY OF THE INSTITUTE OF CONTEMPORARY HISTORY, ACADEMY OF SCIENCES, CZECH REPUBLIC

FIGURE 6. CRITICISM OF OCCUPATION IN THREE LANGUAGES. PHOTOGRAPH COURTESY OF THE INSTITUTE OF CONTEMPORARY HISTORY, ACADEMY OF SCIENCES, CZECH REPUBLIC

federalisation of Czechoslovakia. From 1 January 1969 the state was sub-divided into the Czech Socialist Republic and the Slovak Socialist Republic. The previous Czechoslovak parliament was renamed the Federal Assembly and new national parliaments were created (the Czech and Slovak National Councils). However, these changes were mostly cosmetic given the strong centralising tendencies of the KSČ.

The Warsaw Pact invasion led to a crisis in Czechoslovakia in many respects. Not only did it cause a domestic and international political crisis, but it also prompted much soul-searching among Czech writers and philosophers about whether the national reaction to events was that of pragmatic heroes or spineless cowards and whether given the small size of the state, the people of Czechoslovakia could ever determine their own destiny. These debates are discussed by Stefan Auer and Charles Sabatos in their contributions to this collection. Cowards or heroes they may have been; but, as discussed in the contributions of Libora Oates-Indruchová and Juraj Marušiak, for the Czechs and Slovaks who did not leave the country, the repressive Normalisation period following the Prague Spring posed its own challenges. In the context of Czechoslovakia, Normalisation has come to be understood as the process through which the KSČ came to reassert full control over society. In an essay written in 1979 Šimečka (1990) called it 'the restoration of order' (*obnovenie poriadku*); later, Williams (1997, p. 41) described it as the 'restoration of extreme predictability'.

Accounts in this collection assert that the secret to the success of Normalisation was that it was implemented by the very people who, only months previously, had been the champions of liberalisation. The enthusiasm displayed in the first week following the occupation clearly signals that the general population wished for more democratic freedoms and yet they accepted the return to the status quo with little protest. The main exceptions to this were the student protests of November 1968 and the threats of miners to go on strike in January 1969. The self-immolation of 21 year-old student Jan Palach on 19 January 1969 was a desperate plea for people not to resign themselves to the repression. However, according to Prečan in this collection, the citizens were so disappointed with the failure of leaders to resist the pressures coming from the Warsaw Pact members and especially from Moscow that they could see no point in fighting any longer. Oates-Indruchová and Marušiak detail how the Party authorities applied a range of measures from coercion to bribery to subdue the population. Marušiak's research also highlights how the implementation of Normalisation differed in Slovakia. Party members were all required to attend interviews to renew their membership. The outcome of this process had enormous consequences because of how membership was linked to career opportunities for both members and their children. However, in Slovakia, there were also rewards in terms of career advancement and general improvements in the standards of living which tempted many Slovaks to conform.

Many Czechs and Slovaks felt compelled to leave the country in the 1970s and they supported the dissidents who remained from abroad. The dissident movement in Czechoslovakia cannot be compared with that of Poland or even Hungary in terms of size. The most important opposition initiative was Charter 77 (*Charta 77*). This was originally a petition circulated in 1977 in response to the arrest of members of the psychedelic band Plastic People of the Universe, which challenged the authorities to respect human rights as guaranteed by the state constitution and the Helsinki Accords. Those who signed the petition were punished by the regime in various ways. Some lost their jobs or saw their children refused entry to higher education; others were imprisoned or forced into exile. The tough response to any opposition activity is one reason why the protest movements remained so small; another is the oft-cited pragmatism or cowardice of Czechs, discussed by Stefan Auer in his contribution to this collection. As a consequence, the final collapse of the regime in 1989 was probably influenced more by external events—the domino effect of communist regimes collapsing all around them and Gorbachev's refusal to do anything meaningful to ensure the security of the KSČ—than by domestic pressure for reform, but nevertheless, the mass protests in the streets in November 1989 echoed the demonstrations 21 years previously. This time, however, reform of the system would not suffice; socialism with or without a human face was unanimously rejected in favour of Western style, liberal democracy.

The extent to which the events of 1948 and 1968 influenced Czechoslovak society in 1989 and their relevance today can be debated. After the war Czechs and Slovaks showed clear admiration for the Soviet Union and the communist political system and it is more difficult to argue that communism was imposed on the state than in the case of most neighbouring countries. However, the harsh Stalinism of the 1950s was not what had been anticipated and the reforms in the 1960s, which culminated in the Prague Spring, were an attempt to rectify that. Today anti-communists in the Czech Republic and Slovakia view the events of 1968 as irrelevant, simply tinkering with a system that could never have worked. This was already clear in 1989, when as Prečan argues, it was Havel the dissident that the crowds wanted to see, much more than Dubček the reformer. Nonetheless, the events of 1968, similar to the events of 1938, mark a watershed moment in Czech and Slovak history. The small Czech and Slovak nations were shown that their destiny was not entirely in their own hands and that a hard lesson has not been forgotten. In 1948 and 1968 Czech and Slovak citizens showed their willingness to take to the streets and support political causes they believed in. They may not have stormed any barricades, but their actions were hardly those of an apathetic citizenry. 'Remembering' 1948 and 1968 is not the same as celebrating the events. Rather it is an opportunity to reflect on what happened and why, what mistakes were made and what their consequences were. The contributions to this collection address some of these questions, and based partly on archives that are now open to researchers, they clarify what happened and why. However, it may be that we have to wait another 50 years or more and gain more distance from the communist period before we understand what the legacy of these events truly is.

Overview of the contributions to this collection

This edition opens with an essay which reflects on various aspects of the Prague Spring by Vilém Prečan, co-editor of *Seven Prague Days*, also known as the *Czech Black Book*, the famous eyewitness account of the 1968 invasion. Prečan situates the events of 1968 within the context of the communist period of Czechoslovak history, beginning in 1948 and ending in 1989, and shows how earlier events influenced those which came later. The second contribution, by Stefan Auer, takes an even longer view, detailing how Czech intellectuals have interpreted the non-violent resistance offered by Czechs, both to the Nazi invasion of their country and the Warsaw Pact occupation, and showing how the conventional image of the nation of velvet is open to challenge. Martin Myant's contribution, the only one to directly address the events of 1948, offers a critique of recent historiography of the events of 1948 and proposes a variety of new avenues for further research. These relate not only to the political manoeuvrings of the main protagonists in the February 'Coup' but also to the treatment of ethnic Germans following World War II and the general appetite for socialism in Czechoslovakia after the war.

The next two essays deal with myths which have grown up around the events of 1968. Mary Heimann's research reveals a darker side to Dubček's motives than is generally presented. By piecing together the events which led to Novotný's downfall in January 1968, she shows that Dubček may not have had as strong a commitment to the reform process as he claimed. Similarly, Maud Bracke argues that the way the European Left now remembers the Prague Spring differs quite markedly from how communists in France, for example, perceived events as they were unfolding. She argues that in certain key respects the French left misunderstood the aims of the Prague Spring and it was only in the mid-1970s that the reform project was 'rediscovered' and invested with new symbolic meaning. This could of course be described as cynical, but it also hints at the problem of how events can become larger than the sum of their parts; 1968 certainly falls into that category.

Two essays in this collection are concerned with the academic establishment before and after the events of 1968. Riikka Nisonen-Trnka provides a detailed account of how, even before 1968, members of the Academy of Sciences enjoyed and exploited the academic freedoms they had won thanks to the commercial value of their research to the state. Despite the Cold War rhetoric of the time, collaboration on research projects between scientists in the East and West allowed important breakthroughs to be made. The case of Otto Wichterle's invention of the contact lens is a good example of this. The second essay dealing with academic freedoms, by Libora Oates-Indruchová, focuses on the more difficult times of the Normalisation era. Based on a detailed documentary analysis, she shows exactly how the Party reasserted its authority over academics who had grown used to some freedom. In particular, she focuses on the treatment of scholars in the humanities and social sciences, identified by Party officials as a particularly dangerous breed of academics.

That the events of 1968 have come to be known as the Prague Spring is in itself interesting. Why not the Bratislava Spring or the Czechoslovak Spring? After all, some of the key protagonists, including Dubček and his eventual replacement Husák, were Slovaks and as the pictures included in the collection show, people were mobilised all over the country and not only in the capital city. This collection includes two essays which focus specifically on Slovakia during and after the Prague Spring. Scott Brown discusses the roots of the Velvet Divorce and argues that federalisation, as proposed in 1968, did not sufficiently appease Slovak nationalists who wished for the unbalanced treatment of Czechs and Slovaks within the multinational state to be redressed. While Brown points to similarities in the debates of 1968 and the early 1990s regarding Slovak nationalism and the federalisation of the state, Juraj Marušiak identifies similar continuities between the Normalisation period in Slovakia and Slovak politics in the 1990s. Just as importantly, he also brings out the differences in the implementation of Normalisation between the Slovak-speaking and Czech-speaking halves of the nominally federalised state after 1968.

The collection concludes with an essay by Charles Sabatos which carefully details how Milan Kundera and Václav Havel, two of the best known Czech writers in the West, have interpreted the Prague Spring in their essays and literary works. Given their stature, both in the Czech Republic and abroad, the views of Kundera and Havel inevitably colour how we all interpret recent Czechoslovak history. This discussion of their perspectives of Czechoslovak history is an apt way to close this collection, allowing the reader to come to their own conclusions about how best to remember the events of 1968.

Where possible the essays dealing with 1968 and its dramatic events have been supplemented by photographs.[1] It is said that every photograph tells a story, but the story of how it was taken and how it came to be published can be as interesting as that of the image it captures. Some of these photographs have become iconic images of the twentieth century. An excellent example is the image of *The Bare-chested Man in Front of the Occupier's Tank* (Figure 7). The photograph of Emil Gallo, a Slovak man defiantly facing down a tank, was taken by Ladislav Bielik on 21 August 1968, at the Šafárik Square in Bratislava. This photograph, which was included in the 1968 World Press Photo exhibition collection, was reproduced in newspapers, magazines and textbooks all over the world and is often cited as one of the 100 defining images of the twentieth century. However, the location of the photograph is often mistaken for Prague and in their lifetimes Bielik and Gallo received no credit for the picture. Gallo, who died in 1971, never told anyone what he had done and Bielik, a photographer for the daily *Smena,* lost his job once the Normalisation regime was established and could

FIGURE 7. THE BARE-CHESTED MAN IN FRONT OF THE OCCUPIER'S TANK, BRATISLAVA. PHOTOGRAPHED BY LADISLAV BIELIK, COPYRIGHT PERMISSION PETER BIELIK

[1]Every effort has been made to trace copyright holders and to obtain their permission for the use of copyright. The editor gratefully acknowledges those who granted us permission to reproduce images which capture the events of 1968 and apologises for any errors or omissions. She would be grateful for notification of any corrections.

never claim credit for the images. In the West the picture was widely circulated and accredited to *Deutsche Press-Agentur* or *United Press International*. It is only now thanks to the efforts of Bielik's son, Peter, that this evocative image, together with many other photographs taken by his father, are at last receiving due credit (Bielik 2008).

All but one of the essays in this collection (that of Riikka Nisonen-Trnka) are based on papers presented at a conference held at the University of Glasgow on 3–4 April 2008 to commemorate the sixtieth and fortieth anniversaries, respectively, of the events of 1948 and 1968. The conference was sponsored by the British Association for Slavonic and East European Studies (BASEES), the British Academy, the Centre for Russian, Central and East European Studies (CRCEES), the Czech Centre and the Embassy of the Slovak Republic and allowed academics at an early stage of their careers to present their work alongside some of the most distinguished scholars in the field. While not all contributions to the conference could be included in this collection, the authors are indebted to all those who participated for their comments and criticisms which helped to shape the present contributions.

The conference papers covered a broad range of themes ranging from high political intrigue to social history, and from film and literature to philosophy. Much discussion was devoted to challenging the myths that have grown up around those turbulent times. It was also clear that the conference, and indeed this collection, could have had a far wider remit given that 2008 is the anniversary of many more landmark events in Czech and Slovak history. However, for practical reasons, both the conference and this collection of essays focus on the 'eights' which marked the two key stages in the history of communism in Czechoslovakia. As the events under discussion were within living memory for many delegates, presentations based on archival research which brought new perspectives to historical events could be challenged by those who were 'there' and personally knew some of the key protagonists. This led to fascinating debates about how events are remembered and commemorated and how archives can reveal more than was known at the time. Not only are some archives more accessible than others, there is still a great deal of information which is not yet available to audiences who do not speak Czech or Slovak. The contributions in this collection will, therefore, be of interest to both specialists in the field and readers who are curious to learn more about these events.

University of Glasgow

References

Bielik, L. (2008) *August 1968* (Bratislava, Vydavatel'stvo O.K.O.).
Šimečka, M. (1990) *Obnovenie poriadku* (Bratislava, Archa).
Skilling, H. G. (1976) *Czechoslovakia's Interrupted Revolution* (Princeton, NJ, Princeton University Press).
Williams, K. (1997) *The Prague Spring and its Aftermath: Czechoslovak Politics, 1968–1970* (Cambridge, Cambridge University Press).

Dimensions of the Czechoslovak Crisis of 1967–1970

VILÉM PREČAN

THE EVENTS THAT BECAME KNOWN AS THE 'PRAGUE SPRING' of 1968 are better understood in fact as part of a more complex chain of crisis situations, making up three dimensions of a broader crisis of Czechoslovak society in the late 1960s. This chain of crisis situations began in late 1967 and continued through into 1970. Moreover, in order to grasp the nature of the crisis in its different dimensions, it is necessary to trace its roots back to the beginnings of communist rule in the Czechoslovakia of the late 1940s.

The roots of the Czechoslovak crisis

The fateful week of 19–25 February 1948 encompassed a series of events whose significance was so profound that they became known as a distinct historical category under the name of '*Únor*' (February). The future development of Czechoslovakia and the place of this country in Europe for the next 40 years of the Cold War was definitively decided in that week. 'February' itself, of course, was in a certain sense the culmination of developments which began at Munich in 1938. From the perspective of the subsequent 40 years of the communist era, however, it was only the beginning from which everything began to develop. 'February' marked a discontinuity in Czechoslovak society as the country moved from political pluralism to communist rule. After February and the formation of the government of the reconstituted National Front (*Národní fronta*), there began a period of unlimited rule by the Communist Party of Czechoslovakia (*Komunistická strana Československa*, KSČ) in both state and society; communist power became incontrovertible, as it would turn out, for 41 years. Nevertheless, although the Czechs and Slovaks entered into the Soviet 'protectorate' partly by their own devices, it was not entirely their own fault that they remained there for so long. That would become clear 20 years later.

Tendencies and elements of discontinuity accumulated and intensified for at least another 10 years after February 1948. However, Czech society also demonstrated that discontinuity and continuity are two sides of the same historic process of development and that the long-term contexts of geopolitics, civilisation, and history assert themselves again and again despite takeovers and revolutions and their consequences.

At each of the historical crossroads of Czechoslovak society in subsequent years, the alternatives of political pluralism and political democracy emerged again and again, whenever the opportunity presented itself, as a reminder of the past and a signpost to a normal, independent future. This happened most clearly in the second half of the 1960s in the period which has come to be known as the 'Prague Spring' of 1968.

Two preliminary remarks on the crisis of the 1960s

First, my history of the events of the 'Prague Spring of 1968' takes us rather beyond this date, namely to the spring, even the summer, of 1969. I include in it the signing of the Moscow Protocol, the annulment of the Vysočany congress of the KSČ, the agreement on the temporary basing of Soviet troops in Czechoslovakia on 16 October 1968, the student strike of 17 November 1968, Smrkovský's appeal to metalworkers not to strike on his behalf and Palach's self-sacrificial warning in January 1969, and the feverish attempts to strengthen non-governmental, non-state linkages and structures independent of the Normalising Party-State *apparat*. The definitive end of the Prague Spring lies, as I see it, in the events of August 1969 with the suppression of demonstrations, Alexander Dubček's signature on the legal measure of the Federal Assembly, which was designed allegedly to preserve 'public order' against 'anti-Socialist and anti-social forces'. These events were followed by the public annulment of the statements and the oath of August 1968 in September and October 1969 and the millions of private capitulations during the screening process called *prověrky*.

Secondly, with the benefit of hindsight, we can say that the Czechs and Slovaks did not choose a particularly suitable moment for their struggle for freedom and the right to take the future of their country into their own hands. As historians, however, we know that history is not a game of chess, that the future is always veiled in mist, that people never know what they have actually begun or how it will turn out. Today, indeed, we know everything relevant about the main actors in the events of 1968 in the country, about the people at the top, their ideological makeup and political outlook, and about their lack of preparedness for a conflict with Big Brother USSR, whose reaction to events took them by surprise. In a similar way, we can now see that public pressure took the leadership by surprise after the lifting of censorship. We also know a good deal about the people below, that they too had no idea what awaited them. We know about how they depended on those above and how many illusions they had about them, and despite that, or precisely because of that, they were full of enthusiasm and euphoria from their (cheaply) won freedom, which they eagerly experienced with the prospect of a better future, at a time when history, 'broken free of its chains, charged off into the unknown' (Herling-Grudziński 1995, p. 166).

The three dimensions of the Czechoslovak crisis

The events that played themselves out in Czechoslovakia in 1968 defy attempts to give them a single name; it is difficult to find a simple definition or formula for them. Certainly one reason for this is that the story was so complex, with so many layers and forms, that it is perhaps impossible to find a single common denominator for them all. The name 'Prague Spring' is confusing; initially it was an attempt to employ a metaphor to describe the mood of the spontaneously acting public in 1968, the nascent free discussion, and the growing courage to express openly the burning political issues of the time. This mood had begun to spread throughout Czechoslovakia in the early spring of 1968, and from it followed the hope of a different, more humane communism. The world around Czechoslovakia took note of this new situation, and gave it the poetic appellation which now creates such difficulties for the historian trying to grasp the meaning of the period.

It is possible to talk about 1968 in terms of a crisis in and around Czechoslovakia but it would perhaps be more appropriate to talk about a chain of crises. Of primary importance was the profound systemic crisis of Czechoslovak communism. Its home-grown solution (actually a mere attempt at a solution) soon evoked a crisis in relations within the Soviet bloc, and led to conflict that eventually came to a peak with the invasion and occupation of Czechoslovakia by the armed forces of five states of the Warsaw Pact, led by the Soviet Union, on 21 August 1968. The purpose of military intervention was not to go to war but to create the background for a palace coup to stop the democratising process in Czechoslovakia. In the understanding and language of the Soviet leadership, this was the way to prevent the victory of 'counter-revolution' and the loss of socialist Czechoslovakia.

The conflict within the Soviet bloc and the means of its solution—the movement of a half-million-strong army supported by 6,000 tanks and more than 1,000 aircraft; the clear infringement of a state's sovereignty and the disregard of international law; the lack of clarity about the possible short-term and long-term consequences of this operation for the security, peace, and balance of forces in Europe; the fear of creating a precedent for other, similar steps—all brought about an acute international crisis.

FIGURE 1. TEPLICE. PHOTOGRAPH COURTESY OF THE INSTITUTE OF CONTEMPORARY HISTORY, ACADEMY OF SCIENCES, CZECH REPUBLIC

FIGURE 2. BRATISLAVA. PHOTOGRAPH BY LADISLAV BIELIK, COPYRIGHT PERMISSION PETER BIELIK

Into this crisis were drawn NATO, the UN, and the governments of a number of states ('non-aligned' as well as 'aligned'), together with the public around the world, including communist and left-wing parties in the West.

This, then, is the chain of crisis situations, or in my understanding the three dimensions of the Czechoslovak crisis in the late 1960s. Each of them had its own life, in terms of time and space, and had its own content, and can ultimately be examined independently, providing we are aware of the overall context and the great connections between the events involved. Furthermore each of these processes left its own lasting impression, its own long-term consequences.

The initial story in late 1967 and early 1968 was one episode of a long series of attempts to surmount communist totalitarianism, and was one of the chapters of the still ongoing Cold War, which had also left its mark of hard reality and rules that some call cynical. This story finally came to a close more than 20 years later, with democratic revolutions in Czechoslovakia and in other countries of East and Central Europe: with the declaration of Václav Havel and Mikhail Gorbachev of 26 February 1990, and the intergovernmental Czechoslovak–Soviet agreement of that same day, on the withdrawal of the Soviet troops from Czechoslovak territory.

The systemic crisis of Czechoslovak communism

The fundamental matter in Czechoslovakia in 1968 was the search for a way out of the profound crisis which Czechoslovak society had been plunged into by the Communist Party's monopoly on power, which had been established 20 years before, followed by the Sovietisation of the country, the implantation of a Soviet system in Czechoslovakia in the late 1940s and early 1950s under the direction of Moscow's Czechoslovak satraps. From that, there followed a long, drawn-out illness affecting all spheres of the state and social organisms, including, of course, the economy, the arts and culture, spiritual life, and the status of Slovaks (and Slovakia) and national minorities.

The Czechoslovak road to communist totalitarianism had several essential features, which distinguished it from almost all other East and Central European countries that had found themselves in the position of Soviet satellites. The KSČ had achieved power without the presence of the Soviet armed forces on Czechoslovak territory; the majority of the population had been won over to the idea of socialism (though not only Soviet socialism) long before the communists usurped unlimited power; most Czechoslovaks considered the Soviet Union to be the guarantor of their country's sovereignty and the guarantee against potential danger from neighbouring Germany; non-communist politicians who had been in the Czechoslovak government until the victorious communist 'elegant' takeover of February 1948 were also proponents of a close alliance with the Soviet Union.

The subsequent 20 years 'building of socialism' brought into doubt in numerous ways many (or perhaps all) of the preceding political and intellectual preconditions of Czechoslovak communism, and were in every sense a great lesson for all of Czechoslovak society. The destruction of civil society, the ravaging of the country's political and cultural elite, the absence of civil liberties, the country's many years of isolation from the free world, control by the secret police, mass indoctrination, control over information by communist propaganda and over everyday life in the communist system, all made political opposition impossible. Moreover it also made it difficult to engage in independent political thought, to adopt a rational orientation in various situations, and to search for a way out of the country's problems (assuming, of course, that in a divided world governed by the rules of the Cold War, there was a way out).

The impulses for de-Stalinisation, which had emerged during the Khrushchev period, brought waves of 'thaw' and some liberalisation, as well as a partial opening of contacts with the free world. They made conditions more bearable, and increased faith in the reformability of the system, but ultimately made it less stable. The great economic difficulties that in Czechoslovakia in the early 1960s led to an absolute decline in GDP for the first time since World War II, forced the Party to come up with new economic policies. One clear factor of instability was the Slovak question, which included a social movement against centralism, gaining considerably in strength from 1963 onwards, and affecting the top level of the communist apparatus in Slovakia, too. The belated and reluctantly performed rehabilitation of victims of political violence and unrestrained power during the introduction of Stalinism further increased political tension.

From the beginning of the 1960s dissatisfaction with the state of public affairs was growing. This was apparent not only in various social and intellectual circles but also within the Communist Party and outside it. It stemmed from the clear contradiction between officially proclaimed principles and aims, on the one hand, and real life, on the other, and from the social experience of individual persons and social and professional groups. The accompanying search for solutions to these pressing questions resulted in a universally shared belief in the need for fundamental change. A considerable number of intellectuals, who had been part of the political and arts and culture establishment of Czechoslovakia, were becoming increasingly critical of the Stalinist past, and were turning into supporters of a kind of revisionism, which took the form of a return to some sort of initial ideal of pure socialism 'without deformations', a Czechoslovak variety of socialism. Socialism, while its essence was open to debate with references first to Lenin and then to Marx, was to be preserved, but should comport with the cultural traditions of the country, bearing in mind Czechoslovakia's position in the centre of Europe, and should ensure economic prosperity. Criticism of the past and the present, together with the search for continuity with European and earlier Czech and Slovak intellectual streams, found expression in a remarkable efflorescence of literature and the visual arts, and in particular film.

In the summer and autumn of 1967 the latent systemic crisis became evident. The First Secretary of the Central Committee of the KSČ, Antonín Novotný, who had headed the Party for 14 years and who had mastered critical situations without any of the turbulence seen in Hungary or Poland, came into conflict with the movement wanting to rectify things, with criticism of the so-called 'deformation' of socialism, and with Slovakia. His first solution was an attempt to return to iron-fisted rule: the writers who revolted at the Fourth Congress in late June 1967 were punished with Party sanctions, and the Writers' Union was stripped of its weekly journal, *Literární noviny*, the tribune of social criticism and revisionist views. Novotný accused Alexander Dubček, the First Secretary of the Communist Party in Slovakia (*Komunistická strana Slovenska*), of nationalism. Student demonstrations about living conditions in the Strahov halls of residence in Prague were brutally suppressed by police on 31 October 1967.

In the power struggle within the Party leadership, which these steps had brought about, Novotný lost his position as number one man in the Party and the state hierarchy. On 5 January 1968, Dubček was elected to head the Party, whilst Novotný remained only as president—something he never came to terms with, and for which he planned his revenge. The new leadership felt threatened by Novotný's manoeuvring, particularly when he began to mobilise those in the apparatus who had remained loyal to him.

The 'Prague Spring' begins

The programme of reforms announced by the Party leadership was prepared in the midst of the upheaval following Novotný's deposition. It was both part of the new Party leadership's struggle for unconditional power in the political apparatus throughout the country, and an expression of the attempt to create a new consensus with the population. The reform project, as it was stated 10 years later, was the result of the previous awakening of society and a reaction to this awakening (Havel 1985).[1] It started from a conception of a certain democratisation of the communist system, which allowed for a degree of independence for social actors, and it excluded the use of force in politics. Part of the planned reform was the extension of political

[1] 'The Prague Spring is usually understood as a clash between two groups on the level of real power: those who wanted to maintain the system as it was and those who wanted to reform it. It is frequently forgotten, however, that this encounter was merely the final act and the inevitable consequence of a long drama played out chiefly in the theatre of the spirit and the conscience of society. ... One thing, however, seems clear: the attempt at political reform was not the cause of society's reawakening, but rather the final outcome of that reawakening' (Havel 1985, p. 43).

freedoms for the public and economic reform with elements of a limited market economy.[2]

The decisive step that in the course of a few weeks would change the Czechoslovak political scene was not, however, the Action Programme (which was passed and made public in early April), but rather the lifting of censorship, which took place in practice as early as the second half of January 1968. The appeal to public opinion and the allowing of freedom of speech for journalists in the communist mass media were aspects of the power struggle with Novotný; goodwill towards the media was, apart from this, an important factor in calculations in the competition for influence and position within the new leadership. Formally, preliminary censorship was abolished by a decision of the Presidium of the KSČ's Central Committee in early March.

The overall thaw soon demonstrated how strong the desire for freedom and human dignity had been throughout society, and how great the potential for realising the changes had been. Independent public opinion was being formed and expressed. An infrastructure of organisations and institutions emerged, wresting themselves free from the 'leading role' (that is to say, the dictates) of the Party, and the foundations of a new political and social pluralism and the prerequisites for the renewal of civil society began to take shape. Important aspects of this process were the increasing emancipation of Party members from the apparatus; the intensification of activity by individual persons and groups pushing for extensive personnel changes at all levels of the Party; the announcement of institutional guarantees concerning the irreversibility of the reforms; and—even—the transformation of the Communist Party from a ruling monopoly into a normal political party.

The discussion, however, was still only about the 'renewal of socialism', and this stream of political ideology predominated in public throughout 1968. Nevertheless, individual radical statements and slogans were uttered. On 10 April 1968, the popular magazine *Student* published a paper by the professor of philosophy Ivan Sviták, which he had delivered at Charles University three weeks before. It analysed totalitarian dictatorships, including the Czechoslovak version, and concluded with an appeal:

> If the questions, 'from where?', 'with whom?', and 'where to?' are asked, the concise reply might be 'from Asia to Europe, alone!' This means from a totalitarian dictatorship to an open society, to the liquidation of the monopoly on power, and effective checks over the power elite with freedom of the press and public opinion; from the bureaucratic direction of society, including the arts and culture, 'by cutthroats toeing the official Party line' ... to the implementation of fundamental human rights, at least to the extent of the bourgeois democratic Czechoslovakia. (Sviták 1968)[3]

All the social organisations in existence at the time, interest groups or professional societies of all kinds, including organisations called political parties (non-communist)

[2] Twenty years later, in 1988, in comments made privately at a meeting of the *Listy* Group, Zdeněk Mlynář, a member of the Dubček leadership, would compare the Czechoslovak Communist Party's modest reform plans with the radical measures of the Soviet *perestroika* and say with a sigh: 'Gorbachev gets to remain Secretary General, and I have to remain in exile in Austria' (personal communication with the author).

[3] Also available in Liehm (ed.), 'Jaro 1968', Čítanka pro děti a mládež', Cologne, available at: http://www.blisty.cz/files/knihy/liehm/1968/044.pdf, last accessed 10 August 2008.

that were permitted within the National Front, relatively quickly broke loose from the Leninist–Stalinist model of being mere 'transmission belts'. They then sought to become independent of the *apparat* of the Communist Party, clarified their interests and aims, and manifested an increasingly distinct will to become social entities. People who the regime for some reason had so far lumped into the category of 'unreliable' or 'hostile elements', such as former political prisoners or other groups of Czechs and Slovaks, who were still second or third-class citizens (Roman Catholic nuns or monks of Orders that had been suppressed in the early 1950s, some Church and religious groups), now began to speak up.

New interest groups and civic actions began to emerge spontaneously, but with the intention of establishing themselves on a lasting basis. It was not only the Club of Committed Non-Party Members (*Klub angažovaných nestraníků*) and a number of youth organisations. A Charter of Human and Civil Rights, for example, was discovered, and the founding committee of the Society for Human Rights (*přípravný vybor Společnosti pro lidská práva*) was set up, not 'from above', but as a civic action. Similarly, a Circle of Independent Writers (*Kruh nezávislých spisovatelů*) emerged. Self-management in the original, true sense emerged, and there was work on projects and concrete proposals for how to apply its principles in various spheres of life (for example, in the archipelago of institutions of the Czechoslovak Academy of Sciences and in the running of the individual research institutes). In other words, a whole infrastructure of organisations and institutions emerged, already autonomous or becoming autonomous; the foundations for political and social pluralism were being laid. How firm the foundations of this new and more or less spontaneous pluralisation of Czechoslovak society were had not yet been thoroughly examined. In many respects the military intervention and non-violent civil resistance of August gave the process a strong impulse, and it continued even into the spring of 1969, when it was manifested with extraordinary strength, for example, in the trade unions.

The duality of the socio-political processes (February–August 1968)

In current Czech historical research and in the public discourse on the recent past, the history of the crisis is being both studied and discussed, increasingly with regard to what is often termed its 'dual nature'. On the one hand this concerns the attempt at reform from above and the actions of the Dubčekites; on the other hand it focuses on the social and political movement aimed at emancipation from the rule of the Communist Party and the formation of civil society that underlay the orientation towards a democratic revolution. These two aspects of the crisis were not contradictory, but rather they were mutually dependent on one another. Yet there did exist between them a great deal of tension, and this led to conflict situations, sometimes latent, sometimes conspicuous.

The Dubček leadership, far from being homogeneous (because it comprised people that felt increasingly threatened by reform and were thus seeking agreement with opponents of reform abroad) found itself in a dilemma: on the one hand, while under pressure from public opinion at home, it was bombarded with the criticism from its allies in Moscow, Warsaw and East Berlin; at the same time, by trying to reassure these critics with promises, the Dubček leadership ran the risk of squandering the confidence that it enjoyed at home.

The 'independent public' was mobilised by two fears in particular. The first was that the 'new regime' (or rather those in the Party leadership and *apparat* who were in favour of reform) would only consider the demands of some social entities and see the demands of others as incompatible with the 'leading role of the Party' (even though—both in the Action Programme and in practice—this was conceived less rigidly than at any time in the last 20 years). The second fear was that the reform leaders would give in to pressure from outside. In other words, the current leaders of the Czechoslovak state and Party would be unable to respect, and defend, the right of the Czechoslovak people to decide on internal matters in their own country, and would give preference to the interests of 'socialism' and 'international obligations', that is to say, they would give in to Moscow. Increasingly, the need was felt to put pressure on the leadership to make it respect the will of the public, especially in view of the growing tensions between the 'new regime' in Czechoslovakia and its opponents in the Soviet bloc. The largest mass event before August was the collection of signatures supporting a message to the Czechoslovak delegation, which was meeting the Soviet politburo in Čierná nad Tisou. Among the four 'S's in the message—*Socialismus* (Socialism), *Spojenectví* (Alliance), *Svoboda* (Freedom) and *Suverenita* (Sovereignty)—the last two, Freedom and Sovereignty, had moved more and more palpably to the fore.

The developments of the period between February and August 1968 culminated in the 'Czechoslovak week', from 21 to 27 August 1968, beginning with the late night statement of the Presidium of the Central Committee of the Communist Party of 21 August which condemned the Soviet-led invasion. That was an historic act from the

FIGURE 3. Protestors Surround Soldiers in Brno. Photograph Courtesy of the Moravian Museum

point of view of the history of the Czechoslovak Communist Party up to that point. From its beginning it had always pushed through the 'line' that was dictated, and also approved, by Moscow or by the 'cadres' of the Communist Party, who in the period 1945–1948 really did play the role of the fifth column of Soviet imperialism, and whose leaders had been, for 20 years, Moscow's reliable governors. However, the following seven great days of national resistance against the invasion would have been unthinkable without the preceding six months when an independent public and independent public opinion were formed. The civic and national self-confidence of members of all strata of the population had particularly grown in the course of July and the first three weeks of August. Paradoxically, that week and the seven months which followed were the periods of greatest freedom that the people of Czechoslovakia would experience for the next 20 years.

The top-leadership's clear distancing of itself from the foreign military occupation of the country, and its condemnation of this act as a violation of international law, carried great weight in practical terms too. It gave the popular resistance the hallmark of legitimacy and legality. It strengthened the unity of the popular resistance and the resistance of institutions like the cabinet and the National Assembly. It created a feeling of unity between the common people and the representatives of the state and Party, and in particular, it thwarted the chances that the intervention would enjoy quick political success. (Equally important in this respect was the prompt action of employees at Czechoslovak Radio in broadcasting the leadership's statement to the public in good time before the occupying forces took over the radio station.)

In all other respects, however, the inactivity of the top-level leadership of the country at the most critical time is striking. No decisions or instructions were issued, with the exception of the appeal to remain calm and not to put up any resistance, but to wait until the National Assembly, the cabinet, and the Central Committee of the Communist Party had discussed the situation. Not even more than 40 years after the events do we have the slightest evidence that a single one of the seven men who voted for the statement of 21 August (and the four others who were present, and, although without voting rights, were among the 'progressives' in the central secretariat and agreed with the statement) showed the slightest sign of having considered the possibility of Soviet military intervention beforehand. They neither had a plan for just such a contingency, nor had they thought it would be necessary to retire to a well-equipped government underground shelter from which they might be able to govern the country despite the occupation. (After the text of the statement was approved and the four pro-Moscow men voting against the draft text left the talks, at least three hours passed before Soviet soldiers arrived at the meeting room; of the 'progressive' members of the presidium only Oldřich Černík was absent, having left for the building of the Government Presidium.)

In this critical situation Dubček, the man with *de facto* the most powers in the state, was clueless and impotent. When approached by the secretary of a municipal committee of the Party in Prague, whose presidium had convened after midnight on 21 August and was deliberating over whether to call a general strike for the next day, and whether to call a meeting of the delegates of the planned Communist Party congress,

Dubček made it clear that he could do nothing other than wait until the Soviet representative arrived for talks and the Central Committee met.

Fortunately, instead of relying on the Party leadership, the whole population generally started to rise up: young people, workers, and employees of the radio station, the press, and television; all began to act, spontaneously, without being controlled and managed from above. The civil resistance unconditionally condemned the occupation and demanded the withdrawal of foreign troops, refused to collaborate with the invading units and refused political collaboration of any kind. They demanded that the state and Party representatives who had been taken away by force of arms be permitted to return to office, and they also demanded the continuation of the restructuring of the social system that had already begun. That was the basis on which nationwide unity and solidarity had been formed in a short period. In this resistance movement, members of all generations, social groups, nationalities and political persuasions came together. The movement included constitutional and other top-level institutions, offices, and branches of government at all levels, and, insofar as they were able to act, Czechoslovak diplomats, particularly at the UN Security Council. Another aspect of the nationwide resistance movement was the Vysočany Congress of the Czechoslovak Communist Party and the activities of the lower-levels of the Party *apparat* and its organisations.

Though all this resistance was unarmed, it was not passive. It demonstrated how difficult it was to control a country when all its civil structures decide to ignore an armed aggressor. Also very significant was the role of radio and other modern communications media in the nationwide resistance movement as a real political force,

FIGURE 4. GRAFFITI 'SOVIET OCCUPIERS GO HOME! WE DEMAND THE IMMEDIATE DEPARTURE OF THE OCCUPYING FORCES'. PHOTOGRAPH COURTESY OF THE INSTITUTE OF CONTEMPORARY HISTORY, ACADEMY OF SCIENCES, CZECH REPUBLIC

FIGURE 5. WENCESLAS SQUARE, PRAGUE. PHOTOGRAPH COURTESY OF THE INSTITUTE OF CONTEMPORARY HISTORY, ACADEMY OF SCIENCES, CZECH REPUBLIC

capable of coordinating society without the state (Hoppe 2004; Dienstbier & Lánský 1990).

How the broad movement of the people was pacified

The waning of the activity and solidarity of the general public and their adaptation to the Normalisation conditions of 'real, existing Socialism' was not, in my view, the result of some sort of 'social contract', as has often been suggested. Nor was it a cold, calculated *quid pro quo* act, of relinquishing political rights in return for being granted a decent standard of living. I believe that the private capitulation by which a traumatised and demoralised people adapted externally to the rules of real, existing Socialism ('living in a lie') between 1969 and 1971, was the result of their profound disenchantment and disappointment; it began with the narrow-minded, capitulationist policy of the 'leaders' of the Prague Spring.

Moscow understood, at the latest 48 hours after the start of the military action, that in order to overcome opposition in the most critical phase in the restoration of normality in central Europe, in the sense of the *pax sovietica*, it needed to subordinate and incorporate Dubček and the other 'progressive' political leaders. In other words, the aim of the Moscow leadership was to have their policies carried out with the help of people who had become popular precisely because they had been against the Kremlin, and whose return to state and Party office had been pushed through by the pertinacity of the common people.

The Soviet leadership needed to pacify the Czechoslovak masses as soon as possible to end the non-violent resistance, which was evoking an increasing international response, and they needed to prevent the further internationalisation of the Czechoslovak question. The 'progressive' leaders were, therefore, returned to the people, when, by signing the Moscow Protocol, they had committed themselves to 'restoring order' in the Soviet spirit. They did so unhappily, to be sure, but without much hesitation. Although some of them were tormented by the 'Hamlet question', they launched Normalisation, though still in a moderate form (any other way would have still been impossible in late August 1968) and each of them continued in that manner as long as they were still useful to the Soviet leadership.

Nonetheless, they all remained in office long enough to help prepare the next phase of pacifying the popular movement. Some of them—most strikingly Oldřich Černík and Gustáv Husák—began to play their own game immediately upon their return from Moscow. Others were sure that there was no other solution or that it was still possible to play out a skilful game, and continued to perform their duty and respect 'party discipline' until they were removed.[4] All acted with remarkable political blindness and fully in the tradition of the policy of adopting the lesser evil, which had brought the people of Czechoslovakia so much of the greater evil and countless victims in the previous 50 years.

The mass solidarity and will to resist of the broad strata of the population in August 1968 was ground down step by step. The so-called '*realpolitik*' of the reform leaders blazed the trail and provided an example to the proverbial man in the street, both in matters of high-level politics and in everyday life. The forces willing to restore totalitarian power formed themselves almost before the eyes of the traumatised, disoriented population, and society was gradually pacified by the 'national heroes' Alexander Dubček, Oldřich Černík, Ludvík Svoboda and Josef Smrkovský. The original slogan of solidarity, 'we are with you, so you be with us'—the product of illusions created in the last days of August 1968—sounded more and more like a

[4]This was the way of Alexander Dubček, Josef Smrkovský, and dozens of others.

desperate, urgent reminder ('please be with us!'), until it fell silent, when it met with less and less response and then fell only on deaf ears.

The result was a mood of hopelessness, disappointment and disgust, which gradually overcame all strata of society. In this way the socio-psychological conditions were formed for the restoration of the authoritarian regime without mass conflicts. The population, especially the youth, which resisted the temptation of retiring into their private lives longer than anyone else, still needed to be taught a graphic lesson about whom the streets belonged to. They learned that lesson in August 1969, on the first anniversary of the invasion, when it was not Soviet or allied Warsaw Pact tanks, but the riot squads of the Czechoslovak police, the tank corps of the Czechoslovak Army, Czechoslovak policemen and members of the Czechoslovak workers' militia who, by force or threats, suppressed the memorial demonstration in the large towns of Bohemia, Moravia and Slovakia. At that time, radio, television and the press in Czechoslovakia were already consolidated or 'streamlined', and the lesson taught to the people was celebrated in these same mass media in terms of 'repelling the onslaught of the enemy'.

For the preservation of 'public order' against 'anti-Socialist and anti-social elements' extraordinary legal measures were proclaimed by the Federal Assembly on 22 August 1969, and remained valid until the end of 1969. They were temporary discretionary powers for the police to imprison people for up to three weeks; single judges (rather than the usual judicial boards) were authorised to adjudicate so-called 'political offences'—sedition, seditious libel of the world socialist system, and so forth, as well as all activity that came under the heading of offences against public order—without preliminary hearings, and defence counsels were admitted only to the court proceedings. The labour code was suspended in the case of 'disturbers of the peace', and the civil service was given the right to suspend the activities of organisations or to close them down. Martial law made it possible to expel students, to immediately dismiss teachers from schools of all levels and scholars and scientists from the Academy of Science if they 'disrupted the Socialist social order' or similar cases. Such was the rubbery formulation of this legal measure.

Beneath these full powers for the 'restoration of order' were the signatures of the Leader of the Federal Assembly, Dubček, the Czechoslovak President, Svoboda, and Premier Černík. Exactly one year to the day after the glorious 'Czechoslovak week', everything that had been said in August 1968 or later, everything that had been gloriously proclaimed and gloriously sworn to with the promise of solidarity, was thus conspicuously outlawed. The Soviet lie, defeated during the 'Czechoslovak week', now became the truth in Czechoslovakia, and was now heard time and again from the channels of information, which only the year before had become so famous all over the world for their openness.

From the 'democratisation' to 'democracy'

We know a good deal about where the road led for those who did not capitulate and did not adapt to the rules of the 'restoration of order' (Šimečka 1990); about how the experience of the Prague Spring and its defeat led to a new orientation that crystallised into the knowledge of the indivisibility of freedom and the universal validity of civil and human rights; until it finally found expression in Charter 77, in independent civil activities and civil self-help, in spiritual defiance and resistance. Later in 1988, Jaroslav Šabata, who at the 1968 Vysočany congress had been elected to the Central Committee of the KSČ, who was sentenced in 1972 to six and a half years imprisonment, and who signed the Charter shortly after his release, spoke about the prospects of general emancipation of society.[5]

In view of what the interrupted journey to democracy in 1968 had opened the way to, we would perhaps today agree that those two or three years of crisis in the late 1960s constituted the deepest dividing line in the history of Czechoslovakia since Munich, in the search both for a foreign-policy orientation that would ensure the country's sovereignty and for a way out of the cul-de-sac of totalitarian dictatorship. When, 20 years later, a new chance for freedom appeared, it was not with the programme for the 'rebirth of socialism', but for the recreation of pluralist democratic structures, of democracy for all and without any adjectives, such as 'People's' or 'Socialist', to modify it. As one possibility of development it was perhaps present in embryonic form in the atmosphere of 1968; but this possibility became a reality only as a result of everything that Czechoslovakia and the world went through in the 1970s and 1980s.

No-one and nothing was to remain the same. That became clear, however, only in hindsight, through the social processes of the next 20 years of immobility and cultural malnutrition known as Normalisation. For that explosion of longing for freedom, for that attempt at self-liberation, for those first steps towards curing oneself of what Karl Popper called the 'fatal mental illness of Communism' (Herling-Grudziński 1995, p. 313) which accompanied the communist-led attempt at reform of the system in 1968, Czechoslovak society paid a tremendous price.

A great price, if it can be at all compared, was also paid by the Czechoslovak Communist Party, which carried out (albeit under pressure from Moscow and following its instructions, but with the forces of its own leadership and *apparats*) the restoration of the regime in the form of the real-existing socialism of the 1970s and 1980s: it was excluded from the chance to influence the future (and later to transform itself in a meaningful way, as the communist parties of Poland and Hungary managed to do).

Gorbachev also forfeited Czechoslovakia (assuming it was at all possible to win it over), ultimately—one of the paradoxes of history—as a consequence of his reform attempt, but even earlier, because he did not promptly decide in the name of 'restructuring' (*perestroika*) and the 'new thinking' (*glasnost'*) to condemn the August 1968 military intervention. So as not to interfere in the internal affairs of Czechoslovakia (and not destabilise it), he did not interfere in the affairs of the Soviet Union either, as he was requested in an open letter in September 1989 by one Czechoslovak dissident: 'I ask you, please', wrote Milan Šimečka, 'to intervene in your own internal affairs and with a condemnation of the intervention rid your own country

[5]Interview with Šabata first published in the *samizdat* (*Obsah*, October 1987), subsequently printed in *Listy*, 18, 1, February 1988, pp. 17–26 with the title *Kdy už čas oponou trhne? Rozhovor s Jaroslavem Šabatou.*

of the moral burden of old guilt, which casts into doubt even the hopeful acts of the present'.[6]

Gorbachev did not even support Dubček, who had decided in January 1988 to break his many years of silence and publicly—in a long interview in *L'Unità*, the Italian communist daily—come out in support of Gorbachev's *perestroika* in the Soviet Union, while condemning the Soviet intervention of 1968 and defending his own approach at the time when he was at the head of the Czechoslovak Communist Party.[7] Dubček's defence of the reforms of 1968 met with little response at home. For the Husák regime he naturally remained an enemy. But did he really have something to say about the problems facing contemporary Czechoslovakia? He came, it seemed, from out of the past, in somewhat re-tailored, yet unstylish garb. He was mostly backward-looking and the words he chose now had little relevance to most people. '*Obroda*' (meaning 'revival'), an association of independent former communists, met with a similar fate; it was rejected and persecuted by the regime as enemy number one, and met with little support amongst the public.

Life was, after all, elsewhere, even though it became fully clear only in the last two years of the communist era. Twenty years after the Prague Spring the democratic cards in Czechoslovakia were laid on the table: as Šimečka wrote 'Everything today would have been different if democratic political culture in our country had not been gradually curtailed and eventually destroyed. The revival of a democratic, pluralist political culture is the most important task for the future' (Hlušičková & Císařovská 1994, p. 120). This idea was expanded into the 'Democracy for All' manifesto (Hlušičková & Císařovská 1994), with which the independent Movement for Civil Liberty (*Hnutí za občanskou svobodu*) was established in Czechoslovakia in autumn 1988. Apparently banal truths were summarised here, and then stated publicly as a starting point for political practice. The manifesto was an appeal to society to become involved in politics, because the existing authorities, who were the actual culprits behind the current moral crisis, the undemocratic conditions, the limiting of national and state sovereignty, and the economic and technological decline, were not willing to abandon their totalitarian means of governing. The manifesto expressly contested the legitimacy of the dogma of the leading role of the Communist Party, and held up democratic pluralism as a political principle; it emphasised that everyone should have the same right to share in political power.

The manifesto did not contain the word 'socialism'. That was no accident, and was part of the trend of those days. Václav Havel at the time called the word 'socialism' a 'thoroughly mendacious cipher', a cloak under which the *apparat* of the Communist

[6]The open letter *předsedovi Nejvyššího sovětu SSSR Michailu Gorbačovovi*, dated 7 September 1989, was broadcast by the Voice of America on 10 September 1989. For the full text of the open letter see Kusý (1990, p. 199 f.). Admittedly, Gorbachev remained faithful to his policy of non-intervention in November 1989 too, and was thus indirectly responsible for the collapse of communist rule in Czechoslovakia. The leadership of the Czechoslovak Communist Party, finding itself isolated internationally, and rejected by most of the population in public demonstrations, ultimately relinquished its 'leading role'.

[7]The full text of this interview appeared in Czech in the January issue of the exile journal *Listy (Řím)* in 1988.

Party concealed its monopoly on power.[8] In the polemical *samizdat* article, 'Confusing Socialism', Šimečka (1989) rejected any debate about a term to which he would have to attach a 'thick book of explanations' about what socialism is and is not. And so, when in autumn 1989, all society was set in motion, a repeat performance of the 'revival of socialism' *à la* 1968, whether under the leadership of the Communist Party or without it, could not be a programme for finding a solution to current or future problems facing the country, or, indeed, even a symbol or inspiration for the demanded and expected changes. The day of 21 August, one of the dates of the demonstrations in the streets both in 1968 and in 1989, was not the symbol for the return of the 'revival of socialism', but it was linked clearly with the demand for the restoration of state sovereignty; and, if it recalled something other than Soviet tanks, it was only the activity of the popular-based movement against the August 1968 military intervention.

At the moment when Civic Forum, the representative of the public in revolt, decided not to be merely an actor applying pressure to the communist establishment, but to take part in governing, to enter the establishment and transform it, it was not Dubček who found himself in the most visible place amongst the new representatives, but Havel. At one point, on 7 December 1989, it was even feared during debates amongst the members of the core leadership of the 'Velvet Revolution' that their opponent, the Communist Party, might try and foist upon the public a new version of reform communism, represented by the duo of Adamec and Dubček, as a way out of the crisis, perhaps even with Gorbachev's blessing.[9] Civic Forum could not reject Dubček, primarily because of Slovakia, thus, it found the most suitable compromise solution in making Dubček leader of the Federal Assembly. Dubček bit the bullet and relinquished his chance to stand for the office of President of Czechoslovakia, which he had so badly wanted. And so the Havel–Dubček alliance was interpreted as a symbol of the fact that Havel, the representative of the current, successful struggle for freedom, would accept the office of president from Dubček, the Leader of the Federal Assembly, the representative of the erstwhile, unsuccessful struggle for freedom.

Czechoslovak Documentation Centre/Československé dokumentační středisko

References

Dienstbier, J. & Lánský, K. (1990) 'Rozhlas proti tankům', in Dienstbier, J., Lánský, L., Šilhán, V. & Šimon, B. (eds) (1990) *Srpen 1968* (Prague, Práce), pp. 17–116.

Havel, V. (1985) 'The Power of the Powerless', in Keane, J. (ed.) (1985) *The Power of the Powerless. Citizen against the State in Central-Eastern Europe* (London, Hutchinson).

Havel, V. (1999) *Spisy*, Vol. 4 (Prague, Torst), pp. 1062–65.

Herling-Grudziński, G. (1995) *Deník psaný v noci (1989–1992)* (Prague, Torst).

[8] *Šifra socialismus* (dated 7 June 1988), first published in *Lidové noviny* (*samizdat*), 1988, 7–8, p. 36. See Havel (1999, pp. 1062–65).

[9] *Záznam diskuse na poradě porady členů akční skupiny Koordinačního centra Občanského fóra 7.12. 1989*. Available in Suk (1998, Document 48, p. 127 f.).

Hlušičková, R. & Císařovská, B. (eds) (1994) *Hnutí za občanskou svobodu 1988–1989. Sborník dokumentů*, (Prague, Ústav pro soudobé dějiny AV ČR).
Hoppe, J. (ed.) (2004) *Pražské jaro v médiích* (Brno, Výběr z dobové publicistiky Doplněk).
Kusý, M. (1990) *Na vlnách slobodnej Európy* (Bratislava, Smena).
Šimečka, M. (1989) 'Matoucí socialismus'. [First published in *Alternativa* (*samizdat* journal), 2, April 1989, pp. 52–55. Also available in Hlušičková & Císařovská (1994, pp. 118–21).]
Šimečka, M. (1990) *Obnovenie poriadku* (Bratislava, Archa).
Suk, J. (1998) *Občanské fórum: Listopad—prosinec 1989. 2. díl Dokumenty* (Prague & Brno, ÚSD—Doplněk).
Sviták, I. (1968) 'Hlavou proti zdi', *Student*, 10 April.

1938 and 1968, 1939 and 1969, and the Philosophy of Czech History from Karel H. Mácha to Jan Patočka

STEFAN AUER

THE SIGNIFICANCE OF THE PRAGUE SPRING OF 1968 is best assessed in relation to the other 'magic eights' in Czech history. The nineteenth-century Czech national 'revival' culminated in the revolutionary upheavals of the Spring of Nations in 1848. The First Czechoslovak Republic was established with strong Western support in 1918, only to be betrayed by the Munich Treaty in 1938. Beneš's short-lived experiment with a pro-Soviet democratic regime after the Second World War was defeated with the communist takeover in 1948. Twenty years later still, the attempt to democratise communism was aborted after the Soviet-led invasion in 1968. These snapshots are incomplete, however, without consideration of ensuing developments; we must also pay attention therefore to the 'demystifying nines'. Czech heroism and cowardice, passion and prudence, wisdom and foolishness tend to come to prominence in these crucial dates. The full trauma of Munich in 1938 materialises with the destruction of Czechoslovakia in 1939. The Prague Spring of 1968 stands for hope, socialism with a human face, and people power that seemed to have survived even the full-blown military invasion in August of that year. It took another year for the population to succumb to the new (old) order, and by August 1969 it was clear that the neo-Stalinist policies of Normalisation had succeeded (Tůma 2005, pp. 309–24).

This is not just a numbers game. History matters to contemporaries, but only if they can actively engage with it through meaningful stories that capture their imagination. As Hannah Arendt understood well, keeping history alive amounts to an ongoing struggle against forgetting:

> For if it is true that all thoughts begin with remembrance, it is also true that no remembrance remains secure unless it is condensed and distilled into a framework of conceptual notions

I would like to thank Laura Cashman, Christopher Finlay, Robert Horvath, Adrian Jones, David Vaughan, Anna Bischof and two anonymous reviewers of *Europe-Asia Studies* for their invaluable feedback on earlier drafts of this essay. I also greatly benefited from comments and discussions at the conference in Glasgow 'Remembering 1948 and 1968' in April 2008, particularly with Mary Heimann, Antonín J. Liehm, Vilém Prečan and Avi Tucker. I am indebted to Věra Čapková and Samuel Abrahám for their support in Prague and Bratislava respectively, and to Philip Bull and Peter Russell for all of their help back in Melbourne.

> within which it can further exercise itself. . . . What saves the affairs of mortal men from their inherent futility is nothing but this incessant talk about them, which in turn remains futile unless certain concepts, certain guideposts for future remembrance, and even for sheer reference, arise out of it. (Arendt 1965, p. 220)

Contemporaries make sense of their present times in relation to history. The basic question of national belonging—'Who are we as a community of people?'—requires the evaluation of the decisive moments in that nation's history. In this way, people respond to present challenges and seek to shape their future in relation to past achievements and failures. To the extent that the magic number eight, as a signpost, is anchored in Czech public imagination, its power is very real.[1]

For instance, although surprisingly little of historical significance seemed to have happened in Czechoslovakia in 1988, many Czechs and Slovaks expected something to happen. Milan Šimečka, for example, one of the leading Czech dissidents living in Slovakia, started a diary on New Year's Eve of 1987, confessing that he too succumbed to the veritable obsession with the number eight.[2] He keenly expected 'the end of horrible stagnation' in Czechoslovak society which had depressed him for 20 years (Šimečka 1990a, p. 7). His diary meticulously followed the ups and downs of that year, including the changing political climate in the Soviet Union and a somewhat forgotten event in Bratislava, a religiously inspired candlelit demonstration on 25 March 1988, violently suppressed by the communist authorities. Not surprisingly, Šimečka's account remained rather despondent throughout 1988. The anticipated end of stagnation is only discerned in the very last entry from 28 February 1989. We know now, that what might have appeared as wishful thinking back then unwittingly turned into a self-fulfilling prophecy. Ten years earlier, Šimečka wrote one of the best accounts of the process of post-Prague Spring Normalisation, *The Restoration of Order* (Šimečka 1990b).[3] Characteristically, the study draws parallels between the post-1968 developments and the Czech trauma of Munich. Šimečka opens with his recollection of the humiliating military parade on 15 March 1939, the sense of powerlessness that he observed as a nine-year-old boy. Already then, he also astutely observed the willingness on the part of many of his compatriots to collaborate with the Nazis (Šimečka 1990b, p. 14). With these two studies, Šimečka analysed the way Czechs and Slovaks accommodated themselves to repressive regimes, linking three crucial periods: 1938/1939, 1968/1969 and 1988/1989.

[1]A recent example from popular culture is the 'Magic Eight Film Festival' that took place in January 2008 in Prague. In a similar vein, the main Czech TV channel, *Česká televize*, broadcast a series of programmes devoted to the 'Fateful eights in our history' (*Osudové osmičky v našich dějinách*). At a more official level, the Institute of Contemporary History at the Czech Academy of Sciences organised a series of conferences devoted to Czech crossroads of European history: 1918, 1938, 1948, 1968 (available at: http://1918-1938-1968.cz/content/view/1/3/lang,cz/, accessed 17 April 2008).

[2]Milan Šimečka writes mostly about Czechoslovak rather than just Czech history and there are times when these two perspectives cannot be separated. I use Czech and Czechoslovak perspectives interchangeably in line with the usage of many Czech intellectuals and politicians. It is beyond the scope of this essay to deal with the complexities of the Czech and Slovak relationship. For Slovak discourses of nationalism see Auer (2004, pp. 131–69).

[3]This work was first published in 1979 by the exile publisher Index, based in Cologne.

The question that animates this essay is what kind of narrative best serves a better understanding of the significance of those crucial events in modern Czech history. Have Czechs in their history been prudent, by stoically enduring trials and tribulations inflicted on them by their enemies? Or, in contrast, have they simply been cowardly, seldom showing enough resolve to fight for their liberty and national independence? For people familiar with Jaroslav Hašek's masterpiece *The Good Soldier Švejk*, the problem can be restated in relation to Švejk's ambivalent legacy (Auer 2006, p. 422). In an alteration to Luther's famous doctrine ('*Hier stehe ich und kann nicht anders!*', 'Here I stand and cannot do otherwise'), Švejk's stance can be characterised as 'Here I stand, but I could do otherwise too' (Jandl 2006). Should this attitude be seen as a virtue, or a vice, a pragmatic willingness to compromise, or a sign of moral weakness? There were moments in history when waiting for opportune historical circumstances to realise national ambitions may well have been prudent and justified. Two such moments worth mentioning are 'the "negotiated" revolution in Prague in 1918' (Korbel 1977, p. 4), that gave birth to the Czechoslovak First Republic, and the Velvet Revolution of 1989 (Auer 2006, pp. 415–17). It is less clear whether Czech responses in 1938/1939 and 1968/1969 were virtuous.[4]

To address this question, I will discuss two different versions of the philosophy of Czech history derived from the lessons of the Prague Spring and the trauma of Munich. As a point of departure, I will use two conflicting accounts of Czech history advanced by two influential Czech public intellectuals: the writer Milan Kundera and the dissident philosopher Jan Patočka.[5] This is not an attempt to give a comprehensive account of their respective views, however. Instead, the major motivation for this essay is to engage the dominant images of Czech national mythology and to discuss their impact on Czech history. In this reading, Kundera and Patočka, alongside other writers and intellectuals (Václav Havel, Bohumíl Hrabal, Karel Hynek Mácha and Jan Tesař), simply offer two radically different answers to the perennial question about the 'meaning of Czech history'; answers, which still strongly resonate with Czech society.

There is no way of 'measuring' the relevance of such debates in wider Czech society. However, a number of scholars have observed that Czechs are particularly interested in their history. Ernest Gellner was convinced that 'there can be few nations ... which live on terms of quite such constant intimacy with their own history as do the Czechs' (Gellner 1993, p. 3). Another British anthropologist of Czech origin, Ladislav Holy, later echoed this assessment: 'Czechs tell themselves who they are by projecting contemporary ideas and values on the narrative of the past, which in turn is invoked as

[4]'The unflattering truth' is, as Ivan Sviták suggested to his co-patriots, that 'we, the Czechs, did not fight for the defense of democratic principles; we, the Czechs, miscalculated future events in 1938, 1948, and 1968' (Sviták 1990, p. 87).

[5]Patočka's political philosophy and his personal courage were a great source of inspiration for the dissident movement in Czechoslovakia. Alongside Václav Havel, Patočka was one of the key architects of the human rights movement, Charter 77. Shortly before reaching his seventieth birthday, he became also the first prominent victim of the communist repression of Charter 77, and died of a brain haemorrhage just one week after a series of prolonged interrogations (Vladislav 2007, pp. 95–96). While Patočka's philosophical work is not sufficiently known in the English-speaking world, there are growing numbers of translations and studies. See for example Kohák (1989), Tucker (2000), Findlay (2002), Lom (2002) and Lehmann (2004).

their legitimation' (Holy 1996, p. 82). Even before the collapse of communism in 1989, the importance of national memory was recognised both by the communist authorities and their opponents. Karl Schwarzenberg, the current Czech foreign minister, who was instrumental in the creation of the archive for dissident literature in the former West Germany in 1987, spoke for many Czechs:

> Every creative act [such as the establishment of an archive], that helps to maintain the continuity of our cultural life, is more important for us [Czechs] than larger nations, or such nations which do not find themselves at the crossroads of history. I think that very few people will be able to understand Czech history ... and our failures in decisive moments (it is remarkable that the Czech language derives the word failure [*selhání*] from lying [*lhaní*]), if they do not know that our development towards a freer and a more confident stance was interrupted by ruptures and losses of such exceptional character that they influence our behaviour to this day. (Schwarzenberg 2007, p. 837)

Although Schwarzenberg, writing this from his home in Austria in support of the Charter 77 movement, did not mention specific dates marking these ruptures, we can safely assume that he was referring to 1938, 1968 and most likely also to 1948, when his aristocratic family was forced to leave Czechoslovakia.

Milan Kundera: prudent and peaceful Czechs

One of the persistent themes of Czech self-representation is the image of the nation as a peace-loving people in the centre of Europe who, due to its precarious geographical and historical predicament, learned how to defy adversity by drinking beer and making love rather than war (Figures 1 and 2). Western audiences are

FIGURE 1. Poster Critical of Invasion: 'Enemies of our Friendship of Nations'. Photograph Courtesy of the Institute of Contemporary History, Academy of Sciences, Czech Republic

FIGURE 2. 'NO BEER FOR OCCUPIERS'. PHOTOGRAPH COURTESY OF THE INSTITUTE OF CONTEMPORARY HISTORY, ACADEMY OF SCIENCES, CZECH REPUBLIC

familiar with this theme thanks to literary works by Bohumíl Hrabal and perhaps even more so through their numerous film adaptations. The story of the critically acclaimed film by Jiří Menzel, *Closely Observed Trains*,[6] for example, centres on a young man who struggles to overcome his inhibitions. He reaches his full maturity not merely by overcoming his fear of women, but, more importantly, through his heroic act of resistance against Nazi Germany that costs him his life.[7] The tragedy of the small Czech nation, Jan Patočka would later argue in his philosophical

[6]Jiří Menzel, *Closely Observed Trains*, Czechoslovakia, Filmové studio Barrandov, 1966. In the US the book and film were published and released with the title *Closely Watched Trains*.

[7]The popularity of this film was anticipated by the success of Hrabal's book, which appeared in 1964, at the time when the communist censorship had started to ease. Against the background of these earlier restrictions, Josef Škvorecký commented on the impact of Hrabal's work: 'perhaps it will now be somewhat clearer to the uninitiated why a story combining *ejaculatio praecox* and anti-Nazi sabotage hit the Victorianized and sex-starved Czechoslovak market like a bomb' (Škvorecký 1995, p. ix).

meditations (Patočka 1992b), is that it failed to reach that kind of maturity. In fact, the tragic hero depicted in Menzel's classic film was an isolated figure. Characteristically, the young man in Hrabal's *Closely Observed Trains* (as well as in its film adaptation) observes that only his rather strange grandfather, a professional hypnotist, resisted the Nazi occupation in 1938. Although his hypnotic powers worked for a while, halting the first tank of a long convoy, his resistance ultimately proved insufficient:

> and then the lieutenant gave a signal with his pennant, and the tank changed its mind and moved forward, but Grandfather never budged, and the tank ran over him and crushed his head, and *after that there was nothing standing in the way of the German army*. (Hrabal 1995, p. 6; cf. Auer 2004, p. 194, emphasis added)

In a similar vein, the key message of the more recent film by Menzel, *I Served the King of England*,[8] is that the Czechs are naturally predisposed towards pacifism. As the main character and narrator put it, 'we Czechs, never fight'.[9]

The rejection of violent struggle appears to be a perennial *topos* in Czech popular culture. It can be traced back to the powerful myth of peace-loving Slavs that is said to have originated with the early seventeenth century Czech protestant priest Adam Hartman (Pynsent 1999), and which was later popularised by Johann Gottfried Herder and František Palacký (Auer 2004, p. 113). The best-known nineteenth-century Czech poem 'May' by Karel Hynek Mácha, makes a similar point in the opening stanza:

Čechové jsou národ dobrý!	The Czechs are a kind people!
Nešt'astný, jenž v nouzi lká,	The wretch who sobs in need,
necht' se k Čechovi obrátí,	Let him turn to the Czech,
ten mu rychlou pomoc dá	He will swiftly give him aid;
byt' i Čecha nepřítelem,	Even if the Czech's own foe,
nešetří Čech jeho vin.	A Czech will not heed his guilt.
Čechové jsou národ dobrý,	The Czechs are a kind people,
a Ty Čechů věrný syn!	And you the Czechs' faithful son!
	(Mácha 1836)[10]

Milan Kundera successfully tapped into this tradition when he celebrated the dignified non-violent response to the Soviet-led invasion of Czechoslovakia as being of greater importance than the whole process of liberalisation that preceded it. In this way, it was the 'Prague Autumn' rather than the 'Prague Spring' that gained

[8]Jiří Menzel, *I Served the King of England*, The Czech Republic, Bioscop, 2006.

[9]The film adaptation is more explicit, if not didactic, than the original novel about both the historical background and the Czech national identity. As Menzel later commented after a screening to an American audience: 'We Czechs never fight, each time we hung our heads, we are unable to be responsible for ourself, we dislike elites, we are corrupt and without patriotism. This is sad, but it is like this' (Koch 2007).

[10]It has been argued that Mácha's poem was meant ironically, which is underscored by the character of the opening stanza that amounts, according to Pynsent, 'really to nationalistic trash' (Pynsent 2008, p. 110). As Pynsent also acknowledges, however, very few Czech patriots noticed this ironic quality.

world-historical significance. For Kundera, as he argued in his influential article, 'The Czech Fate' (Kundera 1968), the trauma of 1938/1939 was finally overcome by 1968. In that year, 'Czechs and Slovaks stood for the first time since the end of the Middle Ages once again at the very heart of world history and addressed their challenge to the world' (Kundera 1968, p. 5). Quoting from an earlier play that he authored, Kundera felt vindicated in his earlier assumptions about the Czech national spirit: 'The Czechs never mounted the barricades. Instead they were active in [the gymnastics club] Sokol. Gymnastic exercises proved more beneficial for our nation than ten revolutions' (Kundera 1968, p. 1). With their peaceful resistance to the Soviet occupation, Kundera insinuates, Czechs proved to themselves and the wider world that small is beautiful: small nations, they showed, tend to be better than the large ones. Almost by virtue of their very existence, aggressive, large nations, in Kundera's understanding, are chauvinist and egocentric, while small nations are destined to be prudent, virtuous and highly civilised. 'Oh, poor large nations!' writes Kundera condescendingly, 'the gates to humanity are narrow and you find it so hard to get through them ...'. He continues:

> I am convinced about the great historic mission for small nations in the contemporary world that is at the mercy of superpowers, which seek to mould it in its own image. Small nations, because they constantly seek and create their own character, because they struggle for their own independence, by so doing they protect the entire world against terrible pressures for uniformity. They ensure that manifold traditions and lifestyles can thrive in this world, creating a home for human distinctiveness, peculiarity and wonder. (Kundera 1968, p. 1)

Having visited Paris shortly after the invasion, where he had many interviews and conversations, Kundera surprised himself by being tremendously proud of his nation. He realised, as he put it, that 'there is no nation like us [Czechs] that would show such a degree of steadfastness, wisdom and unity' (Kundera 1968, p. 1). He went on to say:

> Yes, it is true that the Czech nation stood outside the big European conflicts in the last century, but it is also true that it managed at the same time to accomplish a gigantic achievement: to turn itself back from half-literate citizens into a European nation ... Yes, it is true that the Czech nation has not distinguished itself with the spirit of romantic heroism, but it is also true that the other side of this lack of romanticism and heroism is rational soberness, a sense of humour and a critical frame of mind, which this nation also applies to itself making it one of the least chauvinist nations of Europe. (Kundera 1968, p. 1)

Ironically, the argument about Czechs being 'one of the least chauvinist nations of Europe' is not free of chauvinism, as was noted by a number of Kundera's critics early on. Václav Havel ridiculed Kundera's hubristic vision, arguing that his analysis fits in the very same 'tradition of self-admiring revivalist, patriotic illusions from which the author seeks decisively to distance himself' (Havel 1969, pp. 20–23). Whenever Czech patriots lack courage to confront present challenges, posited Havel, they turn towards an imagined past that was presumably characterised by national unity. Whereas Kundera saw in the attempt to humanise socialism a unique Czech contribution to world history, Havel believed that the aims of the Prague Spring were far more modest. The abolition of censorship, for example, simply marked a return to normality, in which the state no longer controlled all aspects of human lives. While Kundera was convinced that the Prague Spring showed the world that 'a socialism in freedom' was possible (Kundera 1980, p. 559), Havel argued that Czechs simply tried to return to normality.[11]

In 'The Czech Fate' written in 1968, Kundera berated his Czech counterparts who left for the West and were reluctant to return home after the Soviet-led invasion of Czechoslovakia. In contrast to Havel, however, Kundera himself emigrated to France in 1975 (where he still lives). According to a Czech *Who's Who* encyclopaedia, Kundera 'is undoubtedly the most successful Czech writer, who is most widely translated and discussed in the world' (Churaň *et al.* 1988, p. 380). Yet, Czech society has an ambivalent relationship with him (as with émigré intellectuals in general) and Kundera does not enjoy as much respect in the Czech Republic as one might expect for a writer with so much popular appeal worldwide.[12]

Kundera's thinking evolved in response to his critics and changing political circumstances, but the underlying argument in his political commentaries has remained the same: the Czech predicament is determined by its precarious location in Central Europe and, just as mortality is the inescapable fact of the human condition (Kundera 1969, p. 24), there is very little that small nations can do to defy the fate allotted to them by history. Understanding this challenge, the Czechs behaved sensibly and responsibly by realising the limits imposed on them by geography and history. Instead of wasting their precious and limited resources in futile heroic gestures, they re-routed all their energy into culture. They sensed that their very survival depended on the survival of their culture. Characteristically, when the Czech people succumbed to the pressures of post-Prague Spring Normalisation and gave up on the ideals of 1968, Kundera blamed the 'totalitarian Russian civilisation' (Kundera 1984, p. 37) but not those Czechs and Slovaks who ended up supporting the policies of Normalisation: 'We were certain that the cultural traditions of the nation (its skepticism, its sense of reality, its deeply rooted incredulity) were stronger than the oriental political system imported from abroad, and that sooner or later they would overcome' (Kundera 1980, p. 558). In Kundera's view, the other culprit responsible for the plight of the small nations of Central Europe was the West, that is Western Europe. In his famous essay, 'The Tragedy of Central Europe' (Kundera 1984), he argued that Europe managed to ignore Czechs, Hungarians and Poles and their hopeless fight for liberty, because Europe no longer believed in itself. Western Europe lost its own sense of purpose. It lost itself in the kitsch of a mass consumer society.

The myth of the prudent, sceptical, peace-loving Czechs that Kundera used to such great effect is problematic for two reasons. First, it does not do justice to the

[11]For a recent lively debate inspired by this controversy see the series of articles in the 2008 volume of *Literární noviny*; in particular, see Pehe (2008, p. 7).

[12]Indicative in this respect are the results of a large project of the main Czech TV station that sought to find *The Greatest Czech* of all time (the Czech spin-off of the BBC *Greatest Britons* show). Kundera ended up as number 85, while Havel received enough votes to secure third place (behind Charles IV in first and Tomas Garrigue Masaryk in second). Available online at: http://www.ceskatelevize.cz/specialy/nejvetsicech/oprojektu_top100, accessed 1 July 2006.

complexities of Czech and Czechoslovak history, which is not free of passion and violence. For example, the famous Defenestration of Prague in 1618, which is said to have triggered the Thirty Years' War in Europe, is no less a part of Czech history than the Velvet Revolution of 1989 (Auer 2006, p. 419). Moreover, communism was not as alien to the Czech culture as Kundera would have us believe (Abrams 2004, p. 6); it had significant domestic roots and was not just a foreign import from Russia. The Czech communists enjoyed popular support already before the Second World War and they gained even more legitimacy thanks to their anti-Nazi and anti-German stance. Czechs also pride themselves on the militant tradition of the fifteenth-century Hussite movement. The second stanza of Mácha's poem celebrates this part of the Czech historic legacy:

Čechové jsou národ statný,	The Czechs are a stout people,
nepřemožen český voj.	Unvanquished is the Czech host.
Necht' se s vítězstvím rozloučí,	Let him say farewell to victory,
proti němuž český boj.	Against whom stands the Czech fight.
Čech kde stojí, krutá bitva	Where a Czech stands, cruel battle
tamt', i mnohý slavný čin.	Is there, and many a noble deed.
Čechové jsou národ statný,	The Czechs are a stout people,
a Ty Čechů věrný syn!	And you the Czechs' faithful son!
	(Mácha 1836)

Secondly, the myth of peace-loving Czechs may blind people to their own inadequacies when responding to tough historical challenges. There were moments in history, such as the Munich crisis in 1938, when the pacifist inclination of the Czechoslovak political leaders arguably represented weakness rather than moral virtue. The relative lack of resistance to the German occupation was overcompensated by the violent expulsion of ethnic Germans after the war, when fighting against the perceived former enemies (not all Germans collaborated with the Nazis) incurred virtually no risks. This is not to ignore numerous examples of individual heroism during the occupation, including a number of Czech pilots who participated in the Battle of Britain,[13] and the assassins of the *Reichsprotektor* Reinhard Heydrich in Prague in 1942. I also do not want to diminish the significance of the Prague Uprising on 5 May 1945. However, my main focus is on the philosophy of Czech history, rather than Czech history *per se*.

Jan Tesař: foolish Czechs

As the Czech historian Jan Tesař argued, the Czech preoccupation with the preservation of peace and the protection of national culture after the invasion of the Czech lands in March 1939 played into the hands of the Nazi leadership that needed the appearance of calm to consolidate its gains. This was not a uniquely Czech phenomenon. Unlike in 1914 when the nations of Europe seemed keen to fight, the

[13]Numbering 88 pilots, the Czech participation in the 'Battle of Many Nations' (Orange 2001, p. 224) was larger, proportionate to population, than the better-known Polish contingent. I am indebted to the anonymous reviewer of *Europe-Asia Studies* for this important reminder.

nationalistic illusion that took over Europe in 1938/1939 was, observed Tesař, 'the myth of peace—peace with a predator, ... peace at all costs. But it was precisely this illusion that paved the way to the most horrific war' (Tesař 1969a, p. 16). While accommodationist tendencies were a Europe-wide phenomenon, Czechs particularly distinguished themselves in turning their patriotic commitments into servitude to the occupying forces. While Czechs thought that through culture they fought for national independence, in reality they unwittingly assisted the Nazis in their own enslavement (Tesař 1969e, p. 16).

The first major public demonstration of Czech national unity *vis-à-vis* the new regime was a peculiar event: the re-burial of Karel Hynek Mácha (Tesař 1969b, p. 16) in 1939. It was peculiar because of its timing and its ambivalent political character. The re-burial took place in the month of May, the 'time of love',[14] but Mácha had died in November 103 years previously—hardly an anniversary! Even more peculiar was its political meaning. While most contemporary participants and observers viewed the re-burial as a courageous act of national mobilisation against the German occupation, the actual event was fully supported by the political leaders who openly collaborated with Nazi Germany. Among the official mourners was the 'Protectorate's titular "State president" Emil Hácha, ... who stood before Mácha's catafalque "in deep emotion" for nearly twenty minutes' (Sayer 1998, p. 25). The funeral oration was held by Msgr. Stašek who passionately declared that, 'we shall remain faithful to your work, your sweat, suffering and blood ... we shall not forget your heartfelt patriotic legacy, and will live up to it honestly and diligently' (Tesař 1969b, p. 16). While Stašek lived up to this ideal, not many of his co-patriots did.

'Faithful we shall remain' (Sayer 1998, p. 25) proved an ambiguous imperative. Faithful to whom? According to Tesař's sceptical assessment, the only aim of the post-March 1939 national programme was the bare physical survival of the nation at any price. This is why the Czech leadership of the protectorate could successfully appeal to patriotic sentiments:

> To be a patriot today requires hard work ... The true love of fatherland manifests itself through work that toughens your hands, and if necessary, you can turn night into day and can toil to the utmost limits of your muscles and your spirit. (Tesař 1969b, p. 16)

What this patriotism obscured was the simple fact that work for the Czech nation also meant work for the Third Reich. This is why the calls of Czech political leaders after March 1939 for calm and quiet work for the nation, their calls for *klid a práci* ('calm and work') (Tesař 1969c, p. 16), proved self-defeating. The Czech's determination to behave sensibly in order to secure the nation's survival ironically contributed to their demise. Tesař argues that this approach, in fact, disempowered the nation, making it easy prey for German aggression.

It is important to note that Tesař produced his critical study about 1939 in 1969, when his nation faced a similar set of challenges. Just as in 1939 the Nazis managed to

[14]Every Czech school child learns the opening lines of Mácha's *May*: '*Byl pozdní večer—první máj—večerní máj—byl lásky čas*' [It was late eve—the first in May—Eve in May—it was love's hour] (Mácha 1836).

co-opt the Czech leadership, who deluded themselves into thinking that this was the only way to ensure the survival of their nation, the Soviet leadership successfully co-opted the elites of the Prague Spring to implement their policies of Normalisation. Emil Hácha, for example, believed that he had to sacrifice his personal honour to save the nation (Tesař 1969d, p. 16).[15] Hácha was later rejected and condemned as a traitor, but it is important to bear in mind that he enjoyed significant support for his stance in 1938/1939 both from the people, as well as the pre-Munich governing elite. As Tesař commented, 'what came to light at the beginning of Nazi occupation was the obvious deficiency of the Czech democratic tradition, which led so many times before and afterwards to uncritical adulation of Czech political representation merely because it was Czech' (Tesař 1969c, p. 16).

Strikingly similar developments took place in 1968/1969. As in 1938/1939, it was assumed that the political elites would be able to rescue as much of the nation's independence as possible through 'sensible' policies of accommodation with the occupying forces. People first believed that all would be well as long as their charismatic leader, Alexander Dubček, remained in charge. Even once Dubček lost his position of General Secretary of the Communist Party, people did not lose hope; he remained influential as the leader of the Federal Assembly. As Vilém Prečan convincingly argued, Moscow's policy of Normalisation was carried out by many of those Czech and Slovak politicians who made their careers on the basis of reformist agendas; their capitulation facilitated the eventual submission of millions of ordinary citizens: 'Private capitulation by which a traumatised and demoralised people adapted externally in 1969–1971 to the rules of real, existing Socialism ("living in a lie") ... began with the narrow-minded, capitulationist policy of the "leaders" of the Prague Spring' (Prečan 2008). In a similar vein, Kieran Williams documented how Dubček's pleading for order in a memorable radio address on 27 August 1968, after his return from the Soviet Union, paved the way for the policies of Normalisation in 1969: 'We truly need order', he pleaded, since 'the sooner we succeed in normalising conditions in the country and the greater the support you give us, the sooner we shall be able to take further steps along our post-January road' (Williams 1997, p. 146). Yet, it would be too simplistic to say that the elites betrayed the trust placed in them by the people. It was rather naïve to maintain that trust after August 1968 and such behaviour was blind to the actual political developments that were taking place. It may well be argued that this deception was partly driven by the kind of national mythology that Kundera articulated (Kundera 1968). As Williams observed, his views demonstrated 'how even notorious sceptics were able to rationalize the retreats of normalization and disarm themselves intellectually: they still accepted Dubček's deal and trumpeted realism (discipline) not just as the way to continue reforms but also as a national virtue' (Williams 1997, p. 183).

It is worth noting that Tesař remained truthful to his critical attitudes towards collaboration not merely as a non-conformist scholar, but also as a courageous citizen after the suppression of the Prague Spring. In fact, Tesař's personal fate seems to suggest that under the circumstances of a repressive state, a historian with scholarly integrity must almost inevitably become a political dissident. As Zdeněk Vašíček

[15]See also Prečan (1979).

observed in a sympathetic biographic sketch, Tesař's approach to history is partly shaped by his concern with his present times and the future. According to Tesař, 'responsibility towards our nation simply forces us to work for its freedom, and we do this, as far as our intellect can take us, by searching for the deepest fundaments that we can possibly uncover' (Vašíček 2000, p. 317). In line with this, during his trial for dissident activities in the summer of 1972, he openly stated that 'the purpose of his life was to fight against the [then] existing dictatorship' (Vašíček 2000, p. 329).[16] It took more than 30 years for Tesař's essays about Czech history to be published again in his homeland (Tesař 2000), though he is still considered something of a maverick amongst professional historians (Zídek 2006).

Both Tesař's assessment of 1938/1939 and Prečan's later analysis of 1968/1969 resonate with a recent irreverent collection of essays in popular history entitled, *České průšvihy aneb prohry, krize, skandály a aféry českých dějin let 1848–1989* [*Czech Stuff-ups or Defeats, Crises, Scandals and Affairs in Czech History between 1848–1989* (Kocian *et al.* 2005)]. According to one of the editors, Jiří Pernes, the Czech people fooled themselves thrice in 1968/1969. First when they believed that socialism was compatible with liberty; and secondly when they expected that the very same Communist Party that had ruled the country with ruthless efficiency for almost 20 years could change overnight and would lead the people to a better and freer tomorrow. 'The Soviet invasion then must have appeared like a great misunderstanding' (Pernes 2005b, p. 284). Thirdly, in line with Prečan's and Williams' argument, after the invasion, Czech and Slovak people lived 'under the illusion that the ideals of the Prague Spring could be preserved as long as they remained sensible and patient (*rozumní a trpěliví*), while at the same time they were doing everything possible to prevent their realisation and serving the occupiers' (Pernes 2005b, p. 285). In a similar vein, Pernes is very critical of 'the biggest stuff-up in modern Czech history, Munich 1938' (Pernes 2005a, p. 122). His conclusion is uncompromising:

> Voluntary capitulation without an attempt of defence is the worst thing that can happen to an individual or a nation. It is worse than death, infinitely worse than suffering in a cruel fight. The decision to succumb to the pressure of four superpowers broke the back of the nation. . . . Ever since, Czechs have substituted philistine rational calculations for courage and in the end they always conclude that it is better to give in to those who are stronger. And they excuse their cowardice by a reference to their small size and weakness. (Pernes 2005a, p. 122)

Such a degree of self-criticism is unusual amongst Czech historians. Perhaps more typical for the current state of debate about the Munich trauma is the study by Jindřich Dejmek, who argues that endless debates about alternatives to the acceptance of the Munich Treaty are pointless (Dejmek 2008). The ironic twist of Dejmek's study is, however, that it appeared in a collection of essays devoted to the great 'what ifs?' in

[16]As a consequence of his defiance against the policies of Normalisation Tesař was imprisoned three times for a total of seven years. The first arrest took place in September 1969. Later on, alongside Václav Havel, Tesař became one of the initiators of the Committee for the Defence of the Unjustly Prosecuted in 1976, and of Charter 77 a year later. On his involvement in Charter 77 see, for example, Tesař (2007). After yet another imprisonment in 1979, he was given the opportunity to leave for the West and ended up emigrating to Germany and later to France.

Czech history (Rak *et al.* 2008). His argument is that there was no 'what if' in 1938, because Beneš simply had to accept the conditions imposed on the nation by the Munich Treaty. Dejmek asserts that decades of meticulous historical research have conclusively demonstrated the fallacy of various alternative scenarios, notwithstanding the fact that journalists and intellectuals, such as Jan Patočka, had continued discussing them (Dejmek 2008, p. 98). Dejmek enumerates the huge disparity of military resources that allegedly existed between Germany and Czechoslovakia (Dejmek 2008, p. 100) and relies on Beneš's original justification for inaction. We know now, Dejmek argues, that Beneš's assessment of the international isolation in which Czechoslovakia had found itself in October 1938 was accurate and that no help would have been forthcoming from either Britain or France, or from the Soviet Union (Dejmek 2008, pp. 97–98). Yet surely, any attempt at writing a 'what if' account of an event should ponder the contingencies of history. Even the changing weather can play an important role. As Katriel Ben-Arie has demonstrated in a compelling study, 'the terrifying Luftwaffe' was far less powerful than the Nazis had claimed (its operational strength being far lower than was then assumed), and its potency would have been severely reduced by bad weather. 'All in all', writes Ben-Arie,

> it seems highly probable that the German armed forces—fighting the weather as well as a superior and well-protected enemy—would have hardly dented the Czech defences. What impact would such a failure have had on the prestige of that frightening and seemingly irresistible Hitler, who had threatened to bomb Prague out of existence if Czechoslovakia dared resist him? What influence would this state of affairs have had upon peoples and leaders elsewhere—in France, in Poland, even in Britain? (Ben-Arie 1990, p. 443)

We do not need to accept Ben-Arie's bold conclusion that Czechoslovakia 'stood a fair chance of withstanding a German onslaught in September 1938, *even if she had to fight all alone*' (Ben-Arie 1990, p. 444, emphasis in the original), to argue that the twentieth century history of Europe could have taken a radically different turn at that point. The political situation in Britain in October and November 1938, for example, might have developed very differently if Neville Chamberlain was not able to deliver his (then) celebrated 'peace for our time' speech. Untouched by such considerations, Dejmek praises the foresight of President Beneš, who in his view correctly anticipated that the Czechoslovak Republic would be restored after the war thanks to 'the great democracies that would not have been able to remain silent' in response to further military aggression of Nazi Germany (Dejmek 2008, p. 108). Thanks to Beneš's diplomatic skills, according to Dejmek, the restoration of Czechoslovakia became one of the war-aims of Great Britain and its allies. What Dejmek fails to take into account is the uncomfortable fact that the post-Second World War independence of Czechoslovakia was incomplete and extremely short-lived.

Jan Patočka: cowardly Czechs

Neither Dejmek's argument about Munich, nor his criticism of Patočka, are new; and neither is exceptional. Most Czech historians, whether they are indebted to Marxist, or positivist methods, tend to be deeply suspicious of Patočka's 'heretical' writings on Czech history. This is partly based on the fundamental misunderstanding of his aims. Whenever Patočka writes about history he writes primarily about morality. In fact, human history can be said to have begun properly at that moment when people became aware of their place in the wider world, when they started questioning their own purpose individually and collectively, when they started thinking about their past and their future. The question about the meaning of history, which Patočka traces back to ancient Greece and its *polis*, is also the question about who we are as individuals and as a political community. It is the question about 'the problematic nature of the being which is free' (Patočka 2002b, p. 205):

> Thus in the historical epoch humankind does not avoid what is problematic but actually invokes it, promising itself from this an access to a more profound meaning than that which was proper to a prehistorical community. In the community, the *polis*, in life dedicated to the *polis*, in political life, humans make room for an autonomous, purely human meaningfulness, one of a mutual respect ... for all its participants and which is not restricted to the preservation of physical life but which, rather, is the source of a life that transcends itself in the memory of deed guaranteed precisely by the *polis*. It is in many ways a more risky, dangerous life than the vegetative humility on which prehistoric humanity depends. (Patočka 1996, p. 63)

Politics is constituted through ongoing attempts to overcome our own limitations. Being aware of our precarious predicament as mortal individuals does not prevent us from being free, rather it makes our freedom possible (Patočka 2002c, p. 314). We must confront the existentialist challenge head on:

> Of course, an important matter is that man always is essentially in a hopeless situation. Man is a being committed to an adventure, which, in a certain sense, cannot end well. We are a ship that necessarily will be shipwrecked. (Patočka 2002b, p. 2)

But Patočka also points out that it makes a huge difference to what extent we are aware of this predicament and how we respond to it. 'A situation is entirely different, depending on whether people who are in a situation of distress give up or do not give up. In a hopeless situation it is possible to behave in very different ways' (Patočka 2002b, p. 2).

How is all this applicable to Czech history and the Czech nation as a political community? Freedom is predicated on the idea that there are always alternatives. An individual 'can find or not find himself in the choice of his life' (Patočka 2002b, p. 205), which means that he cannot escape his freedom and his responsibility. He must always think of himself as someone who has a future, which has no other meaning but that he also has free choices about this future; he has an infinite number of opportunities regarding which course of action to follow. Something similar can be said about a national community. If it is meaningful to talk about a nation and its national history, that conversation must then be animated by the search for its meaning. Even a national community must always think of itself as having an infinite number of opportunities to pursue different courses of action. This is why it is important to consider counterfactuals in history. For historians the classic question 'what could have been, if?' is awkward, silly or meaningless. For Patočka this is the decisive question that can endow a national community with meaning and purpose.

In both crucial moments of Czech history, after the defeat in 1938 and even more so in 1968, Patočka warned against national hubris (Patočka 2006c,[17] p. 541, 2006d,[18] p. 334). Although Patočka repeatedly stressed that a nation needs to project itself into the future, he certainly did not underestimate historical legacies. In fact, he shared Kundera's concerns about the precarious historical and geographical positions of the Czech nation, but he drew a radically different lesson from it. While for Kundera, Czechs had no other opportunity but to realise themselves through their culture, for Patočka, a nation must be constituted by honourable political goals.

Patočka consistently argued that a nation should not see itself merely as a community that shares a common culture expressed through language. If anything, it was the tragedy of the Czech nation that it failed to develop a more inclusive conception of nationalism that would be open to all the people living on the territory of Czechoslovakia. Building on the legacy of the nineteenth century Bohemian philosopher and mathematician Bernard Bolzano, Patočka argued in favour of a nation that is not to be understood as a community of people sharing certain natural attributes, but rather a community that proves itself through its moral actions; 'through its fight against lawlessness' (Patočka 2006e,[19] p. 192), for example. In other words, the nation should be conceived as an ethical community that should pursue ambitious political goals. 'Language differences are no reason for the independent existence of a nation', asserted Patočka in reference to Bolzano. 'Language is the least important prerequisite of national existence' (Patočka 2006e, p. 192). This may appear as an unrealistic proposition for the Czech nation that became virtually ethnically homogenous after the Second World War but Patočka discusses what the Czech nation could have become in order to show what it can accomplish in the future.

Patočka explicitly warned against national mythologising that simply relied on some glorious past, however this past might have been conceived. In a short article entitled 'False theory of nationalism and Slovakia', written in May 1968 (Patočka 1968), that is well before the suppression of the Prague Spring, he urged his Czech compatriots to stop accusing Slovaks of nationalism and to think more critically about their own role in history:

> We tend to assume that the national problem in the Czech lands is no longer pressing after the [post-war] transfer of the German population, so that we no longer need to think about what actually constitutes the nation. Slovakia is here to remind us that this is precisely what we need to revise and that we must thoroughly address many of our lasting taboos. (Patočka 1968, p. 1)

After the onset of Normalisation Patočka once again lost his university appointment, but continued lecturing to a small group of students and colleagues in

[17] Originally published in *Kritický měsíčník*, 1, 1938, pp. 380–81.
[18] Originally published in *Nové knihy*, 44, 30 October 1968, p. 1.
[19] Originally published in *Sociologický časopis*, 5, 1969, pp. 457–72.

clandestine home seminars. This was also the context in which Patočka developed a more comprehensive philosophy of Czech history that challenged the kind of self-congratulatory and pleasing account that became characteristic of Kundera. In a series of lengthy letters written to a German friend under the heading *Was sind die Tschechen?* (What are the Czechs?), Patočka developed a rather idiosyncratic account of Czech history to explain their current predicament. Like Kundera, Patočka argued that the Czechs are a typical small nation and, like Kundera, he stressed that these terms were not quantitative, but qualitative (Patočka 1992b, p. 111). Contrary to Kundera, Patočka saw in Czech smallness the manifestation of its weakness. To put it simply, Czechs are not democrats merely by virtue of their birth; this is not something that just happens to someone because they are Czech. Greatness has to be earned through actions.

According to Patočka, Masaryk presented Czechs with this enormously daring endeavour: to fight for liberty and democracy. This was the challenge that they failed to live up to in 1938/1939 and again in 1968/1969. The tragedy of Masaryk's enterprise was that it was led further by gutless epigones, like Beneš, who destroyed his heritage (Patočka 2006a, p. 413). They presented Masaryk 'not as a question, but as a result' (Patočka 1992a, p. 307):

> They turned him into a meaningless mishmash with statements like 'Masaryk—the philosopher of democracy', 'democracy and humanity' and all these phrases that do not mean anything on their own unless they are endowed with meaning by tough decisions in real situations. (Patočka 2006b, p. 326)

This was Masaryk's challenge to the Czech nation. By creating the country in the most risky circumstances, he presented the Czech people with a challenge. Such a demanding national programme, posited Patočka, 'could not have been realised with comfortable and easy attitudes' (Patočka 2006b, p. 326).[20]

Masaryk's philosophy of Czech history was criticised for being historically inaccurate. But this, contended Patočka, is a misunderstanding. Masaryk developed his philosophy of Czech history '*ne pro praeterito, nýbrž pro futuro*' (Patočka 2006b, p. 327), that is, not so much by looking back, but rather by contemplating the challenges of the future. In a similar way, and contrary to Dejmek, no amount of new empirical evidence can 'disprove' Patočka's contention that Czechs should have defended their liberty more resolutely throughout their history. For example, any purely utilitarian calculation about the likely gains and losses that might have been incurred by Czechs in a possible military confrontation with Germany in 1938 fails to consider fully the nature of the challenge posed by the rise of Nazism. To the extent that Nazism represented the ultimate evil, even a seemingly hopeless fight against it would have been morally justified, or indeed required. The situation was different in 1968. Hardly

[20]Patočka implies, in effect, that Czechoslovakia would have fought for its independence if it had still been led by Masaryk in the autumn of 1938. This we will never know—Masaryk died in 1937. What we know is the fact that even Masaryk sought to play down Hitler's political extremism. In a compelling account of his changing views on democracy, Pynsent demonstrates that in the 1930s Masaryk himself betrayed his earlier ideals, by arguing, for example, that democracy may be compatible with dictatorship (Pynsent 2000).

anyone would argue that an open military confrontation was then the right course of action against the Soviet invasion. Yet here again, that very invasion was partly made possible and easy by Czech weakness that was misconstrued as prudence, or even strength. As Havel, who was otherwise opposed to discussing various 'what ifs' in history, suggested years later, even a tougher rhetorical stand by the Czechoslovak leadership in 1968 might have helped to preserve the achievements of 1968, or could have even prevented the invasion:

> It would have been enough to emphasise continually that we would not surrender, that we stood by our positions, that we would not allow a single foreign soldier to cross our borders. A civilian home guard could have been set up, and it might even have been possible to carry out some kind of military mobilization outside the Warsaw Pact manoeuvres calendar . . . The Kremlin leadership undertook the invasion only because it knew there would be no military resistance here. Even the ageing Brezhnev leadership would have been rational enough not to risk a new Vietnam in the middle of a Europe that was armed to the teeth. (Havel 1990, p. 103)

Readers familiar with Havel, the leader of the Velvet Revolution, might be surprised by such hawkish rhetoric. But Havel, notwithstanding his commitment to non-violent methods in his struggle against communism, was never a pacifist.[21] Likewise, Havel's teacher, the 'velvet philosopher' Patočka (Day 1999) was not as 'velvet' as many of his admirers might have liked him to be. An American philosopher of Czech origin, Erazim Kohák, for example, bemoaned Patočka's 'unfortunate terminological shift'—triggered allegedly by 'the pain and bitterness of the dashing of Czech hopes by the Soviet invasion—and the Czechs' facile accommodation to the new order' (Kohák 1989, p. 113). This is not just a question of style that can be explained away by a temporary relapse to 'the dark idiom' (Kohák 1989, p. 129). There is a strong Heideggerian dimension throughout Patočka's body of work that focuses on *polemos*, that is strife, rather than love and peace.[22] Even Patočka's concept of 'living in truth', which—thanks to Havel—became so strongly associated with the Velvet Revolution of 1989, was developed in engagement with Heidegger's philosophical heritage and the fascination with violence expressed by the likes of Ernst Jünger.[23] Patočka was not the only thinker who developed a firm commitment to freedom on the basis of existentialist philosophising that does not shy away from tough questions about the very meaning of our existence. Clearly discernable in Patočka's thinking, for example,

[21]In 'The Power of the Powerless', where Havel developed his justification of non-violent opposition to communism, he also sharply distanced himself from 'the blindness of European pacifism' that he saw as 'one of the factors that prepared the ground for the Second World War' (Havel 1991, p. 184).

[22]This is something that Kohák finds difficult to accept. As he writes: 'Might not the humble be greater than the mighty? Loving service greater than *Entschlossenheit*, Heidegger's "anticipatory resoluteness"? Though Patočka's questions evoke an echo of recognition, his answers give rise as much to dissent as to assent' (Kohák 1989, p. 135).

[23]It would be ironic if Patočka's philosophical legacy experienced a fate similar to the one he observed with regard to Masaryk's legacy. Paraphrasing Patočka, we should prevent turning him into a meaningless mishmash with statements like '*Patočka—the philosopher of the Velvet Revolution*' '*living in truth*' and all these phrases that do not mean anything on their own unless they are endowed with meaning by tough decisions in real situations (Patočka 2006b, p. 326).

is the inspiration of yet another student of Heidegger, Hannah Arendt. This is not the place to challenge the popular fallacy that Heidegger's influence undermines the democratic credentials of political philosophers (Wolin 2001), but suffice it to say that Patočka's commitment to fundamental values of liberal democracy, such as universal human rights, did not prevent him from contemplating the possibility of the ultimate sacrifice in the fight for liberty.

Conclusion

The aim of this essay has been to show competing versions of the philosophy of Czech history in relation to the momentous events of 1938/1939 and 1968/1969. I contrasted Kundera's argument that Czechs could not live up to their full greatness because of the inimical outside world (if only Russians did not exist!), with Patočka's writings, which proposed that Czechs should start by analysing their own shortcomings and weaknesses. Kundera argued that Czechs are great because they are small. They are great despite the fact that they are condemned by history. In fact, they are great because they are doomed by history, but—sensible as they are—they endure this doom with dignity. Patočka, in contrast, argued that Czechs failed to live up to their potential greatness. Having failed in the crucial moments of their history, Czechs became petty. According to Patočka, Czechs condemned themselves to insignificance because they accepted their defeats with a false sense of dignity. It may well be that Patočka demanded too much from his nation but by posing uncomfortable questions about the meaning of Czech history, he provided an important corrective to the more pleasing and complacent national narratives. To do nothing in 1938 was not the right thing to do. To focus on the preservation of calm and order in 1938/1939 and again in 1968/1969 proved counterproductive. To channel all the energies into the protection of national culture proved insufficient.

La Trobe University, Melbourne

References

Abrams, B. F. (2004) *The Struggle for the Soul of the Nation: Czech Culture and the Rise of Communism* (Lanham, MD, Rowman and Littlefield).

Arendt, H. (1965) *On Revolution* (New York, The Viking Press).

Auer, S. (2004) *Liberal Nationalism in Central Europe* (London, Routledge).

Auer, S. (2006) 'After 1989: Who are the Czechs?', *Nationalism and Ethnic Politics*, 12, 3, pp. 411–30.

Ben-Arie, K. (1990) 'Czechoslovakia at the Time of "Munich": The Military Situation', *Journal of Contemporary History*, 25, 4, pp. 431–46.

Bracke, M. (2003) 'The 1968 Czechoslovak Crisis: Reconsidering its History and Politics', *Contemporary European History*, 12, 3, pp. 373–83.

Churaň, M. *et al.* (1998) *Kdo byl kdo v našich dějinách ve 20. století* (Prague, Libri).

Chvatík, I. & Kouba, P. (eds) (2002) *Péče o duši III* (Prague, Oikoymenh).

Císařovská, B. & Prečan, V. (eds) (2007) *Charta 77: Dokumenty 1977–1989, Přílohy*, 3 Vols (Prague, Ústav pro soudobé dějiny AV ČR).

Day, B. (1999) *The Velvet Philosophers* (London, The Claridge Press).

Dejmek, J. (2008) 'Československo a jeho případná válka v roce 1938: Alternativa k přijetí velmocenské Mnichovské dohody na přelomu září a října 1938', in Rak, J. *et al.* (eds) (2008) pp. 97–108.

Findlay, E. F. (2002) *Caring for the Soul in a Postmodern Age: Politics and Phenomenology in the Thought of Jan Patočka* (Albany, State University of New York Press).

Gellner, E. (1993) 'The Forgotten Beginnings of the Czech National Revival', *Times Literary Supplement*, 3, 16 February.

Havel, V. (1969) 'Český úděl?', *Host do domu*, 15, 15.

Havel, V. (1990) *Disturbing the Peace: A Conversation with Karel Hvížďala* (New York, Knopf).

Havel, V. (1991) 'The Power of the Powerless', in Wilson, P. (ed.) (1991) *Open Letters: Selected Writings 1965–1990* (New York, Alfred A. Knopf), pp. 125–214.

Holy, L. (1996) *The Little Czech and the Great Czech Nation* (Cambridge, Cambridge University Press).

Hrabal, B. (1995) *Closely Watched Trains* (Evanston, IL, Northwestern University Press).

Jandl, P. (2006) 'Hier stehe ich, aber ich könnte auch anders: Der literarische Diplomat Jiří Gruša über Tschechien und Europa', *Neue Zürcher Zeitung*, 16 February, available at: http://www.nzz.ch/2006/02/16/fe/articleDKXFV.html, accessed 19 August 2008.

Koch, A. (2007) 'Nové české filmy nadchly New York', *Mladá fronta dnes*, 19 November.

Kocian, J., Pernes, J. & Tůma, O. (eds) (2005) *České průšvihy aneb prohry, krize, skandály a aféry českých dějin let 1848–1989* (Prague, Barrister & Principal).

Kohák, E. (1989) *Jan Patočka: Philosophy and Selected Writings* (Chicago, The University of Chicago Press).

Korbel, J. (1977) *Twentieth-Century Czechoslovakia: The Meanings of its History* (New York, Columbia University Press).

Kundera, M. (1968) 'Český úděl', *Listy*, 1, 7–8.

Kundera, M. (1969) 'Radikalismus a exhibicionismus', *Host do domu*, 15, 15, pp. 24–29.

Kundera, M. (1980) '1968: Prague, Paris and Josef Škvorecký', *World Literature Today*, 54, 4, pp. 558–60.

Kundera, M. (1984) 'The Tragedy of Central Europe', *New York Review of Books*, 31, 7, 26 April.

Lehmann, S. (2004) *Der Horizont der Freiheit: Zum Existenzdenken Jan Patočkas* (Würzburg, Königshausen & Neumann).

Mácha, K. H. (1836) *Máj*, translated by J. Naughton, available at: http://users.ox.ac.uk/~tayl0010/macha2.html, accessed 13 January 2006.

Orange, V. (2001) 'Book Review of *The Burning Blue: A New History of the Battle of Britain* by Paul Addison and Jeremy A. Crang', *The Journal of Military History*, 65, 1, pp. 223–24.

Palek, K. & Chvatík, I. (eds) (2006a) *Češi I* (Prague, Oikoymenh).

Palek, K. & Chvatík, I. (eds) (2006b) *Češi II* (Prague, Oikoymenh).

Patočka, J. (1968) 'Falešná teorie národa a Slovensko', *Literární listy*, 1, 13.

Patočka, J. (1992a) 'Die tschechische Philosophie in der Zwischenkriegszeit', in Nelen, K. (ed.) (1992) *Schriften zur tschechischen Kultur und Geschichte* (Stuttgart, Klett-Cotta), pp. 292–312.

Patočka, J. (1992b) *Was sind die Tschechen? Kleiner Tatsachenbericht und Erklärungsversuch* (Prague, Panorama).

Patočka, J. (1996) *Heretical Essays in the Philosophy of History*, translated by E. Kohák (Chicago and La Salle, Open Court).

Patočka, J. (2002a) 'Hat die Geschichte einen Sinn?', in Chvatík, I. & Kouba, P. (eds) (2002), pp. 564–86.

Patočka, J. (2002b) *Plato and Europe*, translated by P. Lom (Stanford, CA, Stanford University Press).

Patočka, J. (2002c) 'Před-dějinné úvahy', in Chvatík, I. & Kouba, P. (eds) (2002), pp. 301–17.

Patočka, J. (2006a) 'Rozvrh pojednání Co jsou Češi', in Palek, K. & Chvatík, I. (eds) (2006b), pp. 412–13.

Patočka, J. (2006b) 'Vzpomínka a zamyšlení o Rádlovi a Masarykovi', in Palek, K. & Chvatík, I. (eds) (2006b), pp. 325–38.

Patočka, J. (2006c) 'Úvaha o porážce', in Palek, K. & Chvatík, I. (eds) (2006a), pp. 540–41.

Patočka, J. (2006d) 'Náš národní program a dnešek', in Palek, K. & Chvatík, I. (eds) (2006a), pp. 334–38.

Patočka, J. (2006e) 'Filosofie českých dějin', in Palek, K. & Chvatík, I. (eds) (2006a), pp. 188–200.

Pehe, J. (2008) 'Spor o povahu demokracie', *Literární noviny*, 21 January.

Pernes, J. (2005a) 'Národní prohra aneb Mnichov 1938', in Kocian, J., Pernes, J. & Tůma, O. (eds) (2005), pp. 116–22.

Pernes, J. (2005b) 'Pražské jaro aneb s komunistickou stranou k světlým zítřkům', in Kocian, J., Pernes, J. & Tůma, O. (eds) (2005), pp. 279–86.

Prečan, V. (1979) 'Problémy českého stranického systému mezi Mnichovem 1938 a květnem 1945', in Bosl, K. (ed.) (1979) *Die erste Tschechoslowakische Republik als multinationaler Parteienstaat* (Munich, Vienna, Oldenbourg Verlag), pp. 529–52.

Prečan, V. (2008) 'Dimensions of the Czechoslovak Crisis of 1967–70', *Europe-Asia Studies*, 60, 10, pp. 1659–76.

Pynsent, R. B. (1999) 'Die Dalimil-chronik als polymythischer Text (Dalimil-Fichte-Havel)', in Behring, E., Richter, L. & Schwarz, W. F. (eds) (1999) *Geschichtliche Mythen in den Literaturen und Kulturen Ostmittel- und Südosteuropas* (Stuttgart, Steiner), pp. 199–231.

Pynsent, R. B. (2000) 'Masaryk's "Path of Democracy" or: The Democratic National Socialist Ideal', *The Masaryk Journal*, pp. 35–57.

Pynsent, R. B. (2008) 'Characterizace v Máchově Máji', in Pynsent, R. B. (ed.) (2008) *Ďáblové, ženy a národ: Výbor z úvah o české literatuře* (Prague, Karolinum), pp. 105–28.

Rak, J., Čornejová, I., Vlnas, V. *et al.* (eds) (2008) *Co kdyby to dopadlo jinak? Křižovatky českých, dějin* (Prague, Dokořán).

Sayer, D. (1998) *The Coasts of Bohemia: A Czech History* (Princeton, NJ, Princeton University Press).

Schwarzenberg, K. (2007) 'Dokument č. 6/87 (15 January 1987), Poděkování Karlu Schwarzenbergovi za poskytnutí prostoru v Scheinfeldu pro Československé dokumentační středisko nezávislé literatury', in Císařovská, B. & Prečan, V. (eds) (2007), Vol. 2, pp. 837–38.

Šimečka, M. (1990a) *Konec nehybnosti* (Prague, Lidové noviny).

Šimečka, M. (1990b) *Obnovenie poriadku* (Bratislava, Archa).

Škvorecký, J. (1995) 'Foreword', in Hrabal, B. (1995).

Sviták, I. (1990) *The Unbearable Burden of History* (Prague, Academia).

Tesař, J. (1969a) 'Vlastenci a bojovníci 1: President "Zachránce"', *Listy*, 2, 11, 20 March.

Tesař, J. (1969b) 'Vlastenci a bojovníci 3: Průvod kolem hrobů', *Listy*, 2, 13, 3 April.

Tesař, J. (1969c) 'Vlastenci a bojovníci 4: Klid a práci', *Listy*, 2, 14, 10 April.

Tesař, J. (1969d) 'Vlastenci a bojovníci 6: Realisté a "Nezodpovědní"', *Listy*, 2, 16, 24 April.

Tesař, J. (1969e) 'Vlastenci a bojovníci 8: Svědomí národa', *Listy*, 2, 18, 7 May.

Tesař, J. (2000) *Mnichovský komplex. Jeho příčiny a důsledky* (Prague, Prostor).

Tesař, J. (2007) 'Dokument p 10/4 (March 1978), Analýza, jak dále rozvíjet činnost Charty 77 a intenzivní komunikaci s veřejností, předložená k interní diskusi', in Císařovská, B. & Prečan, V. (eds) (2007), Vol. 3, pp. 248–57.

Tucker, A. (2000) *The Philosophy and Politics of Czech Dissidence from Patočka to Havel* (Pittsburgh, University of Pittsburgh Press).

Tůma, O. (2005) 'Poslední bitva pražského jara aneb srpen 1969', in Kocian, J., Pernes, J. & Tůma, O. (eds) (2005), pp. 309–24.

Vašíček, Z. (2000) 'Historik, který odmítl svědčit: Příběh Jana Tesaře', *Soudobé dějiny*, 7, 3, pp. 315–37.

Vladislav, J. (2007) 'Dokument P 4/8 (January–March 1977), Z otevřeného deníku', in Císařovská, B. & Prečan, V. (eds) (2007), Vol. 3, pp. 81–96.

Williams, K. (1997) *The Prague Spring and its Aftermath* (Cambridge, Cambridge University Press).

Wolin, R. (2001) *Heidegger's Children: Hannah Arendt, Karl Löwith, Hans Jonas, and Herbert Marcuse* (Princeton, NJ, Princeton University Press).

Zídek, P. (2006) 'Kauza Jan Tesař', *CS Magazín*, available at: http://www.cs-magazin.com/2006-12/view.php?article=articles/cs0612145.htm, accessed 1 July 2006.

New Research on February 1948 in Czechoslovakia

MARTIN MYANT

HISTORICAL RESEARCH ALWAYS REFLECTS THE PRESSURES of the period in which it is produced. It is influenced both by the availability of information and by how aspects of the past seem relevant to the present. The period since 1989 has created huge scope for a new perspective, or new perspectives, on Czechoslovakia's development in the first years after the Second World War, culminating in the communist takeover of February 1948, often referred to as 'the February events'. This essay aims to look at new contributions to the history of that period, asking how far they have led to a better understanding of the period and setting them against the political pressures of the post-1989 period. The focus is restricted to the Czech Republic, leaving aside the somewhat different process of reinterpretation in Slovakia.

The open questions

As covered in previous work (Myant 1981), the period 1945–1948 saw Czechoslovakia emerge from World War II with a coalition government. There were four Czech parties—the National Socialists (*Československá strana národně socialistická*), the People's Party (*Československá strana lidová*), Social Democrats (*Československá sociálni demokracie*) and the communists (*Komunistická strana Československa*)—and two Slovak parties, the Democratic Party (*Demokratická strana*) and the communists (*Komunistická strana Slovenska*). These six parties formed the 'National Front' (*Národní fronta*) and no parties outside that structure were allowed. They were all nominally committed to a programme of revolutionary social and economic changes; this included close alliance with the Soviet Union—the West was widely seen as having failed the country with the Munich Agreement of 1938—nationalisation of almost all of industry and the expulsion of much of the substantial German minority. Elections in 1946 confirmed the communists as the largest party, with 40% of the Czech and 30% of the Slovak votes making 38% overall, and the same coalition continued under the communist Prime Minister Klement Gottwald. President Edvard Beneš was closer to the National Socialists, but tried to stand above party politics.

Research for this essay was undertaken with the help of a small grant from the Carnegie Trust for Universities in Scotland.

From mid-1947 the coalition was gripped by increasingly deep divisions over a wide range of internal policy issues, with the communists either standing alone or backed only by the Social Democrats. Division culminated on 20 February 1948 when the ministers of the remaining three parties offered their resignations in protest at the failure by the communist Minister of the Interior to implement a government decision reversing personnel changes in the police force. The communists portrayed this as a step towards removing them from government and reversing the direction of post-1945 policies. They mobilised mass support and exploited the positions of power they held to establish an effective monopoly of power. This was achieved by nominally constitutional means. The key event was President Beneš's acceptance of a new coalition government under firm communist domination on 25 February 1948.

Controversy begins once those bare bones are filled out with explanations for events and their outcomes. Previous work can be divided by period and political perspective. In the West, where work was dominated by émigré writers, major themes included the communists' apparent dishonesty and determination to take power and whether Beneš had broken his word when he accepted the ministers' resignations. Within Czechoslovakia approaches passed through an early dogmatic phase into the beginnings of doubts about the Communist Party's policies (Belda *et al.* 1968), including speculation on how far Czechoslovakia was pursuing its 'specific' road to socialism. Historians were very active in 1968 and many suffered from the purge of the following years. This meant that in the 1970s and 1980s there was a division between 'dissident' historians, who continued to develop new ideas and address new themes, and the 'official' historians with some access to sources, but whose published work contributed little of value.

In the post-1989 period new sources became available and the atmosphere of open dialogue and free international exchange of opinions should also have created scope for posing new questions. The biggest advances have come from access to archives while the posing and answering of new questions has been patchy. The prominent 'dissident' historian Jan Křen set what he saw as the tasks for future historical research in a way that seemed free from political pressures (Křen 1990, pp. 41–42). He saw an abundance of available information, but gaps on some themes remained. These included: the expulsion of Germans; the nature and fate of conservative forces; how thinking changed and how peoples' mentalities and everyday life changed; a possible 'decline in feelings for democratic values'; and programmatic ideas for a non-communist socialism and the implications of the newly acquired mass base of the Communist Party set alongside a leadership coming from emigration in the Soviet Union. With this research agenda, Křen was directing attention away from the struggle for political power alone. He also recognised the need for access to the Soviet archives.

As the following sections demonstrate, political pressures have been important, sometimes encouraging and sometimes discouraging the posing of important questions. The political atmosphere has contributed to the new emphasis on researching the expulsion of Germans, particularly because of pressures from the changed international environment. A strong desire to condemn the communist past and to expose the 'crimes of communism', well reflected in the popular media, has focused attention on repressive aspects of the past and made it less attractive to follow the leftward movement in society and the popular base that the communists enjoyed.

The February events themselves have widely been characterised as a 'putsch', a term firmly favoured by Václav Havel when president. This again directs attention onto the use of force and repression and away from the place of the February events within a broader social transformation over the preceding years. However, this has not been the only force setting the agenda. It may have discouraged the addressing of some of Křen's questions, but professional historians were building on past research that itself raised questions requiring a more nuanced view of the period, particularly in relation to the communists' strategy. Nevertheless, gaps remain in bringing together diverse themes into a synthesis that can set the period in a wider span of Czechoslovak history.

The expulsion of Germans

The expulsion of the German minority represented an enormous change in the make-up of society and might therefore be judged as being at least as important as the communist victory. Indeed, it emerged as 'without question the most discussed theme in Czech history after 1989' (Kopeček & Kunštát 2003, p. 293). Justifications at the time included notions of collective guilt, of restoring the Czech nation to its historical territory and, more pragmatically, of creating a secure state in the face of a possible future threat from Germany which was considered a serious danger by Czechs of almost all political persuasions. Published Czechoslovak sources had given practically no information on how Germans were living or how they experienced either the forced expulsions of mid-1945 or the more organised transfers from January 1946. The first press reports of bad treatment of Germans came after concerns were expressed by British and US sources (Kaplan 1990, p. 133). More public information over the following years came from German sources and was dismissed as both exaggerated, as estimates of deaths did seem to be excessive, and as serving the political purposes of diverting attention from Nazi atrocities and discrediting post-war Czechoslovakia.

This was therefore a theme that needed to be treated with great care or, perhaps better, left alone. For many years it was not a popular question for historical study inside Czechoslovakia, where there was little desire to question the policy of expulsions, and there were few doubters concerning the general policy direction among the generation that had lived through the period. However, there were pressures for serious study among professional historians before 1989. There were uncomfortable personal memories and stories of excesses on the Czech side, and it was difficult to explain away all the injustices as reflections of the post-war atmosphere. While the National Socialists made no distinctions among Germans, the communists nominally did, but were soon advising anti-fascists to leave. In the end only 5,071 Germans and Hungarians were granted Czechoslovak citizenship in 1948 (Kaplan 1990, p. 158), a fraction of those identified as anti-fascists by the very restrictive criterion of membership of communist or social-democratic parties.

This led to questions being raised about the nationalist thinking that had emerged out of the war and occupation, which in turn led to questions concerning the moral status of the Czech nation if it could not confront possibly uncomfortable elements in its past. The result was the publication of a small amount of work by 1968 and some subsequent discussion in dissident circles. However, in view of the difficulty of consulting new sources, much of the dissident discussion was only at the stage of recognising that there were difficult questions that should be explored (Černý *et al.* 1990). There was also a pressure for reinterpretation once the post-1945 period was set within the longer span of Czech history. 'Germans' could not be simply characterised as oppressors since the two nationalities had lived and developed together for centuries, bringing the benefits of outside contacts to the Czech side. This issue of a 'partnership of conflict' was covered in a work by Křen (1989) which was published in the West before it became available to a wider Czech audience.

After 1989 the issue gained more direct political significance. The German Federal Republic became a friendly, rather than an enemy state and the voice of Germans who felt they had been wronged became a potential obstacle to diplomacy and international recognition. Havel set the scene with a comment made before he had become president, to the effect that an apology was owed to the expelled Germans. This was not a popular view and caused considerable offence to much of the generation that had lived through the occupation. Civic Forum (*Občanské forum*) argued, in a statement issued on 3 January 1990, that an apology was not the answer.

Havel returned to the theme on several subsequent occasions and his approach was echoed by some other politicians. For example, Petr Pithart (1994, p. 11) suggested that Czechs should admit their moral mistake but explain to a presumably reasonable German side that there could be no revision of property confiscations undertaken before the communist takeover. Many felt this encouraged demands from the *Sudetendeutsche Landsmannschaft*, an organisation in Bavaria representing the expelled Germans and calling for a restoration of their property. Its influence on German politics was unclear, with formal support from the Bavarian Christian Social Union (CSU) and its leader Edmond Stoiber, but this was given minimal publicity to other audiences in Germany for whom returning to the outcome of the Second World War was not a popular theme.

The persistent target of criticism was the 'Beneš decrees' which deprived Germans of Czechoslovak citizenship, confiscated their property and legalised their expulsion. The terminology here has political connotations as, in the period in 1945 before the re-establishment of a parliament, all laws were passed by decree, and subsequently ratified when formal constitutional structures had been re-established. Moreover, as works from earlier periods had made clear and as was re-emphasised in subsequent Czech accounts, the policy of expulsion had developed over the preceding years with a number of inputs. Its author was not Beneš alone and it was far from clear exactly how ideas developed in emigration would be applied on the ground. The policy was also incorporated into the Potsdam Agreement on 2 August 1945, providing formal approval from the allies.

This context inevitably politicised interpretations of the expulsion of Germans. Czech views spanned a spectrum (Kopeček & Kunštát 2003) from condemnation, based largely on moral principles, to critical support, based largely on a pragmatic view of what was most desirable in a specific period. Protagonists of the 'moral' position often implicitly saw the need to confront the pragmatic issues, highlighting anti-Nazi activity, or at least apathy, among the German population (Mandler 2002, p. 4; Mlynárik 2002, pp. 4–8). However, there is not enough evidence to support the view that the great majority of Germans would not again, after 1945 as in the 1930s, have supported the destruction of a Czechoslovak state if backed by an aggressively nationalist Germany.

However, the 'moral' position was well represented in parts of the media. In the lead-up to parliamentary elections in 2002 it provoked a very public response from a group of prominent historians who saw an attempt to revise Czech history 'in the interest of returning central Europe to before 1918' (Pravec 2002, p. 8). At a press conference on 7 May 2002 under the title 'Historians against the rape of history', Jaroslav Pánek, director of the History Institute of the Academy of Sciences, presented 15 'theses' on Czech–German relations in the twentieth century in an effort to counter the 'spontaneous historicism' of journalists and politicians and their 'manipulated accounts of history' (Pravec 2002). Their theses were also open to some challenges (Kopeček & Kunštát 2003, pp. 309–10), but this politicisation of interpretations accompanied and encouraged, rather than obstructed, a desire for deeper research and openness to alternative approaches.

From the early 1990s there was a powerful focus on reconciliation and working jointly with German colleagues, including joint meetings, joint bilingual publications and the translation of some important works, especially that of Seibt (1996).[1] Joint investigations led to a rough consensus on the numbers of deaths in some way linked to the expulsion process: the figure was estimated at between 15,000 and 30,000 (Staněk 2005, p. 327). Cooperation became a permanent feature of research on this theme, further stimulated and financed after the two governments signed a joint declaration in January 1997 in the hope of somehow drawing a line under the past.

Cooperation and mutual respect did not require formal consensus. Nevertheless, a reasonable basis was provided by Křen (2002, p. 4), joint chair of the commission of Czech and German historians. His position included a recognition that the German minority overwhelmingly backed Hitler; that the expulsions were approved by the great powers, but that fact could not be used to divert responsibility as the idea was developed and pressed from the Czechoslovak side; and that the expulsions did involve significant loss of life and that was nothing to be proud of. However, he argued, it was very difficult to see how a stable and peaceful state could have been developed while keeping the German minority. Removing the Germans, albeit in as humane a way as possible, was the best option.

Research on more specific events was already proving possible in work under preparation before 1989. It became clear that there was information on how the German population had been treated and that led to a growing body of local research, plus more serious general studies (Staněk 1991, 1996). It was, in some cases, possible to match up personal accounts from the German side with Czech archival sources. An example was the issue of the 'massacre' in Ústí nad Labem on 31 July 1945 (Kaiserová & Kaiser 1995, pp. 227–29; Staněk 1996, pp. 131–37, 2005, pp. 151–56). Reports from the German side, albeit based on second-hand rather than eyewitness accounts, referred to up to 2,000 deaths. The desire for good relations with Germany pointed to the need for an honest and thorough investigation.

The events were sparked by an explosion in an armaments store which Czech sources suggest killed 27, mostly Germans. Subsequent violence in the town led to German

[1]Originally published as *Deutschland und die Tschechen* (Munich, 1993).

deaths which Czech sources estimate at least 43 and probably approaching 100. This is based on substantial investigations after 1989, including evidence from available sources on who was missing from work, on German bodies burned in the neighbouring crematorium and on eyewitness accounts from the time, written to support an investigation that was kept secret. It remains unclear who carried out the massacre, which started well away from the explosion, but the culprits probably included incoming Revolutionary Guards, Czechoslovak and Red Army soldiers and some recent settlers. The local Czech population, itself small by the end of the war, was probably not involved and the situation was brought under control by Czech civilian authorities.

The explosion was played up by the government and media at the time as evidence of the underground Nazi organisation *Werwolf* and as confirmation of the need to expel the German population as quickly as possible. Defence Minister Ludvík Svoboda, coming to investigate on 1 August 1945, concluded that 'it is necessary for once and for all to dispose of the fifth column and we can take as our example the Soviet Union', referring to the policy towards the Volga Germans (Staněk 1996, p. 135).

Research gradually revealed more details of Czechoslovak 'excesses'. In many cases no reports were made at the time, but about 50 incidents were investigated in 1947 and early 1948 with 164 individuals under suspicion (Staněk 2005, pp. 105–06). This included one incident close to Žatec in North-West Bohemia (Staněk 2005, pp. 114–29) for which the country's political leadership accepted the need to reopen mass graves, albeit with a determination that there should be an absolute minimum of publicity that could harm the country's reputation in the West. It appeared that about 800 Germans had been killed by Czechoslovak army units, egged on by the conviction, which was in clear conflict with the government policy referred to below, that all Germans were potential enemies in a possible future war so that 'the only good German is a dead German' (Staněk 2005, p. 118).

No criminal charges were brought for this or other 'excesses'. The official line was that regrettable incidents were the result of the atmosphere of the time. A presidential decree, confirmed by a law in May 1946, ensured an amnesty for acts of resistance during the occupation, and acts of conflict in the immediate following months which would not be acceptable in peace time. Some attempts were made to reopen cases after 1990, but they had little chance of leading to convictions and were soon abandoned.

This and similar evidence raised questions about the role of the central authorities. These were partly answered by a study of the 'wild' expulsions of mid-1945 (Staněk & von Arburg 2005–2006) which showed that they received strong encouragement at the highest political levels and were organised first by the army, as the only Czechoslovak authority in predominantly German areas, and then increasingly by civilian authorities as they were established. The aim was to take advantage of a sympathetic approach from the Soviet authorities to transfer as many Germans as possible across the frontier, largely into the Soviet occupation zone. An estimated 750,000 Germans were expelled in this early period (Staněk & von Arburg 2005–2006, p. 374).

Everything was done to minimise publicity so as not to alienate the Western powers who were considered to be reluctant to support the policy of mass expulsion. Even quite important instructions were often carried by word of mouth alone (Staněk & von Arburg 2005–2006, p. 471). Evidence of a continuing danger from the German population was played up, partly to convince the Czech population and partly to impress the Western allies prior to the decision at Potsdam in August. This sets the context for the public portrayal of the Ústí nad Labem incident which was followed by a marked acceleration in the pace of expulsions. This also puts the question of 'excesses' in a slightly different context. retribution against former occupiers and collaborators was common in European countries, but here there was an additional aim of encouraging the German population to leave.

There are still open questions about the German population in the post-war Czech Republic, but the years since 1989 have seen a major change. Professional historians have started to tell a story that can be reasonably complete and acceptable to the mainstreams on both the German and Czech sides. Nevertheless, the place of this story within Czech development remains under-explored, leaving open questions about its impact on economic and social development and on political conflicts. There is an obvious view that repression in 1945 may be linked to repression from 1948 onwards, a discussion set in motion in the 1970s in émigré and dissident circles (Danubius 1990) which then inspired some of the research referred to above (Staněk 1996, p. 15). The links would be difficult to draw, partly because the kinds and methods of repression were substantially different. Another theme has been to blame Beneš for setting in motion a nationalist revolution that led to the communists' victory and a 'retarded' national consciousness, or a moral weakness that led to an acceptance of totalitarianism (Staněk 1996, p. 182). Again, the relevance of such broad abstractions remains to be demonstrated.

A more direct link to February 1948 may be found through considering the involvement of all the parties in, or at least their passive acceptance of, the policy of mass expulsions. This appeared as a common endeavour and as a popular nationalist policy. Beneš was fully involved in implicit support for the 'wild' expulsions, although it is unclear how well informed he was of conditions on the ground. He was also an enthusiastic propagator of the notion of collective guilt of the whole German population. He and others saw the Soviet Union as their natural ally and the Western powers as more reluctant friends. Even when there was evidence of 'excesses', the National Socialists backed away from exploiting the issue politically to accuse the communists of imminent totalitarianism (Staněk 2005, pp. 94–101).

Although the majority of those who came under investigation probably were communists, some were from other parties and there was no political mileage in raising issues that could harm the country's reputation in the West, or weaken any party's reputation among the Czech population. It can be added that all parties had supported the law granting amnesty for acts of resistance and post-war violence. Thus the important point is that the policies towards the German population made it very difficult to develop and propagate a clearly anti-communist and pro-Western strategy. However, it is remarkable how work on the expulsion of Germans has remained isolated from work on developments in Czech politics, highlighting the lack of an overall, synthesising framework.

Thinking, mentalities and socialist programmes

There is a continuing gap in research on mentalities and thinking, possibly an unattractive theme in the post-1989 atmosphere. Indeed, the most substantial work has come from the USA (Abrams 2004) where it has also broken with that country's traditional Cold-War interpretation of post-1945 Czechoslovak history by seeking to explain why the communists won rather than just condemning them. Abrams has examined cultural and church publications—an area somewhat removed from state control—to build up a picture of a strong shift towards the left in general (rather than towards any particular party).

A similar kind of picture emerges from looking at the fate of advocates of liberal and pro-capitalist views. For example, a study by Drápala (1999) on 'the fate of liberalism' focused on the political career of Helena Koželuhová, a journalist from the People's Party and one of the most prominent protagonists of a greater reliance on the free market. Her prospects were poor, due not just to society's shift to the left, but also to the strength of other elements from the country's past, including conservative Catholic views that had a strong influence within her own party. Similarly there was little support for the most 'pro-capitalist' vision for an economic system, proposed by Jiří Hejda, a leading National Socialist economist who had previously been director of a major engineering company. His proposal was for nationalised enterprises to become joint-stock companies with 51% state ownership. The remaining shares could be traded (with the share price providing an indicator of the firm's performance) or sold to foreign companies (some of whom had apparently expressed an interest). He made clear that he was 'obviously for a reasonable management of the economy and therefore against liberalistic laissez faire' (Hejda 1991, p. 253). Such was his conclusion from the experiences of the inter-war period. Nevertheless, specific policy proposals met a very negative response at the time and he was partially disowned by his own party.

A study by Lenka Kalinová (2004) builds up a picture of a widespread acceptance of the benefits of a substantial state role, even if its exact nature was not clear. Beneš, she demonstrates, was moving firmly in this direction before Munich, and also towards the need for alliance with the Soviet Union. These trends found a reflection in the post-war period in a development of economic and social policy thinking that reflected world, and particularly British, thinking and practices, while still based on a determination to build from Czechoslovak traditions and experience.

Thus, a specific Czechoslovak road to socialism was much more than a communist tactic. Indeed, frequent sympathy for the communist position was mixed with misgivings, for example from cultural life where disillusionment seemed to be spreading through 1947 as party rhetoric became more belligerent (Kalinová 2004, p. 95). Kalinová also argues that the communist emphasis on eliminating private property led to less emphasis on building the foundations of a modern welfare state, although that did also face various practical obstacles.

This redirection of attention towards the broader context of changes helps set the 1945–1948 period in the context of a broader sweep of history and to set the communist victory in the context of a leftward move in society's thinking. It also points to further questions about the nature of the communists' support, about possible alternative socialist strategies and about the strength of attachment to forms and institutions of democracy.

'Conservative' forces

The non-communist part of the political spectrum was diverse and divided. However, the post-1989 political atmosphere has encouraged some acceptance of the 'standard' position from post-February émigré writers. In this view, they were determined fighters against communist attempts to undermine democracy. A partially alternative interpretation, put most clearly by Kaplan, points to the failure of those opposed to the communist victory to recognise the true nature of that party's determined drive for a monopoly of power. In this view, therefore, they were rather poor defenders of democracy who could have done better. In view of the international situation, they could not have altered the broad outcome, but 'they did not need to lose quite so badly' (Kaplan 1996, p. 540). There is some flexibility in interpretations here, depending on whether the perceived mistake was a misinterpretation of communist strategy only from mid-1947 or over the preceding years as well. The former view could help better explain the general unpreparedness as the communists' potential opponents were partly taken by surprise. The latter view is harder to sustain. It lays the basis for studies that point out mistakes, missed opportunities and naïve actions (Kocian 2002), but still leaves questions about what may lie behind them.

The depth of these unanswered questions was highlighted by Eva Schmidt-Hartmann (1994), using published memoirs of non-communist politicians to demonstrate serious inconsistencies in their claims to have been charting an alternative to the communists' positions. The public face of these politicians was to accept the direction the country was following both internally and in foreign policy. Above all, they accepted the alliance with the Soviet Union as the foundation for foreign policy, and post-war internal changes as the foundation of the new Czechoslovakia. Their failure to mobilise any significant public support in 1948 was, therefore, not due to mistakes at the time, but had deeper roots.

The relationship with the Soviet Union was central to Beneš's position. It derived in part from scepticism about the reliability of the West, based on experiences in the inter-war period, over Munich, and in diplomatic activities during the Second World War and in the post-war period. As chronicled by Kaplan (1990), Czechoslovakia had disputes with all its neighbours, even including hopes of gaining significant territory from Germany, and the Soviet Union was the most important potential benefactor. The experience of the expulsion of the German minority pointed in the same direction. Scepticism towards the Soviet Union was tempered by the need for a strong ally against Germany, by hopes that Stalin would continue to want good relations with the West, and by an assumption that there would be a trend in that country towards greater democracy. The experience of the Second World War, it could be hoped, would encourage the Soviet Union to favour strong and friendly neighbours, with a democratic Czechoslovakia an attractive candidate.

At least part of this was accepted across most of the political spectrum. It remains an open question whether, with the new state consolidated and its borders decided, the resigning ministers saw the Soviet Union as less essential and saw scope for a more exclusively pro-Western orientation. This could have marked a fundamental difference from Beneš's view. There is so far no evidence of any serious rethinking along those lines. However, this kind of issue and the difficulties in confronting the central issues of the country's post-war development, rather than in individual mistakes, is likely to provide the key to understanding the failure of the right of the post-war Czech political spectrum. They had a conception of defending democracy, but that was not enough when they were appearing reluctant on other issues that appeared important to much of the population (Myant 1981, Chapter 5).

Communist strategy and aims

Křen's list of themes that are yet to be pursued in detail did not emphasise communist strategy and tactics inside Czechoslovakia. This was well-researched before 1989 and set at the centre of studies of that period. However, much new information has come from work by Karel Kaplan, a historian with a long pedigree, who emigrated to Germany in 1976 and returned to the Czech Republic after 1989. He has been cautious about joining in polemics with other historians and developing new frameworks or posing those questions that might set the period in a different context. Rather, his contribution has been to pursue as exhaustively as possible the established themes of how political forces viewed each other, set their strategies and related to organs of power (Kaplan 1996).

He argues that, up to mid-1947, the coalition worked reasonably well. It required concessions from all sides, but seemed to function. The big break came with the changed Soviet view of the world: they feared loss of influence in Eastern Europe and responded by consolidating their bloc. This is consistent with the limited information available on reports that were received by the Soviet authorities. The latter seemed broadly satisfied, albeit with concerns that the Soviet message was not being put effectively enough to the public (Marjinová 1997). There is nothing to conflict with Soviet hopes of a friendly Czechoslovakia based on its existing political structures, but nor is there evidence of a rejection of the alternative, of a communist monopoly of power which, in the Soviet view, was obviously the ideal political form. The Soviet side may simply have kept options open. However, by 1947 they were worrying that the communists would be forced out of the government, as in France and Italy, and the country would become an ally of the West. The emphasis shifted to concern over whether or not the Czechoslovak communists were taking an unnecessary risk by trusting in parliamentary elections and whether they should be consolidating positions of power in the state apparatus and armed forces.

The communist response points to some differences and doubts within the Party leadership. Gottwald had won considerable respect from politicians of other parties as a man who behaved correctly in both personal and political relations and seemed to accept compromises when he had to. However, he and others in the Communist Party clearly were convinced of a danger from the West. Moreover, they would never really challenge Soviet policy, nor voice any doubts publicly. In September 1947 the Soviet leadership initiated the Informbureau of nine communist parties, a body that incorporated the key parties from Eastern Europe plus the Italian and French parties and was used as an agency for consolidating the Soviet bloc. It served as a platform for criticising first the French and Italian parties and subsequently the Yugoslav party. Gottwald was not enthusiastic when this new body emerged and felt under attack for alleged 'parliamentary illusions' (Kaplan 1996, pp. 197–98), but he accepted some of the language required by the Soviet leadership about 'class enemies', 'bourgeois' politicians and 'imperialists' which created a clear tension in relation to internal coalition politics. He was always cautious of setting Beneš up as an enemy and although the Soviets regarded him as 'pro-Western' it remains unclear exactly what Gottwald really thought.

He still seems to have seen the elections, due in May 1948, as the decisive battleground. The aim of winning 51% of the votes had been set in general terms in January 1947 but in the new international situation, this became even more urgent. However, Gottwald was not panicked when the radical Minister of Agriculture Julius Ďuriš warned that 51% was not assured and that mass action should be organised to decide the election result 'before the elections' (Kaplan 1996, pp. 325–26). Gottwald seemed confident that the parliamentary arithmetic would work out, even without a 51% majority, and saw no way to make the result certain before the elections.

Gottwald saw the key to success in transformations within the coalition parties. The communists had close allies, and in some cases informers, throughout other parties who provided them with information and helped to influence those parties' policies. These were now encouraged to create organised groups that would either gain control of their parties or join a communist-backed election list. Approaches were also made to prominent non-Party figures, such as the Foreign Minister Jan Masaryk, who had ambitions to become president, but he was more likely to join a Social Democrat list.

The Gottwald strategy contained two further elements. The first was a mobilisation of public opinion around demands for further nationalisations, approval of the new social security system and further agricultural land reform. These came to a head in the congresses of works councils and of farmers' representatives that took place during the February events. When the congresses were originally planned it was still unclear exactly how they would influence the question of power. Ďuriš's radical alternative went beyond Gottwald's to foresee mass mobilisation leading to the establishment of 'dual power' (Kaplan 1996, pp. 345–46), albeit still without precise specification of the next stage.

The second element was a strengthening of the communist position in the police force, with Party members forming over 50% of uniformed police (or so they told the Soviet leaders) and the dominance of a special, well-armed unit that patrolled the frontier. It was not clear how this would contribute to the communists' victory, but plans took shape for a police presence at all election meetings with the potential to take legal action against those making statements judged to be 'anti-state' (Hanzlík 1997, pp. 210–13). They could, however, make little progress in the army. They reassured the Soviet leaders that one third of the generals were with them, but these were mostly specialists rather than commanders.

There was also a more radical desire in the police and security forces to settle matters quickly with a putsch. Indeed, there were a number of provocations (finding alleged links between spies and leading politicians) that seem to have originated within the security services. There is no evidence of prompting from the domestic Party leadership or from Soviet agents, but the communist press took these cases seriously and gave them full publicity. Communists in government defended the integrity of the police and security forces, exasperating their coalition partners. There is no evidence on whether they felt at all embarrassed, or whether they genuinely welcomed such activities, but there is good reason to believe that the Party leadership was not in control. Potentially the most dangerous case was an assassination attempt in September 1947 on three ministers, including Masaryk, which was investigated at the time thanks to the strong National Socialist position in the criminal police (rather than the security police). There was probably involvement from former communist partisans and security personnel. Investigations continued after February 1948, with the last attempt in 1957, suggesting that the authorities may genuinely not have known who was behind the attempt. It can be added that investigations also failed to confirm communist propaganda that it was a provocation by their political opponents.

Thus it is difficult to speak of a single communist strategy in late 1947 and early 1948. There were distinct, but overlapping, conceptions of the exact aim and of how to achieve it. One approach focused on elections, but increasingly sought means to influence their outcome, at least to ensure communist dominance. Others sought to use some of the same means to transform the power structure without regard to elections and that meant more decisively eliminating other political forces from any chance of sharing power. All approaches from the communist side, and particularly the most radical, served to frighten other parties and hence to isolate the communists in government, without actually making victory more certain or the road to victory any clearer. All of that changed on 20 February when the ministers of three coalition parties (the Czech National Socialist and People's Parties and the Democratic Party from Slovakia) resigned, leaving the majority of the government, made up of communists, Social Democrats and non-Party ministers, in post.

The February events

'New' evidence on the February events has come from Kaplan and others who have carefully sifted through Czechoslovak archival sources, and from some important hints on Soviet thinking during the February events and over the preceding years. However, there are still large gaps in our information on the thinking and interpretations of people involved, or not involved, at the time and even on the thinking of the key actors. There is also scope for different interpretations depending on how February is seen to fit with the developments of the immediately preceding years.

All evidence on the thinking behind the resignations of the ministers of three coalition parties confirms a lack of preparation and that the decision was taken by a very narrow circle: it was a surprise to their own parties and to their own MPs (Kaplan 1996). The balance of evidence supports the view that Beneš was not consulted in advance and Masaryk was furious at the 'culpable naivety' of 'the fools, idiots' (Kaplan 1996, p. 445); he saw their hope of some kind of help from the USA as ludicrously unrealistic (Kaplan 1996, p. 523). Remarkably, there had been some discussions with the US ambassador, Laurence Steinhardt, who was pleased that the ministers were taking a firm stand, expecting it to raise Czechoslovakia's prestige in the USA (Kaplan 1996, p. 352). He was confident they would win, as he thought the Soviet side would give priority to good relations with the West, and would therefore put pressure on Gottwald to calm down. Happy to believe implausible claims of a substantial decline in communist support,[2] he looked forward to Czechoslovakia leaving the Soviet sphere of influence.

The key Soviet influence came from Deputy Foreign Minister Zorin who arrived in Prague as the crisis broke. Somewhat thin evidence had been used to support the view that he came threatening an armed intervention to resolve the crisis. Alternative evidence suggests Gottwald may have asked for at least some Soviet troop movements to frighten the opposition, which Zorin flatly rejected, telling Gottwald to 'be harder' and use his internal strength while reporting back that Gottwald was trying 'to avoid any sort of tough measures in the fight against reaction' and was 'in the grip of parliamentary illusions' (Murašková 1997, 1998; Šiška 1998a, p. 10, 1998b, p. 10).

This theme provoked some heated debate (Gibianskij 1998, 1999; Kaplan 1998) perhaps partly because it could be seen shifting the focus from Soviet pressure onto internal Czechoslovak responsibility for the outcome of February. The question of possible Soviet military intentions remains unclear. Zorin has not been shown to have ruled it out in any eventuality, and Gottwald felt able to warn Beneš that there is always the Soviet Union. The exact impact of Zorin's visit on events therefore remains unclear, but he probably pushed Gottwald away from emphasising constitutional means and more towards a 'putsch'. The details were decided on the ground.

Gottwald was initially surprised by the resignations and took a few hours to gather his thoughts. He then formulated the response of insisting that Beneš should accept the resignations, replace the resigning ministers with ones Gottwald was proposing and resist calls for early elections; this was a solution in line with the constitution (Kaplan 1996, pp. 323 and 347). It also proved massively popular with a large part of the public (Myant 1981, Chapter 9), as indicated by demonstrations, a near unanimous vote in favour of the communists' position at the Congress of Works Councils, near unanimous participation in a token general strike and telegrammes and resolutions to Beneš with 5,237 supporting the communists' position against 150 for the other side.

Repressive measures were not particularly important at first, but strengthened after the Congress of Works Councils with arrests of several hundred political opponents over the following days. The reason for the shift is unclear. There may have been a freelance element, but it was backed from above, as indicated by an insistence that ministers and MPs were not to be arrested (Kaplan 1996, p. 404). Indeed, a secret list of arrests was drawn up, suggesting some preparation for a real 'putsch', but it was not implemented. It is conceivable that the leadership took seriously state security claims to have found evidence of a planned putsch by the National Socialists. It is also possible that greater repression seemed necessary to bring the crisis to an end, possibly as pressed for by Zorin and reflected in a strong line taken by *Pravda* on the same day, intended as a call to Gottwald to get on with the job. Demonstrations of public

[2]The National Socialist leaders appeared convinced that the communists would suffer a substantial drop in votes in the forthcoming parliamentary elections. This may be the source of a claim that an opinion poll actually showed a likely drop in communist support of about 10% since the 1946 parliamentary elections. In fact, a poll was undertaken in January 1948, but the returns were not counted and reported until later in 1968. They suggested only small changes from 1946. Estimates based on changing party memberships, with all of them recording growth, similarly pointed to little substantial change from the 1946 election outcome (Myant 1981, p. 192; Abrams 2004, pp. 188–89).

opinion need not have brought any conclusion if the president simply sat tight and refused to appoint new ministers to the vacant posts, as the National Socialists hoped.

The communist tactics continued to suggest that they were combining two different approaches. Gottwald wanted a constitutional solution, but this was not his only option. He was able to avoid a full-scale putsch, with mass arrests and internment of opponents, but he reached 'the boundaries of a putsch' (Kaplan 1996, p. 487). However, arrests to ensure the paralysis of potential political opponents clearly crossed the boundaries of a constitutional process.

There was early reluctance to 'arm the workers', despite pressure from the Party's 'radicals' (Kaplan 1996, p. 365). The creation of the Peoples' Militia was only approved later in the crisis as a small and inadequately armed force, unable to get help from the army and in some cases even parading without arms (Kaplan 1996, pp. 445–46). Its main practical contribution seems to have been an attempt to ensure, by brute force, victory for pro-communist elements within the Social Democrat Party. In this it failed. Indeed, it remains unclear whether repression contributed to Beneš's decision to accept the resignations and to other ministers' decisions to remain in the government. (The possible negative impact on Masaryk is discussed below.)

However, repression did set the change in the nature of power. Having once silenced the opposition, it was unthinkable to return to the old form of coalition or to allow genuinely contested elections with no certainty over their outcome, although that was even given passing consideration after February. Thus, although a monopoly of power may not have been the sole and clear aim of the Party in the immediately preceding years, the communists' ideological position meant that they had no reservations about imposing their dictatorship when the opportunity presented itself. Indeed, a firm line was probably a requirement for impressing the Soviet leadership. It seems to have been some months after February 1948 before Gottwald felt reassured that he was in the Soviet leadership's good books again. An initial Soviet report on the Czechoslovak communists' 'mistakes' criticised practically the whole post-war approach (Marjinová 1997, p. 467). Stalin passed on praise in September 1948, for the first time (Kaplan 1996, p. 521).

Jan Masaryk

A discussion of new work on the February events cannot be complete without a consideration of the death of Jan Masaryk, the theme that has attracted probably the greatest volume of media attention, alongside remarkably little concern from professional historians. Masaryk did not join in the resignations and was set to continue in the post-February government when his body was found in the courtyard under his flat on 10 March 1948, only hours before the new government was to be presented to parliament.

The investigation was almost immediately taken over by the security police who were untrained in criminal investigation—and therefore perhaps unaware of the importance of checking the position and state of the body, or whether anyone else had been in the flat at the time—and reached a speedy verdict of suicide. This was announced in parliament even before a medical examination of the body, although the report from that examination subsequently gave no grounds for doubting the original verdict. Those closest to Masaryk gave, and continued to give, further circumstantial evidence supporting the view of suicide. His personal secretary helpfully accumulated and provided negative comments on the range of alternative explanations (Sum 2003). Stories were nevertheless soon circulating suggesting murder and even naming the culprits. This was an attractive verdict, particularly in the USA, with unequivocal condemnation for anyone who would question it (Ulč 1982, p. 818).

The case was reopened in 1968 and, before its suspension in mid-1969, a substantial investigation had looked at a wide range of possibilities, concluding that 'no significant fact has so far emerged that provided evidence for murder' (Kettner & Jedlička 1990, p. 182). That book, giving details from the investigation, was ready for publication in 1970, but the authorities preferred to destroy the copies.

The case was reopened again in 1993 by the *Úřad dokumentace a vyšetřování zločinů komunismu* (Office for the Documentation and Investigation of the Crimes of Communism) and considerable efforts were expended to find new evidence. That investigation ended in 1995 without a clear result and with doubts over whether new evidence was reliable. The case was further reopened in 2002 and new evidence was provided by an expert witness who had studied photographs of the position of the body when it was found. This allegedly proved that Masaryk must have been pushed.[3] This appeared very difficult to prove, not least because the body may have been moved at any point (Šiška 2004, p. 19). Nevertheless, the investigators this time concluded in December 2003 that the evidence justified the conclusion that Masaryk had been murdered. The state prosecutor in Prague concurred with this conclusion, but without further elaboration and indicated that there was no prospect of any prosecutions.

Indeed, no serious progress was reported in identifying suspects. The favoured chief suspect in this, as in several previous accounts, was Augustin Schramm, a man assassinated in May 1948 (Boháč 2004). In fact, evidence linking Schramm to Masaryk's death had always been thin. His name first appeared in a report in West Germany in 1965, built around the claim that Schramm had been assassinated by agents sent from the West who knew that he had murdered Masaryk. However, the most complete account of his role, based on the investigations in 1968, found very little to associate him with Masaryk's death while a number of testimonies ruled out such a link. The case against him seemed to be based largely on supposition, invention and inaccurate information. Schramm had had the job of verifying claims by individuals of participation in partisan groups during the wartime resistance and that could have created enemies keen to see him dead (Kettner & Jedlička 1990, pp. 143–54).

The point about Jan Masaryk's death is that it can crystallise a whole number of judgements. It is a substitute for a more substantial historical investigation and discussion. The alternatives of suicide or murder, presumably involving the Czechoslovak or Soviet security police, have substantial implications for interpretations of the early post-war years. Suicide suggests that Masaryk felt depressed by events, powerless and maybe ashamed of staying on in the government. It suggests failure and that he was no threat to anyone. The communists could have wanted him to stay in office as a cover while they consolidated power. This would be consistent

[3] 'ÚDV: Jan Masaryk byl zavražděn', *Hospodářské noviny*, 14 March 2002.

with his behaviour and statements during February 1948. He indicated both privately and publicly that he was 'going with the people' when he joined the general strike and agreed to participate in Gottwald's post-February government (Kaplan 1996, p. 507). At the same time, he could not betray 'the name and ideals of his father, or even himself' (Sum 1996, p. 6) which the repressive measures used against the communists' opponents would have implied.

Murder changes his standing completely, obscuring from view his positions before, during and after February 1948. It also fits with a more negative view of the communist period as a whole, supporting condemnations of brutality from start to finish and providing a narrative for the following years that begins with a symbolic tragedy. However, a serious view would reject the Czechoslovak communist leadership as likely culprits. They could only be enthusiastic about his role in the preceding days and could well have been as stunned as they claimed over his death. It is also reasonable to assume that any written evidence in Czechoslovak sources would by now have come to light. However, the Soviet leadership could have had a motive, not least as Masaryk would have been a character with minimal appeal to Stalin (Boháč 2004; Sum 2003, p. 262). It can be reiterated that the assassination attempt of autumn 1947 remains to be explained. There is, then, scope for seeking further information here, but a role for Soviet agents would not be decisive for overall interpretations of the period. Indeed, Masaryk's death has been largely ignored in the substantial works of professional historians, attracting attention only in the light of wider media coverage.

Conclusion

New information on February 1948 and on the preceding years has helped to answer some previously unanswered questions. However, new knowledge also serves to highlight the continuing blank spaces. Three interrelated themes can be mentioned.

The first concerns the issue of public attitudes and perceptions. There clearly was a substantial move to the left in popular thinking and this set a context for all parties' activities. There is a serious gap in the kinds of personal memoirs that would show how this affected behaviour. It remains remarkable that during the February events public support for the communists' position was so strong and opposition so weak. This presumably did not represent support for a monopoly of power for one party. The point was that the communists were able to appear as representatives of a dominant trend in society. This theme remains under-researched and somewhat sidelined by a focus on issues of pure political power alone.

The second concerns the failure of the political parties that suffered defeat. The resignations in February 1948 were a mistake that proved catastrophic, but it is unclear how far that was a one-off mistake and how far it reflected deeper problems in those politicians' more general failure to understand how the thinking of much of the Czechoslovak population had been shaped by the preceding years, making it extremely difficult to develop a convincing alternative. There are also gaps in our knowledge of how potential supporters viewed the situation. The failure of leadership, with some resigning ministers heading off to holiday homes and recreational activities rather than behaving as if they wanted public support, could not have helped. It still remains remarkable that active opposition to the communists' position was so weak, leaving open questions about the thinking that led to immobility of that large part of the population that did not welcome the communist victory.

The third concerns the communists' approach and the contradiction between the steps Gottwald took to follow a constitutional road alongside the extent of repressive means used to establish a monopoly of power. Gottwald has received an understandably negative press in recent years, but even an unflattering account of his life leaves open questions (Pernes 2003). It can be added that he, and a number of close colleagues, behaved in the period 1945–1948 as if he rather liked cooperation with other parties. It provided a framework for political stability and for the post-war revolutionary changes. It was something he was good at, as a man who communicated well, could earn trust and liked getting on with a job in hand. He was not a natural demagogue, still less a theoretician, and nor were many of those around him. Despite some rhetoric from an earlier period, he did not necessarily relish revolutionary politics as traditionally understood.[4]

Křen's question about the nature of the mass party may also be relevant. The mass of new members and supporters, all of those who gave unequivocal backing during the February events, were not committed Marxist–Leninists who might see an armed uprising as a necessary step to break with a capitalist past, although that was the view of a minority. Not enough is known about their thinking, but a possible indication could come from the memoirs of one young official at the time whose background was in a combination of nationalist and socialist thinking and an admiration for T.G. Masaryk. He remembers a significant lack of enthusiasm over clearly repressive measures (Císař 2005, p. 249). A 'radical' solution, breaking ties with Beneš and the symbols of the country's past, would have risked narrowing the Party's base.

To this could be added possible fears over the international situation. Gottwald apparently asked Zorin about the credibility of rumours of possible US armed intervention and was told they could be dismissed. However, a breakdown of order, some doubts within the Party's own ranks and the continuing uncertainty over the army could have been a prospect Gottwald feared. These would have been tactical considerations. He never indicated any awareness of the dangers of a one-party state and even occasionally speculated that parties would voluntarily merge to produce just one. Moreover, despite cases in the 1930s of reluctance in the face of Comintern policies, he never expressed any sort of public opposition to Soviet policies. To have done so would have been unthinkable for him personally and for his position within

[4]In his maiden speech to parliament on 21 December 1929, Gottwald responded to the claim that he was taking orders from Moscow with the words: 'we go to Moscow to learn from the Russian Bolsheviks how to wring your necks' (available at the Czech parliament's website: http://www.psp.cz/eknih/1929ns/ps/stenprot/007schuz/s007003.htm, accessed 10 August 2008). This has very frequently been used as an indication of his political philosophy. It should be treated more cautiously. The phrase appeared in the context of Gottwald responding to interruptions from his parliamentary critics and the report of the parliamentary session indicates that the flamboyant language, in this and other parts of his speech, was met with laughter from some MPs. It is an indication that Gottwald, newly elected to the position of Party leader at the age of 33 following Comintern backing, was capable of reproducing the belligerent rhetoric of the Comintern in that period. It had little to do with the actual activities of the Party at the time and should not, in the absence of other evidence, be taken as proof of enthusiasm for the use of violence. Indeed, it is out of line with Gottwald's normally rather dull style in speeches and articles from both earlier and later years.

the Party. This ultimately overruled any concerns that he may have had over the possible benefits of a purely constitutional road.

Thus there are points of detail still to be resolved. Some may never be resolved. They are important for setting 1948, and the subsequent communist period, into a longer time-span of Czech and Czechoslovak history. So far, Czech historiography has not produced such a synthesis. It would need to provide an explanation for the communist victory in 1948, including its popularity and the weakness of opposition, set against the background of the experiences of the preceding years. It should also set the scene for the nature of the ruling party in the following years, including the two diverse communist traditions as displayed in the loyalty of the Stalin period and normalisation—and even in the continuing strength of a Communist Party after 1989—and in the reform communism of 1968. Both need to be related to the kind of party, and society's approach to socialist ideas, that was shaped in part by the 1945–1948 period.

University of the West of Scotland, Paisley

References

Abrams, B. (2004) *The Struggle for the Soul of the Nation: Czech Culture and the Rise of Communism* (Lanham, MD, Rowman & Littlefield Publishers, Inc).

Belda, J., Bouček, M., Deyl, Z. & Klimeš, M. (1968) *Na rozhraní dvou epoch* (Prague, Svoboda).

Boháč, L. (2004) 'Jan Masaryk a podceněné vyšetřování', *Listy*, 2.

Černý, B., Křen, J., Kural, V. & Otáhal, M. (eds) (1990) *Češi Němci odsun* (Prague, Academia).

Císař, Č. (2005) *Paměti. Nejen o zákulisí Pražského jara* (Prague, SinCon).

Danubius (Ján Mlynárik) (1990) 'Tézy o vysídlení československých Nemcov', in Černý, B., *et al.* (eds) (1990), pp. 55–90.

Drápala, M. (1999) 'Zavržení liberalismu v Čechach a Helena Koželuhová: K ideologickému profilu poválečné republiky (1945–1948)', *Soudobé dějiny*, 6, pp. 7–44.

Gibianskij, L. (1998) 'Otevřené otázky zůstávají', *Soudobé dějiny*, 5, pp. 318–19.

Gibianskij, L. (1999) 'Dokumenty k Zorinově pražské misi v únoru 1948', *Soudobé dějiny*, 6, pp. 534–44.

Hanzlík, F. (1997) *Únor 1948—výsledek nerovného zápasu* (Prague, Prewon).

Hejda, J. (1991) *Žil jsem zbytečně. Román mého života* (Prague, Melantrich).

Kaiserová, K. & Kaiser, V. (1995) *Dějiny města Ústí nad Labem* (Ústí nad Labem, Město Ústí nad Labem).

Kalinová, L. (2004) *Východiska, očekávání a realita poválečné doby. K dějinám české společnosti v letech 1945–1948* (Prague, Ústav pro soudobé dějiny Akademie věd České republiky).

Kaplan, K. (1990) *Pravda o Československu 1945–1948* (Prague, Panorama).

Kaplan, K. (1996) *Pět kapitol o Únoru* (Brno, Doplněk).

Kaplan, K. (1998) 'Dosavadní a nové poznatky: Předběžné závěry', *Soudobé dějiny*, 5, pp. 319–20.

Kettner, P. & Jedlička, I. (1990) *Proč zemřel Jan Masaryk?* (Prague, Horizont).

Kocian, J. (2002) *Československá strana národně socialistická v letech 1945–1948* (Brno, Doplněk).

Kopeček, M. & Kunštát, M. (2003) '"Sudetoněmecká otázka" v české akademické debatě po roce 1989', *Soudobé dějiny*, 10, pp. 293–318.

Křen, J. (1989) *Konfliktní společenství. Češi a Němci 1780–1918* (Toronto, Sixty-Eight Publisher).

Křen, J. (1990) *Bílá místa v našich dějinách* (Prague, Lidové noviny).

Křen, J. (2002) 'V takové nouzi, abychom museli bouchat pěstí do stolu, určitě nejsme', *Právo*, 13 April.

Mandler, E. (2002) 'Češi a Němci po druhé světové válce mohli žít společně', *Hospodářské noviny*, 9 May.

Marjinová, V. (1997) 'Od důvěry k podezíravosti. Sovětští a českoslovenští komunisté v letech 1945–48', *Soudobé dějiny*, 4, pp. 451–67.

Mlynárik, J. (2002) 'Vítězové se mstili metodou poražených', *Hospodářské noviny víkend*, 9 May.

Murašková, G. (1997) 'Únorová politická krize roku 1948 v Československu a sovětský factor. Z materiálů sovětských archivů', *Soudobé dějiny*, 4, pp. 468–78.

Murašková, G. (1998) 'Únorová krize roku 1948 v Československu a sovětské politické vedení', *Soudobé dějiny*, 5, pp. 314–17.

Myant, M. (1981) *Socialism and Democracy in Czechoslovakia, 1945–1948* (Cambridge, Cambridge University Press).

Pernes, J. (2003) *Takoví nám vládli Komunističtí prezidenti Československa a doba, v níž žili* (Prague, Nakladatelství Brána).

Pithart, P. (1994) 'Logika, která neplatí, a pravda, které neutečeme', *Hospodářské noviny*, 17 June.

Pravec, J. (2002) 'Historici odmítají překrucování dějin', *Hospodářské noviny*, 9 May.

Schmidt-Hartmann, E. (1994) 'Demokraten in der Sackgasse: Das Bild der kommunistischen Machtübernahme in den Memoiren besiegter tschechischer Politiker', in Schmidt-Hartmann, E. (ed.) (1994) *Kommunismus und Osteuropa: Konzepte, Perspektiven und Interpretationen im Wandel* (Munich, R. Oldenburg Verlag), pp. 203–20.

Seibt, F. (1996) *Německo a Češi: Dějiny jednoho sousedství uprostřed Evropy* (Prague, Academia).

Šiška, M. (1998a) 'Únor měl předurčeného vítěze', *Právo*, 21 February.

Šiška, M. (1998b) 'Zorinova mise v únoru', *Právo*, 28 February.

Šiška, M. (2004) 'Nekonečný příběh o smrti Jana Masaryka', *Právo*, 6 March.

Staněk, T. (1991) *Odsun Němců z Československa 1945–1947* (Prague, Naše vojsko).

Staněk, T. (1996) *Perzekuce 1945* (Prague, Institut pro středoevropskou kulturu a politiku).

Staněk, T. (2005) *Poválečné 'excesy' v českých zemích v roce 1945 a jejich vyšetřování* (Prague, Ústav pro soudobé dějiny Akademie věd České republiky).

Staněk, T. & von Arburg, A. (2005–2006) 'Organizované divoké odsuny? Úloha ústředních státních orgánů při provádění "evakuace" německého obyvatelstva (květen až září 1945)', published in 3 parts in *Soudobé dějiny*, 12, pp. 465–533; 13, pp. 13–49; pp. 321–76.

Sum, A. (1996) *Osudové kroky Jana Masaryka: Výběr dokumentů ke 110. výročí narozeniny Jana Masaryka* (Prague, Sekce archivní správy MV).

Sum, A. (ed.) (2003) *Otec a syn II. svazek syn Jan* (Prague, Pragma).

Ulč, O. (1982) 'Review of Myant', *American Historical Review*, 87, pp. 817–18.

The Scheming *Apparatchik* of the Prague Spring

MARY HEIMANN

IN THE LAST WEEK OF AUGUST 1968, AS UNFOLDING FOOTAGE of the Soviet and Warsaw Pact invasion of Czechoslovakia was being shown to an astonished world, the reputation of the country's leader, Alexander Dubček, began to be fixed in collective political memory. *The Times*, like most other Western newspapers, presented the First Secretary of the Czechoslovak Communist Party (*Komunistická strana Československa* (KSČ)) as a gentle, decent man; a leader as devoted to his countrymen as they so manifestly were to him. True, Dubček had at first been hesitant to embrace radical reform; but, once persuaded of the need to liberalise and democratise the communist system, he had become one of 'liberal' or 'progressive' socialism's staunchest and most enthusiastic supporters.[1]

The first book-length political analysis of the Prague Spring to appear in print, Pavel Tigrid's *Why Dubček Fell*,[2] sharply distinguished Dubček from the usual Party 'cynics, opportunists and tacticians' on the grounds that Dubček was a genuine 'believer' in communism, a man who 'never lost his faith, not even on 21 August 1968 when he was abducted by force, denounced as a counter-revolutionary and his whole future put in the balance' (Tigrid 1971, pp. 11–12). In the first biography of Dubček to appear in English, and which was subsequently reissued several times, William Shawcross made much the same point: this product of the 'Party apparatus' was different from 'other *apparatchiks*' because he had somehow managed to retain his 'ingenuous sympathy and humanity' (Shawcross 1970, p. 64). Even a critical review of the Shawcross biography complimented the author on having evoked Dubček's 'sensitivity' and 'profound humanity' and added that Dubček was a man who, 'for a politician', possessed 'almost too much decency and loyalty'. Yet this same personal integrity made Dubček

To Des McGhee, Lynda Holmes and David McKee; and with thanks to Robert Pynsent, David Goodall and Dinos Aristidou for commenting on various draft versions.

[1]See, for example, 'Moscow Keeps Up the Pressure', *The Times*, 20 August 1968; 'Russians Step In Before Purges Sweep Away the Yes-Men', *The Times*, 22 August 1968; 'Pride and Prejudice in Prague', *The Times*, 23 August 1968.

[2]Although the book first appeared in print, in 1969, as *La chute irrésistible d'Alexandre Dubček*, this was a translation, by Jean Bloch-Michel, from the English version, whose own publication was delayed until 1971. This is why the English, rather than the French, version is cited here.

> an almost mythical symbol personifying the longings of the Czechs and Slovaks, and in a sense of people in other parts of the world, for social justice and decency in public life, so that it need no longer be said 'politics is a dirty game'. ('Moravus' 1971, p. 203)[3]

As Miklós Kun has aptly pointed out, 'the Czechoslovak events of 1968, like all historic times, created their own stereotypes very early'. Accordingly, 'Dubček was an honest and sincere man, but a weak and indecisive politician' (Kun 1999, p. 69).[4] The portrait has proved remarkably resilient, colouring, if not dictating, interpretations of the Prague Spring in all but a handful of highly specialist works. Hans Renner, for example, in his *History of Czechoslovakia since 1945* (published in 1989) blames the failure of the Prague Spring on Dubček's supposed political innocence. What was needed, he explains, in a 'post-Stalinist satellite state in the Brezhnev era' was 'a leader with a lot of political experience, cunning, the ability to act quickly, and the necessary toughness; all qualities which the kind and decent Dubček did not have' (Renner 1989, p. 52). Even the most recent single-volume history of Czechoslovakia to have appeared in English echoes the refrain, arguing that 'it is essential not to underestimate Dubcek's sincere commitment to Communism and to the Soviet Union' (Dowling 2002, p. 107), yet fails to explain the puzzle of how a supposed idealist like Dubček should have managed to climb to the top, first of the regional Slovak Communist Party (*Komunistická strana Slovenska* or KSS) and then of the state-wide KSČ, without being compromised by a system he himself exposed as thoroughly corrupt.

Just three political analyses in print either hint or suggest that Dubček, far from being the political innocent of post-1968 legend, could be as cunning a strategist as the rest: Vladimir V. Kusin's brilliant *Intellectual Origins of the Prague Spring* (1971), which was produced in the immediate aftermath of the Czechoslovak crisis; Zdeněk Mlynář's insightful *Night Frost in Prague* (1980), which was published 30 years ago by a disaffected Presidium insider; and Kieran Williams' *The Prague Spring and its Aftermath* (1997), perhaps the most penetrating of the three, which appeared a decade ago from an academic press. But the clearest and most damning indictments of Dubček's political machinations are to be found, ironically enough, in his own posthumously published autobiography, *Hope Dies Last* (1993) which, when read attentively and checked against information held in the secret police (*Státní bezpečnost* or StB) archive in Prague, quite clearly reveals the pattern of his rise to power in Slovakia (a topic left out of both Mlynář's and Williams' accounts, and only lightly touched upon by Kusin) and confirms their suspicions (or, in Williams' case, informed arguments) about his second rise to power in Prague.

In general histories of Czechoslovakia—to say nothing of broader accounts of post-war Europe, the Cold War, or the history of Socialism—the replacement of Antonín Novotný by Alexander Dubček as First Secretary of the Czechoslovak Communist Party on 5 January 1968 is routinely presented as the start of the 'Prague Spring', the moment when the dark forces represented by Novotný's 'Stalinist' old guard were

[3]I am grateful to one of the anonymous readers of the present essay for bringing the review of Shawcross by 'Moravus' to my attention.

[4]Originally published in Hungarian as *Prágai tavasz, prágai ősz: 1968 fehér foltjai* in 1998 by Akadémiai Kiadó.

vanquished by the supposed light of Dubček's 'humane socialism' or 'Socialism with a Human Face'. As specialists may already know (but general readers do not), the real story started a good eight years earlier; and under Novotný, not Dubček. Given the persistence of what might be called the myth of Dubčekian exceptionalism, it seems worth setting the record straight by focusing, directly and explicitly, on the question of Dubček's reputation.

In 1960, the year in which Czechoslovakia was formally declared a Socialist Republic, the ruling KSČ was one of the most authoritarian communist parties in Europe and its relationship with the Soviet Union among the closest. Reminders of the debt of gratitude owed by the Czechs and Slovaks to their Soviet liberators from the Nazis were to be found in every part of the country, including in Slovakia, which had not been occupied until the last stages of the Second World War. Ideologically correct names, the most obvious of which were Lenin, Stalin and Gottwald,[5] had been given to streets, squares, tram stops and factories throughout the country. Prague's embankments along the *Vltava* (Moldau) river had become the Gottwald, Marx and Engels embankments; Zlín, home to the Bat'a shoe empire, renamed 'Gottwaldov'; the Škoda plant in Plzeň the 'Lenin' and the iron works at Vítkovice the 'Klement Gottwald' works.

From all important vantage points of Prague city centre—including the Old Town Square, the top of Wenceslas Square, and the middle of Charles Bridge—could be seen, on the crest of Letná hill, a colossal granite statue of the 'Generalissimo of the world proletariat', the largest such representation of Stalin to be found anywhere in the world. On another of Prague's seven hills, Vítkov, an equally grotesquely oversized statue, that of the equestrian Hussite warrior Žižka, marked the place where a monument to the Czechoslovak Legions had been turned into a mausoleum for communist dignitaries and decorated with a suitable mix of proletarian, Hussite and communist themes. Inside, Gottwald's corpse, which had already been visited by over a million people, was carefully measured every day for humidity by a team of embalming experts trained in the Soviet Union. At the far end of the monument, a chapel-like space had become a special hall to honour the Red Army; decorated with Socialist Realist mosaics of Soviet soldiers, it even contained—in the place where a holy water stoup would be found in a church—a stand containing a few grains of soil from the Socialist motherland.

Despite the air of fossil-like permanence which prevailed throughout the Socialist Republic, there was growing dissatisfaction within both the state-wide KSČ and its frankly subservient junior partner, the Slovak Communist Party (KSČ). As Zdenek Mlynář, one of the principal architects of the Prague Spring, afterwards recalled, a whole generation of committed Stalinists who had joined the Communist Party just after the Second World War, typically when they were in their twenties or thirties, were on the brink of middle age and the most influential part of their careers. Many of those who, as promising young candidates, had been sent for special training in Moscow at just the time that Khrushchev's reforms were taking hold in the Soviet Union, found the Czechoslovakia to which they returned old-fashioned and excessively authoritarian.

[5]After Klement Gottwald, Czechoslovakia's first communist president (1948–1953). It was Gottwald who had presided over the most elaborate and sensational political show trials to take place in the post-war Eastern bloc, the Slánský and associated trials of late 1952.

While they continued to justify the hard-line Stalinism of their youth as having been necessary to uproot Czechoslovakia's 'bourgeois traditions', now that 'class warfare' had officially been declared to have ended in the 'victory of the working class', there no longer seemed good reasons to prolong the mood of 'vigilance' (Mlynář 1980, pp. 10, 28–29).

Despite the constant trumpeting by the Communist Party of the 'achievements of socialism', everyone could see that the economy was lurching from crisis to crisis; that there were chronic shortages; and that the quality of goods was often shoddy. Month after month, confidential situation reports from the StB regions into which the country was divided diligently recorded the overheard complaints of housewives and others about the scarcity or poor quality of food and other staples. At politically sensitive times, such as just before elections, such reports were drawn to the direct attention of the First Secretary of the KSČ, accompanied, as often as not, by clandestine public opinion surveys compiled from private letters which the StB would steam open, typically in batches of about 17,000.[6]

What was beginning to trouble economists within the Party was the growing suspicion that five-year economic plans, which concentrated on heavy industry as political showpieces rather than responses to demand, might be what was unbalancing the economy and leading to the constant shortages of consumer goods. Now that the Soviet Union had been reconciled with Tito, the possibility of choosing the 'Yugoslav option' of introducing elements from the capitalist system to 'strengthen socialism' was no longer politically unthinkable. A final matter for concern being voiced within both the KSČ and KSS was the apparent indifference towards socialism on the part of the young; children of the revolution who—although too young to have imbibed the 'bourgeois' values of the interwar First Czechoslovak Republic—nevertheless seemed unmoved by clarion calls enthusiastically to embrace socialism.

It was not so much Khrushchev's 'secret speech' of 1956, in which Stalin was first denounced to the Party faithful, which began to change the direction of the KSČ leadership, but rather the Soviet leader's addresses to the Twenty-Second Congress of the Soviet Communist Party, which was held in Moscow in October 1961. This time, Khrushchev not only renewed and extended his denunciations of Stalinism; he did so at a public meeting at which Antonín Novotný, First Secretary of the all-important KSČ (and, since 1957, simultaneously President of Czechoslovakia) was in attendance. The Congress was immediately followed by the removal of Stalin's embalmed body from its resting-place next to Lenin in the mausoleum in Red Square, in order to signal formal displeasure at the 'Personality Cult' of which he had become the prime symbol. This unambiguous sign from the Kremlin put Novotný in a tight corner. On the one hand, he could not afford, like the Chinese Communist Party, simply to ignore Moscow's lead, but must be seen to be liberalising; on the other hand, he could not yet permit thoroughgoing Czechoslovak reforms, since any attempt to 'de-Stalinise' would inevitably lead to the pointing of accusing fingers at men who were still part of his

[6]Archiv Ministerstva vnitra České republiky (Archive of the Ministry of the Interior of the Czech Republic, hereafter cited as AMV), A 2/1-670, 'Poznatky z průzkumu veřejného mínění obyvatelstva, získané kontrolou listovního poštovního styku ve dnech 7.– 12.6 1954', ff. 1–3; 'Zpráva o závadových zjevech v průběhu předvolební kampaně', ff. 1–7.

Presidium—most notably Gottwald's remaining appointments, Viliam Široký, Karol Bacílek and Brunno Koehler—as well, perhaps, as himself.

In a political system in which one of the few ways for the ambitious to get ahead was to disgrace and oust the Party leader, there was no shortage of political rivals willing to jump on the reformist bandwagon as a means of promoting their own careers. Alexander Dubček (1921–1992), who had been trained in Moscow, had risen through the ranks of the KSS and was rewarded for 14 years of loyal service by being appointed Secretary for Industry in the Central Committee of the KSČ, was among the first to sense the new possibilities. When, just after the Twenty-Second Soviet Communist Party Congress, the hitherto impeccably conformist Dubček was asked to accompany Novotný to an international congress of Communist Party leaders held in Bucharest, nothing more was anticipated than the usual round of dull speeches. As it happened, however, the Chinese delegates' criticisms of Khrushchev's anti-Stalinist policies became so sharp that, in an unexpected departure from protocol, Khrushchev called together an unscheduled meeting of all foreign delegates. Since there was no time to prepare a formal speech and have it translated into Russian, a language in which Novotný was not at home, Dubček, who had grown up in the Soviet Union and spoke perfect Russian, was suddenly given the floor. Quick as a flash, he used the occasion to defend Khrushchev's reforms, simultaneously ingratiating himself with the Soviet leadership and pushing Novotný into precisely the corner he had been so artfully managing to avoid since the first winds of change had begun to blow from the Kremlin in 1956. Small wonder that, as Dubček afterwards complained, Novotný systematically tried to 'cut him down', demoting him from his position as secretary in the state-wide KSČ to that of secretary in the regional KSS, and avoided taking him to further congresses (Dubček 1993, pp. 98, 83).

Novotný needed to buy time with further token gestures of 'Khrushchevisation' until his position within the Presidium could be sufficiently strengthened to allow him to introduce more sweeping economic reforms and, with them, some political changes. At a meeting held on 15 November 1961, he therefore laid what he described as two 'weighty' problems before his comrades in the Central Committee. The first was what to do about the Stalin monument at Letná whose 'megalomania and bombast' and 'main figure' he now declared to be in conflict with the 'political convictions of our Party' and the 'purity' of the 'brotherly relationship' between the Czechoslovak and the Soviet peoples. The second problem was what to do about Gottwald's embalmed body, whose symbolism, Novotný now proclaimed, 'hardly corresponds with the traditions and feelings of our people' and whose message was not 'in harmony' with a 'Leninist understanding of the role of the personality and the collective nature of leadership' (Novotný 1961).[7]

Among the resolutions which the KSČ Central Committee adopted in late 1961were calls to remove Gottwald's body, cremate it, and bury the ashes in the memorial hall at Vítkov 'in the same way as was done with all other leading warriors of the Party'; to rename all factories and streets which were called after Stalin; and to appoint a 'politico-expert commission' to prepare 'plans for the best use of the site where the Stalin monument now stands' (Novotný 1961). It was this resolution which led, in

[7]Novotný's speech was published in *Rudé právo* on 21 November 1961 and was reproduced in full (in English translation) in Slánská (1969, pp. 57–58).

1962, to a remarkable public spectacle: the destruction, on orders from the KSČ leadership, of the Stalin statue on Letná hill. Although Novotný's evident hope had been to deal with the matter quickly and without fuss, it took a full two months of jack-hammering, with crews working night and day, to reduce the monolith to rubble (Deitch 2000, p. 37). Gottwald's remains were disposed of more discreetly: his corpse was cremated and the ashes buried at Vítkov in a private ceremony for no more than 15 or 20 high Communist officials.[8]

Making grand gestures to symbolise the 'abolition' of the 'Cult of Personality' in the Czechoslovak Socialist Republic, however much expectation they may have aroused, was relatively risk-free for the Novotný regime. A much more difficult problem was posed by the Soviet example of rehabilitating the victims of the Stalinist political trials and denouncing those held to have been responsible for extorting 'confessions' and fabricating 'crimes'. Czechoslovak Minister of the Interior and Deputy Prime Minister Rudolf Barák appears to have been the first to plan to use the evidence which his commission had uncovered during the period 1955–1957 to implicate most of the current leadership in the Czechoslovak show trials of the 1950s, including the Slánský trial, and thus to seize power for a rival group within the KSČ. Novotný swiftly had Barák removed from the Presidium and the KSČ and sentenced to 15 years in prison on trumped-up charges of embezzlement. He even arranged, in classic 1950s style, for a special exhibition of the deputy prime minister's 'expensive suits and shirts', along with 'foreign banknotes, pictures and art objects' to be set up for the television cameras in order to discredit him with the public (Mlynář 1980, p. 58). Having rid himself of his most immediate rival, Novotný concentrated on laying the ground for his future security by seizing the opportunities left by the deaths of Gottwald's immediate successor, Antonín Zápotocký (in 1957) and Václav Kopecký (in 1962), to staff the Presidium with three men—Jiří Hendrych, Drahomír Kolder and Michal Chudík—who were at once free of the taint of the political trials and personally indebted to him (Mlynář 1980, pp. 68–69).

At the KSČ's twelfth Party Congress in late 1962, Novotný put forward draft proposals for a new version of the Communist Party statutes. The primary purpose of this move appeared to be to cement his own position as leader of both Party (as First Secretary of the KSČ) and State (as President of the Republic). After the draft proposals met with criticism, he circulated an ominous-looking appendix to the draft listing all 'negative' points and opinions which had been raised during discussion.[9] By the beginning of 1963, Novotný had secured his position sufficiently to feel that he could not only risk Khrushchev-style reforms but, like Khrushchev himself, stand to benefit from them. He therefore set up a new commission of enquiry into the Slánský trial and associated political show trials, under the direction of Drahomír Kolder, a regional Party secretary in Ostrava who owed his position to Novotný's patronage. This time, the purpose of the investigation was to enable Novotný to claim the mantle

[8] '*Takoví jsme byli*', 1962 (Česká televize, 1996).

[9] Státní ústřední archiv v Praze, Archiv ÚV KSČ (hereafter cited as ÚV KSČ), fond 00/12, box sv. 1, 'XII. Sjezd KSČ' (1962), a.j. 10 'Informační zpráva o některých zvláštních a negativních připomínkách a názorech z diskuse k návrhu stanov KSČ', příloha iv, f. 1.

FIGURE 1. ALEXANDER DUBČEK. PHOTOGRAPH COURTESY OF VILÉM PREČAN

of reform, simultaneously winning the approval of the current Soviet leadership and the loyalty of reform-minded members within his own Central Committee.

In February 1963, the Kolder Commission reported to the Presidium that the Slánský and associated show trials of the 1950s had fabricated evidence, extorted confessions, and in every way conformed to the pattern of the discredited Stalinist trials of the 1930s. The sensational revelations were passed on to the Central Committee in April 1963 and to the general public in late August. The Kolder Commission, of which Dubček was also a member, although sweeping in its rehabilitation of the Czech communists, was more cautious in the matter of the Slovak show trials of so-called 'Slovak bourgeois nationalists'. Vladimír Clementis, Gustáv Husák, Ladislav Novomeský and other Slovak communists who had been victims in these trials, although granted civil rehabilitation, were not restored to full Party membership (Kaplan 1990, pp. xvi–xvii; Dubček 1993, p. 86). This gave Alexander Dubček, who had been made First Secretary of the KSS in May 1963, and knew that Novotný had reason to suspect him, the opportunity to play the Slovak card.

From about the same time that Dubček, as a member of the Kolder Commission, had information which implicated Novotný as an outspoken supporter of the Slánský and other political trials, *Kulturný život*, the weekly journal of the Party-approved Union of Slovak Writers, was suddenly allowed to go beyond the bounds of censorship then permitted in the Czech-speaking regions of the country. In no time, even *Pravda*, the official mouthpiece of the KSS (not to be confused with the Soviet Communist Party's equivalent of the same name), began to press for a reinvestigation of the 'Slovak bourgeois nationalist' trials. At the Slovak Writers' Congress in April, Ladislav Novomeský (who, together with Gustáv Husák, was one of the most prominent victims of the 'Slovak bourgeois nationalists' trials), was allowed to speak in defence of Clementis; and Miroslav Hysko went so far as to accuse Prime Minister Široký, known to be one of Novotný's closest allies, of having been the main instigator of the trumped-up charges (Dubček 1993, p. 89).

When Novotný challenged Dubček to explain why the Slovak press was not being kept under tighter control, Dubček replied that 'the Party' felt that 'rehabilitation in Czechoslovakia' was 'going too slowly' in comparison with the Soviet Union, an argument which he knew Novotný 'could not openly reject' (Dubček 1993, pp. 90–91). Although he was still keeping his cards close to his chest, Dubček appears to have been banking on widespread Slovak resentment of a whole range of issues, from the 'Slovak bourgeois nationalist' trials of the 1950s and curtailing of autonomy in the 1960 Constitution, to the widespread belief that the Czech-speaking regions received favourable economic treatment and that Novotný was personally insensitive to Slovak distinctiveness. Once Czech communists had begun to notice and to follow the Slovak communist press, Novotný had little choice but to allow the three remaining Gottwald appointments whom he could no longer afford to save—Široký, Bacílek and Koehler—to be sacked, and to call for a new commission, known as the Barnabitky Commission, to reopen the files on the Slovak political trials (Kaplan 1990, p. xv). The Presidium's disgraced members, all of whom had been Novotný supporters, were duly replaced by three men untainted by association with the Gottwald years: Jozef Lenárt, Martin Vaculík and Alexander Dubček (Mlynář 1980, pp. 68–69).

When, in 1963, the very first year of the Czechoslovak Socialist Republic's third Five-Year Plan, GNP declined by 2%, it was impossible to hide the discrepancy between the government's expectations and the actual workings of the economy. Faced with the prospect of economic collapse, the Novotný leadership was suddenly more open to the arguments of reform economists that some restrictions imposed by the command economy be removed and the Stalinist model that gave priority to heavy industry be partly reoriented towards consumer-friendly light industry (Williams 1997, p. 22). The idea of reintroducing carefully circumscribed pockets where market forces would be allowed to determine supply and demand was most closely associated with the name of Ota Šik; but it was also supported by a variety of other economists, as well as by newly appointed Presidium members Oldřich Černík and Lubomír Štrougal (Skilling 1976, p. 120). The 'New System of Economic Management' was therefore adopted as official Party and state policy between 1964 and 1966.

In October 1965, just as the reform movement in Czechoslovakia was beginning to gather a head of steam, Khrushchev was ousted from the leadership of the Communist Party of the Soviet Union and replaced by an unknown quantity, Leonid Brezhnev. It is an indication of the degree to which Novotný and the KSČ leadership had come to feel committed to the Khrushchev leadership that the KSČ Presidium responded to the news with the unheard-of step of sending a letter to the Soviet leadership to express 'surprise' at the 'sudden' changes in Moscow (Mlynář 1980, p. 70; Dubček 1993, pp. 100–01; 'Moravus' 1971, pp. 207–08). Novotný further signalled his preference for the reformist wing represented by the deposed Khrushchev by making friendly gestures towards Yugoslavia and Romania; by declining to engage in anti-Chinese polemics; and by making tentative approaches to the West Germans (Williams 1997, p. 54; Navrátil 1998, p. 44, note 15; 'Moravus' 1971, p. 208). Since it was not clear at the time how long Brezhnev would last, it is possible that Novotný's Presidium was simply backing the wrong horse; but the unusually bold gesture suggests that, at least in economic matters, it was genuinely persuaded of the need for Czechoslovakia to 'de-Stalinise'.

In Slovakia, meanwhile, Dubček took advantage of the controversy aroused by the findings of the Kolder Commission and the ongoing Barnabitky investigations by recommending that Gustáv Husák be readmitted to the Party, and making sure that the suggestion was included in the Barnabitky report submitted to the KSČ Central Committee on 19 December 1963 (Dubček 1993, p. 94). As well as tacitly acknowledging injured Slovak nationalist feelings, and so boosting his popularity in Slovakia, Dubček's gesture indirectly challenged Novotný's reputation and authority, thus helping Dubček further to strengthen his own position. Armed with the damning indictments of the Barnabitky report, Dubček kept up the pressure on the central KSČ leadership by allowing a number of carefully selected Slovak grievances to be aired within KSS circles: that L'udovít Štúr, traditionally dismissed as 'bourgeois', had nevertheless contributed to the Slovak National Awakening; that 'Stalinist' accounts of the Slovak Uprising of 1944, which suggested that only communists and the Red Army had been involved, represented a 'dogmatic oversimplification'; and even that Czech motives underlying the trials of 'Slovak bourgeois nationalists' might have been coloured by a 'nationalist deformation' of their own. As Vladimir Kusin found, as a result of Dubček's tacit toleration of these views, by 1965 the sense of Slovak nationalist grievance had grown so strident that a conference held by Slovak historians in Banská Bystrica was permitted to take as its sole theme 'The Slovaks and their National Evolution' (Kusin 1971, p. 70).

Dubček, who had thus far not risked publicly identifying with either side of the Slovak debate, made his first overt gesture in favour of reform by taking part in celebrations, held at Uhrovec on 30 October 1965, to commemorate the 150th anniversary of Štúr's birth. He then made sure that the fact that he had been born in the same house as Štúr became widely known (Dubček 1993, pp. 106–07, 7). Even when Novotný came to Slovakia to put in an official appearance at celebrations in Martin to commemorate the establishment of the *Matica slovenská* (Slovak Foundation) he found himself outmanoeuvred. Dubček, who did not attend the event himself, was nevertheless able to make capital out of Novotný's having supposedly behaved 'like a bull in a china shop' by declining to accept gifts of a fur coat and Slovak embroidery on behalf of his wife. Although the story could just as easily been used to demonstrate Novotný's refusal to be bribed, it was instead presented as an example of his supposed contempt for Slovak national feeling, a rumour which Dubček then allowed to be blown up into a major political scandal

(Pithart 1990, pp. 109–10;[10] Dubček 1993, pp. 114–15). Small wonder that Novotný, as Dubček later contemptuously expressed it, was 'convinced that someone somewhere in Slovakia was constantly conspiring against him' (Dubček 1993, p. 106); or, as the Ministry of Interior archives reveal, that he began to keep a close eye on members of the Slovak Communist Party.[11]

At the thirteenth Congress of the KSČ (31 May–4 June 1966), it was officially declared that since 'socialist social relations' in the Czechoslovak Socialist Republic had been 'characterised by the elimination of class antagonism', the future development of socialism in Czechoslovakia should be 'directly linked' to the 'spread of socialist democracy' and the 'participation of all working people in government management' (Mencl & Ouředník 1968, p. 24). The ensuing round of meetings and discussions gave Dubček the opportunity to advertise himself to the KSČ as the perfect compromise candidate to take over from the old guard in Prague. In a masterly speech, ostensibly simply a report on conditions in Slovakia, he managed to present himself as all things to all people. Dubček supported his own constituency by pushing for further investment in Slovakia; he showed how up-to-date he was by praising the new economic thinking; yet at the same time he based his claims to recent Slovak economic successes in terms of fulfilment of traditional five-year plans.[12] Insisting upon the implementation of 'full equality' between the 'fraternal' Czech and Slovak nations as promised in the Košice political programme of 1945, he spoke with equal resoluteness on the centrality of 'proletarian internationalism'. Even when Dubček applauded the Central Committee's admission of past 'mistakes' with regard to 'Slovak bourgeois nationalism' and the 1944 Slovak Uprising, he did so in 'practical fulfilment' of Gottwald's post-war promises of 'genuine brotherly unity' between the Czechs and the Slovaks. Similarly, although he hinted darkly at the 'misuse' of nationalism by 'past régimes', he spoke equally ominously of the current dangers presented by 'antisocialist forces'.[13]

It was not so much what Dubček said which mattered, since his statements were vague, inconsistent and contradictory, but rather the way that he said it. Dubček's contributions, unlike those of most of his colleagues—and particularly the long-winded Novotný—were mercifully short, relatively free of clichés, and included some refreshing suggestions, such as that the Communist Party should stop launching campaigns 'against' particular evils but rather 'in favour' of positive 'good'.[14] Above all, Dubček hinted to the KSČ leadership (to whom he took the trouble to speak in Czech rather than in Slovak), that his own friendlier, more open style of leadership

[10]Pithart originally published the work in 1980, but abroad (in Cologne) and under a pseudonym (J. Sládeček). It was first officially published, in Czechoslovakia and under Pithart's real name, in 1990, after the fall of the communist regime. The earlier version was published under the pseudonym of J. Sládeček, *Osmašedesátý* (Cologne, Index, 1980).

[11]AMV, A 2/2-1019 (counter-intelligence reports from the Ministry of Interior to President Novotný dated 5 November 1965; 12 November 1965; 19 November 1965; 29 November 1965; 4 December 1965; 20 December 1965; 29 December 1965), microfiche.

[12]ÚV KSČ, Fond 00/13 (XIII. Sjezd KSČ 1966), sv. 5, ar.j. 56 'Diskuse', 'Dubček, A.', ff. 9, 5.

[13]ÚV KSČ, Fond 00/13 (XIII. Sjezd KSČ 1966), sv. 5, ar.j. 56 'Diskuse', 'Dubček, A.', ff. 5, 4–5, 12, 10.

[14]ÚV KSČ, Fond 00/13 (XIII. Sjezd KSČ 1966), sv. 5, ar.j. 56 'Diskuse', 'Dubček, A.', f. 10.

was already being tested, and shown to work, in Slovakia, where the economy was said to be improving and there was markedly more participation in political life by the young, ethnic minorities, and other formerly disaffected groups. There was no reason to suppose, he hinted, that—given the right leader at the helm of the KSČ—the experiment could not work just as well throughout the rest of the republic.

By 1967, as Dubček later recalled, a 'direct clash' between communist functionaries impatient for further reforms and those believed to be holding 'progress' back had become inevitable (Dubček 1993, p. 112). The confrontation finally came out into the open at the Fourth Writers' Congress, held in June 1967, at which former Stalinists like Milan Kundera, Pavel Kohout and Ivan Klíma publicly joined forces with non-Party writers such as Václav Havel in opposing censorship, however discreet the technique. In their defence they cited Aleksandr Solzhenitsyn's recent (and far more rebellious) letter to the Soviet Writers' Union's own Fourth Congress, parts of which were read aloud to the assembled gathering. Ludvík Vaculík, in a sweeping harangue which distinguished what he called Czechoslovakia's 'power system' from actual 'socialism', demanded to know why 'we cannot live where we wish' and why a 'decent apology' had not yet been given to those who had been formally rehabilitated of political crimes. He rounded off his diatribe with the angry accusation that 'not one human problem' had been 'solved' during the previous 20 years:

> from such elementary needs as housing, schools and economic prosperity to the more subtle needs which the undemocratic systems of the world cannot provide: a feeling of one's full worth in society, a feeling that politics is subordinate to ethics, a belief in the meaning of humble work, the need for confidence among people, the advancement of education for the people. (Vaculík 1968, p. 7)[15]

Unsurprisingly, the Presidium of the Central Committee of the KSČ found unacceptable such 'outright attacks and slanders'—not only against the 'socialist system', but also the 'domestic and foreign policies of our republic' and 'the communist party' (Navrátil 1998, pp. 11–12). They singled out Vaculík, Havel and others for special condemnation. In time-honoured fashion, the radicals were accused of being fed their lines by the CIA, this time via the exiled 'agent' Pavel Tigrid, editor of the radically reformist *Svědectví*, several hundred copies of which had recently been smuggled into Czechoslovakia from France. Because the leadership of the Writers' Union proved reluctant to discipline its own members, Novotný, Hendrych and others proposed a number of disciplinary measures at the September 1967 Central Committee Plenum: that the Union's weekly, *Literární noviny*, henceforward be edited by the Minister of Culture and Information; that comrades Ivan Klíma and Ludvík Vaculík be expelled from the Party; that Pavel Kohout be issued a warning; and that disciplinary proceedings be started against Milan Kundera (Navrátil 1998, pp. 11–12). Although Dubček later claimed to have 'opposed this step', as Kieran Williams has pointed out, the disciplinary measures were endorsed by the whole of the

[15]The 1967 speech was first published in 1968, as part of the official proceedings of the Writers' Congress which appeared in print as *Sjezd Svazu československých spisovatelů (Protokol), Praha 27.–29. června 1967* (Prague, SSČS, 1968), pp. 131–62.

Central Committee, Dubček and Černík distinguishing themselves from the others only in that they expressed the opinion that the causes of the young writers' rebellion ought also to be considered. The sanctions could, in any case, have been much more severe—including court cases and prison sentences—had the Novotný regime really been as authoritarian as its predecessors had been; or as Dubček afterwards liked to pretend (Williams 1997, p. 55; Dubček 1993, p. 113).

Novotný's next move was to reassert the Communist Party's authority by issuing a report, to be announced as a joint statement of the Central Committee, outlining the Party's 'place in the political system'. In his opening speech, Novotný emphasised that 'only the Communist Party' and not 'just any group' can 'oversee and direct the social process, and where necessary set right shortcomings and mistakes which may arise during its development' (Mencl & Ouředník 1968, p. 24). Dubček, who was now emerging as one of the principal thorns in Novotný's side, proposed that the statement include elements of 'self-criticism' by the Party leadership; that the line between government and Party be stated more clearly; and that a new Action Programme be prepared. At the plenary session of the Central Committee which was supposed finally to approve the report, held on 30–31 October 1967, Dubček again took the opportunity publicly to criticise the report, calling for greater self-criticism on the part of the leadership, changes in how the Party directed its affairs, and greater autonomy for the KSS (Dubček 1993, pp. 115–16).

To Novotný's astonishment, Dubček was soon being backed by Josef Smrkovský, a convinced Stalinist, but who had been persecuted during the Slánský trial; as well as two regional secretaries from Moravia (Oldřich Voleník and Josef Špaček), who may have held a grudge from the Moravian purges surrounding the Šling affair. František Kriegel, a doctor who had worked in the rabidly pro-régime Father Josef Plojhar's Ministry of Health from 1949, but had been disgraced as a Jew during the Slánský years and had just rejoined the Central Committee in the previous year (1966), added his own indictments, claiming that in a third of Party organisations in northern Moravia there was not a single member under the age of 25; and that the Union of Youth and the Pioneers were in crisis (Mencl & Ouředník 1968, p. 19).

An incident then occurred which added considerable heat to the already lively debates about the disenchantment of the young. At the university dormitories at Strahov in Prague, which had been opened in 1965 and to great fanfare, students were becoming increasingly discontented about the frequent power cuts which prevented them, as they complained, from being able to study. The leaders of the Party-approved Union of Youth (*Svaz československé mládeže* or SČM), led by Pavel Dvořák, having already made several appeals, held a meeting on 31 October 1967 to discuss how best to press the authorities to do something.[16] When the electricity failed yet again, in the middle of their evening meeting, they decided to march together, there and then, to the *Hrad* (or Castle, the presidential residence) to complain. When the regular ('Public Security') police (*Veřejná bezpečnost* or VB), already nervous because of the expected

[16] 'Strahov 1967' (broadcast 8 January 2003) in Večeřa, J., director, 'Osudové okamžiky' (Česká televize, 2003).

arrival of a Soviet delegation,[17] were confronted with the sight of students marching in the streets holding lit candles and chanting 'We want light!' and 'We want to study!', they misinterpreted the slogans as politically subversive. At Neruda Street, on the way to the Castle from the Old Town Square, the student march was met by a wall of police bearing riot shields and truncheons. Without asking questions, the police began to beat the students and arrest them.[18]

The brutal police reaction not only outraged the students, whose official youth organisation, the SČM, demanded an inquiry; but also their parents, who were, of course, Communist Party members. News of the Strahov incident reached the KSČ Central Committee at about eight o'clock on the evening of 31 October 1967, just as its session was slowly drawing to a close. For the first time, a majority, taking quick advantage of the fiasco, criticised Novotný's draft statement as 'formulaic' and 'inadequate' and, in an unprecedented step, insisted that it be sent back for 'redrafting and fresh consideration' in December. As Dubček later recalled, there could have been 'no clearer signal' of Novotný's 'declining authority'. The Central Committee was 'itself surprised' by its 'sudden power'. The 'crisis of leadership was now obvious to everyone' (Dubček 1993, pp. 116–17).

Seizing the moment, Dubček launched his first open attack on Novotný by suggesting that the tasks of 'central leadership' (in other words, the post of First Secretary of the KSČ) and those of 'management' (in other words, the office of President of the Republic) be 'carefully separated'. Novotný, completely caught off guard by the attack, rejoined with a speech which was not only less temperate than Dubček's but, fatally, reminded his listeners that the KSS was supposed to be subordinate to the KSČ.

By alienating a large part of the hitherto politically irreproachable student body from the police, the Novotný leadership gave those within the Party who were pressing for reform yet another means of discrediting the conservative wing. The magazine *Reportér* opened the battle with an article by Jiří Ruml with the provocative title '*Více světla—nejen pro Strahov*' ('More light—and not just for Strahov'). Combined with the controversy which ensued from Dubček's speech and Novotný's rejoinder to it, the Strahov incident became so inflamed that even the National Assembly, which normally rubber-stamped whatever the Party leadership recommended, spoke up to condemn the police action and demand an inquiry. Since the implication of such disobedience was that the KSČ leadership was out of touch, not only with the regions, but also with the lower Party echelons and the government, Novotný, in serious need of reinforcement, disappeared to Moscow for several days.

Upon his return (10 November 1967), evidently having found some sympathy from Brezhnev, Novotný set up a five-man committee within the Presidium (composed of

[17]Kieran Williams found that the VB were keeping an especially close watch on students because of the unprecedented numbers (some 6,000) who had been allowed to travel to the West in the previous year (Williams 1997, p. 56).

[18]AMV, A2/3-2133, 'Písemnosti ke strahovským událostem'; 'Zpráva o událostech, které proběhly 31.10.1967, vypracovaná na základě svědectví přímých účastníků', f. 144 [internal pagination, ff. 1–2]; 'Zpráva tiskového tajemníka vlády o studentské demonstraci v Praze na Strahově dne 31.10', ff. 66–70 [internal pagination, ff. 1–5]; interview with Pavel Dvořák, Pavel Janda and others in 'Strahov 1967' (2003), Večeřa, J., director, 'Osudové okamžiky' (Česká televize, 2003).

himself, Hendrych, Chudík, Michal Sabolčík and Lenárt) to look into Dubček's 'national deviation'. Dubček, however, who was growing confident of his new influence within the Presidium, joined forces with Oldřich Černík, Jaromír Dolanský and Drahomír Kolder to press for a separation of the offices of President and First Secretary. Although initially opposed by the remaining six voting members of the Presidium (Hendrych, Chudík, Lenárt, Bohuslav Laštovička and Otakar Šimůnek), Dubček managed to break Novotný's majority in the Presidium by hinting to Hendrych that, should the posts of President and First Secretary be separated, Hendrych would stand to take over as First Secretary. The bait evidently worked, since Dubček found that, when he was called in front of the commission called to examine his 'nationalist deviation', Hendrych 'chose to remain entirely neutral', cleaning his glasses several times and taking a lot of notes, but not committing himself to disciplining Dubček. The Slovak Presidium, which could have taken the matter further, also declined to do so, with only Michal Chudík showing himself to be on Novotný's side by being ready to persecute Dubček (Dubček 1993, pp. 118–21; Jakeš 1996, p. 37).

By winter, the split within the Communist Party, between a faction allied with KSS First Secretary Dubček and another with KSČ First Secretary Novotný, had become such an open secret that it was beginning to cause a scandal throughout the socialist bloc. On 8 December 1967, Novotný invited Brezhnev to Prague, presumably to shore up his support once again. This time, in addition to Novotný, Brezhnev spoke to Dubček, Hendrych, Lenárt and Dolanský, which evidently persuaded him that Novotný was unable to control his Party. Since Novotný previously had also shown himself capable of acting independently of Moscow, and had made clear in 1965 that his personal allegiance was to Khrushchev rather than to Brezhnev, there no longer seemed any good reason to try to save him. Although the often-repeated tale that Brezhnev declared '*Eto vashe delo*' ('It's your business') to the KSČ Presidium is almost certainly apocryphal, the effect of the Soviet leader's failure overtly to support Novotný, or to appear to care which of the grey men in the Presidium took over from him, came to much the same thing (Mlynář 1980, p. 71; Dubček 1993, p. 122; Skilling 1976, p. 179).

When, at the next Central Committee session (19–21 December), Dubček again raised the issue of separating the functions of President and First Secretary, the discussion ended in a deadlock with those for and against the proposal remaining evenly split. Discussions resumed after the Christmas recess, during which time Miroslav Mamula, chief of the Central Committee's infamous Department VIII, and Jan Šejna, Party chief of Military Security, considered staging a putsch against the Dubček contingent but were evidently blocked by a rival, anti-Novotný contingent within the Ministry of Defence.[19] Finally, during meetings which lasted from 2 January to 5 January 1968, the balance tipped against Novotný sufficiently for it to be

[19]AMV, microfiche A/213–2327, 'Jan Šejna—mimoriadna informácia', ff. 1–8, A9–796–1 'kniha jednacího protokolu založena v arch. ve Spiš. Podhradě'; A9–796–2 'Záznam' (24 September 1969); A/3–237 'Jan Šejna', ff. 1–12. See also Dubček (1993, pp. 123–25). Department VIII had won its sinister reputation through involvement in interrogations surrounding the Slánský show trial.

suggested first that Dubček and Lenárt (both Slovaks), be proposed to take over from Novotný as First Secretary of the KSČ; and, finally, on the morning of 5 January, that Dubček alone be proposed. The Central Committee then passed a resolution which stated that, since the 'separation of the two highest posts' is a 'logical part' of the 'democratisation process in the state and political spheres', it approved Comrade Antonín Novotný's 'personal request', as President of the Czechoslovak Socialist Republic, to be 'released' from the post of First Secretary of the KSČ Central Committee (Navrátil 1998, p. 35).

Although Dubček proved effective in uniting opinion against, and eventually ousting, Novotný as head of the state-wide Party, this was not the same thing as having a secure position in the Presidium, let alone either the will or political backing to undertake reforms of the kind with which his name later came to be so closely associated. Just like Novotný before him, Dubček began by making a statement of his new leadership's intentions to right the wrongs of the past, while at the same time taking care to pledge nothing more concrete than what could be read into the usual political clichés. At a speech given at an agricultural congress on 1 February 1968, for example, he promised to 'develop a resolute approach to overcoming everything outdated' and to produce an Action Programme which would be 'linked with a purposeful approach to the detailed elaboration of the key problems of socialist progress' so as to 'enable us to do a good and prompt job of preparing the agenda of the Fourteenth Congress of our Communist Party of Czechoslovakia' (Dubček 1968, p. 41). Although Novotný had been 'defeated', the 'system' which he represented had not (Skilling 1976, p. 183).

Since Dubček's first priority, like that of Novotný before him, was to retain his hold on power, it is not surprising that he sought to do this in the same way as other communist leaders: by surrounding himself with comrades who could be counted upon to remain loyal to him, while simultaneously attempting to rid himself of known enemies and rivals. What increasingly distinguished Dubček's methods from those of Novotný, Zápotocký and Gottwald before him, however, was his tendency to use rank-and-file Party opinion, rather than the backing of the Moscow leadership, as the principal lever with which to enforce desired changes in the leadership of the KSČ. In his time as First Secretary of the KSS, Dubček had learned from experience that it was possible, simply by judiciously removing restrictions on censorship, to mobilise enough public and Party opinion to topple even the First Secretary of the KSČ. He now used the same methods to discredit his enemies and weaken the bloc in the Presidium which remained against him. Thus, within weeks of taking office, General Jan Šejna, who had plotted against him, was exposed by the military prosecutor's office as a black marketer. Instead of staging a show trial, Dubček left it to the media who were suddenly and unexpectedly given free rein to publish the news of Šejna's sensational escape to the West (Dubček 1993, p. 138). Journalists, completely unused to having to use their own judgement, were alarmed at not being told explicitly where the boundaries lay; but, as Kieran Williams has found, even when the editors of *Rudé právo*, the KSČ official daily, repeatedly invited Dubček to their offices to give them some guidance, he steadfastly refused to do so (Williams 1997, p. 68). Before long, with the help of the Ministry of the Interior, they had traced Šejna's connections with Novotný's son, which more than suited Dubček's purposes. A summary report of the case, running to 67 typed pages, was then sent to the government by the Minister of Interior, Josef Kudrna.[20]

On 4 March 1968, aware that Novotný was thoroughly discredited, the Presidium began formally dismantling the system of censorship. The immediate result was that on 8 March the press for the first time printed demands that Novotný step down as president. Within weeks, there were further such calls from students, artists and other groups whose consciousness of the possibilities had been raised through 'mass meetings' held in Prague by 'cultural' and 'political' officials. Soon, there were additional calls to remove Michal Chudík, one of Dubček's oldest enemies, from his position as chairman of the Slovak National Council; to fire Prime Minister Lenárt; and to remove the leading officers of the Trade Union Council, the Union of Czechoslovak Youth (SČM) and the Union of Czechoslovak Journalists, together with 'sharp criticism' of the attorney general and of the ministers of Defence and the Interior; in other words, the same men who, in December 1967, had considered deposing the Dubček wing of the Presidium (Dubček 1993, p. 139; Mlynář 1980, p. 102).

In order to keep the spotlight firmly focused on the scandals of the past, in which the Novotný regime was thoroughly compromised, and to keep the grievances of those who had been purged in the 1950s at fever pitch, on 14 March the Presidium announced that it would speed up the rehabilitation of those who had been unjustly persecuted. On 15 March, it further accepted a demand from the Slovak National Council that Czech–Slovak relations be organised in accordance with the principles of federation. Censors at the Publication Board then published criticism of their own bosses, together with the Minister of Interior, for not yet having 'responded' to 'the public criticism of censorship'. One of Dubček's most dangerous enemies, Jiří Hendrych, was singled out for special condemnation, being held personally responsible for having led them 'astray' on various occasions, most notably over the disciplining of *Literární noviny* (Remington 1969, p. 54). Having allowed his principal rivals to be mauled by the press, Dubček took equal care to reward the generals at the Ministry of Defence who had resisted Novotný's attempts to remove him (Dubček 1993, p. 125).

Although Alexander Dubček, the very symbol of the Prague Spring, is usually portrayed as a deeply and sincerely convinced 'liberal', the pattern of his rise to power—first within the KSS and then within the KSČ—suggests that he used popular grievances to establish his own power base within the Presidium rather than to adopt 'reformist' positions from conviction. As his half-admiring, half-contemptuous colleague, Zdeněk Mlynář, hinted, only such an analysis can make sense of why Ota Šik, a reformist but who was associated with Novotný, was kept out of his Presidium, while notorious conservatives, like Kolder and Štrougal, but who were unfriendly to Novotný, were retained (Mlynář 1980, pp. 104–05).

Techniques which suited Dubček's means of consolidating power—first within the KSS and then within the KSČ—and which won for him the brief (and, as things

[20]AMV, microfiche A/24–963, Sekretariát MV plk. Demjana, Správa pasů a víz (5 March 1968), unpaginated; A/3–237 'Informace pro vládu k případu trestné činnosti Jana Šejny a Jaroslava Moravce' (11 March 1968), ff. 1–67.

turned out, only temporarily helpful) reputation of being a reformer, were not considered so benign by those neighbouring socialist regimes whose own leaders, in the more traditional Novotný mould, could just as easily have been toppled by the same methods. Only Brezhnev, who knew Dubček's past record of obedience and loyalty to the Soviet Union, remained, outwardly at least, confident of Dubček's political soundness and reliability, appearing to understand that Dubček needed to establish control over the Presidium before he would be able to return things to normal. By 18 March 1968, after censorship in Czechoslovakia had been all but abandoned and the press was filling with grievances and accusations directed at high communist officials, even Brezhnev could not stop the East German authorities, afraid that their own Party and population might follow suit, from banning travel to Czechoslovakia, together with any reporting about the situation there.

On 21 March 1968 Novotný, by now blocked at every turn, announced his decision to step down as President of the Czechoslovak Socialist Republic. Ludvík Svoboda, the pro-Soviet war hero who had proved so helpful to the KSČ in February 1948 but afterwards had his own troubles during the Slánský trials, was put forward to replace him. To those reformists in the KSČ and KSS who had come to see Novotný as the symbol of all the evils and injustices of the 'Stalinist' era, his departure seemed almost too good to be true, a fairy-tale happy ending. Within months, they were to discover that the two prime symbols of the Prague Spring—Dubček and Svoboda—would be the first to begin the return to the *status quo ante* known as Normalisation.

As things turned out, Dubček was to remain at the helm of the KSČ for only another eight months. Svoboda, meanwhile, was to remain President until 1975 when, aged 80 and having already been too ill to carry out his functions for more than a year, he finally had to be forced—through the application of constitutional law—to retire. Like Svoboda, Dubček did not begin dismantling the Prague Spring reforms because he had to; he did not even begin 'normalising' because it was necessary to preserve communist rule in Czechoslovakia. Rather, like other *apparatchiks* shaped by the same political system, he began oppressing colleagues and fellow citizens because to do so offered his only hope—however slim—of being able to hang on to power.

University of Strathclyde

References

Bil'ak, V. (1991) *Paměti Vasila Bil'aka* (Prague, Agentura Cesty).
Deitch, G. (2000) *For the Love of Prague* (Prague, Baset Books).
Dowling, M. (2002) *Czechoslovakia* (London, Arnold).
Dubček, A. (1968) 'Speech at Agricultural Congress (1 February 1968)', *Rudé právo*, 2 February, reproduced in Remington, R. (ed.) (1969).
Dubček, A. (1993) *Hope Dies Last: The Autobiography of Alexander Dubcek*, edited and translated by J. Hochman (New York, Harper Collins).
Fejtö, F. & Rupnik, J. (eds) (1999) *Le Printemps tchécoslovaque 1968: Interventions* (Brussels, Éditions Complexe).
Jakeš, M. (1996) *Dva roky generálním tajemníkem* (Prague, Regulus).
Kaplan, K. (1990) *Report on the Murder of the General Secretary*, translated by K. Kovanda (Columbus, Ohio State University Press).
Kaplan, K. (2000) *Kořeny Československé reformy 1968*, 2 vols (Brno, Doplněk).
Kun, M. (1999) *Prague Spring—Prague Fall: Blank Spots of 1968*, translated by H. Csatorday (Budapest, Akadémiai Kiadó).

Kusin, V. (1971) *The Intellectual Origins of the Prague Spring: The Development of Reformist Ideas in Czechoslovakia* (Cambridge, Cambridge University Press).
Mencl, V. & Ouředník, F. (1968) 'What Happened in January', in Remington, R. (ed.) (1969).
Ministerstvo vnitra České republiky (2001) *Generál Jan Šejna—předmět zájmu vojenské kontrarozvědky* vol 8. (Prague, MVČR).
Mlynář, Z. (1980) *Night Frost in Prague: The End of Humane Socialism*, translated by P. Wilson (London, C. Hurst & Company). [Originally published in German as *Nachtfrost* (1978).]
'Moravus' (1971) 'Shawcross's Dubcek—a Different Dubcek', *Survey*, 17, 4, 81, pp. 203–15.
Navrátil, J. (ed.) (1998) *The Prague Spring 1968: A National Security Archive Documents Reader* (Budapest, Central European University Press).
Novotný, A. (1961) 'Speech to the KSČ Central Committee of 15 November 1961', *Rudé právo*, 21 November.
Pithart, P. (1990) *Osmašedesátý* (Prague, Rozmluvy).
Remington, R. (ed.) (1969) *Winter in Prague: Documents on Czechoslovak Communism in Crisis* (Cambridge, MA, MIT Press).
Renner, H. (1989) *A History of Czechoslovakia since 1945*, translated by E. Hurst-Buist (London and New York, Routledge).
Shawcross, W. (1970) *Dubcek* (London, Weidenfeld and Nicolson).
Skilling, H. G. (1976) *Czechoslovakia's Interrupted Revolution* (Princeton, NJ, Princeton University Press).
Slánská, J. (1969) *Report on my Husband*, translated by E. Pargeter (London, Hutchinson).
Tigrid, P. (1971) *Why Dubček Fell* (London, Macdonald and Co.).
Vaculík, L. (1969) 'Speech to the Fourth Writers' Congress of the Czechoslovak Communist Party', in Remington, R. (ed.) (1969).
Williams, K. (1997) *The Prague Spring and its Aftermath: Czechoslovak Politics 1968–1970* (Cambridge, Cambridge University Press).

French Responses to the Prague Spring: Connections, (Mis)perception and Appropriation

MAUD BRACKE

LOOKING AT THE VAST LITERATURE ON THE EVENTS OF 1968 in various European countries, it is striking that the histories of '1968' of the Western and Eastern halves of the continent are largely still written separately.[1] Nevertheless, despite the very different political and socio-economic contexts, the protest movements on both sides of the Iron Curtain shared a number of characteristics. The 1968 events in Czechoslovakia and Western Europe were, reduced to the basics, investigations into the possibility of marrying social justice with liberty, and thus reflected a tension within European Marxism. This essay provides an analysis specifically of the responses by the French left—the Communist Party, the student movements and the *gauchistes*—to the Prague Spring, characterised by misunderstandings and strategic appropriation. The Prague Spring was seen by both the reformist and the radical left in France as a moderate movement. This limited interpretation of the Prague Spring as a liberal democratic project continues to inform our memory of it.

Grand narratives of '1968'

One way to understand the continental scope of '1968', I propose, is by interpreting it as the culmination point of a set of challenges posed to the various traditions of European Marxism. The Prague Spring was in this sense the Czechoslovak variant of a European-wide phenomenon in the 1960s, namely, the emergence of hybrid, creative new strands of Marxist interpretation. In countries such as Italy, France, Czechoslovakia and Yugoslavia, the emergence of 'heterodox' or 'revisionist' interpretations of Marxism as of the early 1960s was related to generational change, the end of the post-war era and the weakening of political identities which based their legitimacy on anti-fascism and a specific interpretation of World War Two—such as state communism in the East and Soviet-aligned communism in the West. It was,

[1] In the English-language literature, 'the sixties' as an object of study usually refers primarily to the industrialised Western world. Developments in Eastern Europe are either not included or when they are analysed they often do not have a significant impact on the overall line of argument. A recent example is Schildt and Siegfried (2006).

further, a belated effect of the multiple disruptions of 1956, namely the de-Stalinisation process and the Hungarian revolution and its suppression.[2]

'1968' confronted the various traditions of the Marxist left in Europe with an issue it had long forgotten: liberty. A key and shared issue for all Prague Spring protagonists was how to marry social justice with liberty. The notion of liberty here included national liberty and national sovereignty, both with regard to the Soviet Union and in terms of relations between the Czech and Slovak nations; intellectual and creative liberty, including also the protection of individual liberties *vis-à-vis* the state; political liberty, involving the central questions of overcoming the Stalinist past and establishing a form of political pluralism; and socio-economic liberty, including managerial autonomy, self-management for workers and the organisation of factory councils. Also in France, the re-emergence of liberty in Marxist debates and practice was a central feature of the 1968 events. This was clear not only from the students' and anarchists' fierce opposition to the Communist Party's authoritarianism, but also from the new left's investigations into libertarian interpretations of Marxism, and from the centrality of the notion of *autogestion* in the search for self-management and self-control of industrial workers.

Yet, these common themes shared by the 1968 protests in East and West are revealed only with hindsight; they are an analytical device rather than a reality actually experienced at the time. Responses to the Prague Spring by the various actors of the left in France in 1968 were characterised by misreadings, as the events were systematically and strategically interpreted through the lens of the dramatic domestic political developments. Misunderstandings of the Prague Spring occurred in all West European countries, but in Italy, for instance, the left as a whole showed itself more genuinely interested in the events and debates in Czechoslovakia (Bracke 2007, pp. 167–75). France is an interesting case for contradictory reasons—on the one hand, the lack of genuine engagement with the Czechoslovak developments, and on the other hand, the broad instrumentalisation of these events in the context of the radical social and political battles at home. Before turning to these French perceptions, I will highlight a few aspects of the origins and developments of the Prague Spring which can illustrate the central concern of marrying social justice with liberty.

'Against the dehumanising forces of capitalism, fascism and Stalinism': the nature of the Prague Spring

Most of the recent literature on the 1968 events in Czechoslovakia has either not engaged with the political nature and ideological roots of the Prague Spring (dealing primarily with the conflict with the Soviet Union, or analysing power struggles within the Czechoslovak Communist Party (*Komunistická strana Československa*, KSČ) while dealing only to a limited extent with ideological debates in society at large),[3] or has attempted to interpret the political agenda of the critical writers and playwrights such

[2]On the importance of the 1956 events to the emergence of dissident Marxism in Czechoslovakia, see Kusin (1971, pp. 19–27).

[3]This is the case for, for example, the studies by Mark Kramer and Kieran Williams (Kramer 1998, pp. 111–71; Williams 1997).

as Václav Havel and Ludvík Vaculík from a liberal, pro-Western perspective.[4] However, what is absent from recent narratives is a discussion of the kinds of Marxism to which the protagonists of the Prague Spring adhered.[5] The most radical dimensions of the Prague Spring, I suggest, have been 'forgotten', not only because of the ideological ramifications of today's debates on Central and East European (CEE) history, but also because many observers in Western Europe at the time had an interest in presenting it as a liberal democratic project, as will be illustrated below for the case of France.

In his 1971 study of the intellectual origins of the Prague Spring, Vladimir Kusin proposed that, reduced to its simplest dilemma, the Prague Spring was about developing 'a socially just form of democracy' (Kusin 1971, pp. 1–2). It was a context in which the nature of both socialism and democracy were being investigated, in a debate that, while not fully free, was significantly less constrained than it had been previously. However, what complicates our historical reading of the debates on socialism and democracy is the fact that the discourse of the 'deepening' or 'perfecting' of 'socialist democracy' was one that had been employed by the communists in power during the Novotný period. From the late 1950s those breaking away from this discourse, such as Zdeněk Mlynář and Ota Šik, wished to reclaim both the words socialism and democracy because they firmly believed that these stood for something very different to what Czechoslovak neo-Stalinism had to offer. Yet, the confusion of terminology made it harder for their contemporaries in Czechoslovakia, as well as for analysts ever since, to distinguish between political views aimed at preserving the status quo, and those aimed at upsetting it.

In addition, it may be objected that it was only due to (self-)censorship and (self-) discipline that the reform projects were couched in Marxist discourse, thus disguising an unspoken wish to abandon Marxist analysis. Censorship began to be relaxed in February 1968, and by late March censors had effectively ceased to exercise control, thus giving way to the emergence of 'public opinion as a powerful force' (Skilling 1976).[6] Admittedly, it is reasonable to assume that the formal abolition of censorship did not produce overnight the effect of an entire nation daring to and being capable of openly questioning the foundations of its political system and discourse. However, to present this as the only reason for the explicitly socialist nature of the reform ideas is to dismiss the importance of the Marxist tradition in Czechoslovakia. It will be illustrated here that for the various protagonists of the Prague Spring, Marxist discourse was not merely a tactical device, but rather a matter of critical investigation of its purpose and usefulness.

Clearly, important differences existed between the various actors in terms of how they related to Marxism, not least between on the one hand, the reform communists in the leadership of the KSČ such as Alexander Dubček and Oldřich Černík, and on the

[4]See for example Keane (1999). However, in earlier work, Keane has interpreted Havel and Charter 77 as expressing the ideals of democratic socialism (Keane 1985, pp. 7–9).

[5]A useful exception is Tucker's discussion of the philosophical foundations of the Czech dissident movement post-1968; he asserts that it would be a mistake to understand Czech dissidents as 'ardent anti-communists' (Tucker 2000, pp. 9–10).

[6]For more on the end of censorship and the development of the press, see Skilling (1976, pp. 196–201).

other hand, the intellectual leaders of the more critical movement of cultural revival, such as Václav Havel and Ludvík Vaculík.[7] Nonetheless, all these Prague Spring protagonists shared a core of political values and intellectual legacies. A commitment to Marxism and a dislike and rejection of free-market capitalism were central characteristics of Czechoslovakia's political and intellectual cultures, and had been since the 1930s. The influence of Marxism as a political culture in 1960s Czechoslovakia was not directly affected by the de-legitimation of Stalinism. The rejection of Stalinism was unambiguous among the leaders of the revival movement, in public opinion at large, and even among the reform Communist Party leaders—although, to be sure, a set of taboos remained in place which impeded an actual historical analysis of Stalinism. Still, cleansing Czechoslovak society and politics from the many remnants of Stalinism lies at the heart of the Prague Spring and was indeed one of the key unifying elements of often diverging agendas. However, for the leaders of the reform and revival movements this did not mean that rejecting Stalinism could be equated with rejecting Marxism and socialism.

Re-interpretations of Marxism in Czechoslovakia found their origins in the years following 1956 in the debates among philosophers, writers and playwrights. As argued by James Satterwhite, a generation of philosophers and political theorists started utilising Marxism against the Party leadership—first cautiously, but towards 1968 in more explicit terms (Satterwhite 2002, pp. 115–34). Writings by Karel Kosík and Ivan Sviták were especially innovative and politically influential. Kosík theorised the centrality of everyday, practical exchanges in man's existence and consciousness and attempted to create links between Marxism, phenomenology and existentialism. The influence of the French existentialists as well as Georg Lukács were evident through his notion of 'dialectics of the concrete'. Praxis was given a humanist meaning reminiscent of Lukács, understood as a creative way of living in the world. This discussion implied a fundamental critique of the Communist Party, though on the basis of a fresh Marxist analysis. Kosík discussed Communist Party ideology as a set of self-sufficient views, estranged from reality. Marxism, by contrast, was in his view the philosophical expression of the experiences of the working classes, a much more authentic reflection of actual, concrete life experiences. In the context of the Prague Spring, Kosík's emphasis on praxis and agency came to be interpreted as a powerful call to dissidence and action.[8]

Innovative artists, intellectuals and writers, who were key in preparing the ground for the Prague Spring in the decade preceding it, also used Marxist methods to develop a critique of communist rule, by emphasising the political nature of artistic creation. Furthermore, the debates in the Writers' Union at the end of 1967, which directly prompted a change in the power relations within the KSČ leadership and facilitated Dubček's coming to power, reflected a re-investigation of Marxist methods as well as social concerns. Critical writers such as Antonín J. Liehm developed an attack on

[7] I follow here the broad consensus in the literature on the Prague Spring as consisting of two dimensions: a top-down, Communist Party-led reform movement, and a more spontaneous bottom-up movement of cultural and intellectual revival.

[8] See for example his article 'Naše nynější krize', published in *Literární listy* in April 1968 (Kosík 1968).

socialist realism in the arts, and new plays and novels no longer dealt primarily with Party heroes but with ordinary people with everyday feelings and dilemmas. Resistance to artistic dogma and calls for freedom of expression were the channels through which the Communist Party rule was criticised more generally. However, these were not calls for a 'neutral', value-free, or non-political form of art; quite to the contrary, the critics all emphasised the political role of art, in its duty to represent the concrete living conditions of ordinary people. As posed by Liehm, socialism needed to rid culture of 'two Diktats', those of power and those of the market, of arbitrary government and of liberalism. He further proposed that the political system should guarantee not only the individual freedom of creation, but also access to culture for all sections of the population in equal measure (Kusin 1971, pp. 57–58).

Socio-economic liberty was debated through the ideas of self-management and factory councils. As early as 1957, a number of economic experts, among them future Prague Spring protagonist Ota Šik, started to invoke Marx against (neo-)Stalinism, as well as to positively reassess aspects of Yugoslav 'revisionism'. By the mid-1960s, the Institute for Economics, led by Šik, had become a creative laboratory for economic reform blueprints. Among the advocates of reform there was no general call for the abandoning of the planned economy; rather, debates and propositions were more complex, and can be summed up, as suggested by Skilling, as an investigation into 'planned market socialism' (Skilling 1976, pp. 119–25). It was proposed that production plans should be more accurate and realistic, less prestige-oriented, less centralised, more diversified and devolved, and they should involve low-level decision making with participation from the various parties in the production units. One of Šik's collaborators, Čestmír Kožušník, critically explored the notion of socialisation of the means of production, and came to argue that ownership by the state did not mean collectivisation and that 'social ownership' should benefit all of society, the employees foremost (Kusin 1971, p. 86). Furthermore, the factory council experiments were central to economic reform in Czechoslovakia and also to debates in other East European countries and to the left in Western Europe. There was broad agreement among the reformers—including Šik and Mlynář among others—that making the planned economy more efficient should be accompanied by making it more democratic, by allowing for input into the organisation and planning of production not only by managers, but also by employees. While the April Programme announced the creation in the factories of 'democratic organs' representing the views and interests of the workers, it was only in June that a network of factory councils was established by the KSČ throughout the country. However, a tension existed between more democratic views on what the factory councils should be, proposing authoritative organs through which workers would exercise a form of self-management, and a more technocratic view, which preferred to see workers' control limited by managerial authority. While those focusing on greater managerial autonomy sought inspiration in Western social democracy, those privileging the theme of grassroots participation in the factories looked at alternative communist models, such as that of Yugoslavia (Skilling 1976, pp. 433–41). In the working class, the search for alternative ways of organising power relations on the factory floor was articulated through arguments in favour of greater trade union autonomy against the Soviet model of union subordination *vis-à-vis* the Party (Grémion 1985, pp. 40–42).

While economic reform proved hardest to implement in practice, political reform was the area in which disagreements were most explicit, particularly in the weeks preceding the invasion. Most influential here was Zdeněk Mlynář, whose thinking from the late 1950s onwards centred on the role of the Party, both in relation to the masses and to the state. In the mid-1960s his ideas moved on rapidly, as he abandoned the vague notion of the 'masses' and developed a more complex vision of civil society as the locus of power. Modes of political representation became the key question, and as it was accepted now that there were different, sometimes conflicting, interests in society which all needed to be represented adequately,[9] the debate came to hinge upon the issue of political pluralism. Notions of representation and participation were not limited to the Party. Other structures were envisaged, especially on the local and workplace levels, such as Mlynář's notions of 'National Committees', which would have autonomy over a number of policy areas at the local level, and the 'working teams', which were to elect councils in workplaces (Kusin 1971, pp. 107–08, 115).

Critiques of both the East European one party practice and the West European multiparty system were important. Věnek Šilhán for example, director of the Research Institute of the Economics of Industry and Construction and a strong advocate of economic and political reform, stated that the multiparty concept had also become obsolete in Western Europe. Free elections and the rotation of power between different parties in no way guaranteed the adequate representation of different interests, he argued (Skilling 1976, p. 439). Mlynář's blueprint included the reinstatement of the National Front, no longer as the ossified mockery of pluralism which it had become under Stalinism, but as the centre of power, defining overall policy. It was to be made up of representatives of the Communist and other parties, as well as representatives of various social organisations, including trade unions and women's organisations. Yet, the role to be played by the Communist Party in this new political system remained the sore point. What was clear, however, was that in the context of rising political awareness, a majority in public opinion saw the development of a more democratic form of socialism as crucially dependent on the Communist Party's unambiguous abandonment of its power monopoly. According to an August 1968 opinion poll, 81% of respondents favoured the two formally recognised parties—the National Socialist Party (*Československá strana národně socialistická*) and the People's Party (*Československá strana lidová*)—becoming 'really autonomous' of and 'equal partners' to the KSČ (Skilling 1976, p. 545).[10]

Despite the increasingly outspoken critiques of the KSČ reform leadership between April and July by the politicised sections of society, public opinion, according to polls taken between February and August, while increasingly critical of the Dubček leadership, did continue to believe that the reforms would strengthen democracy.[11] The most visible expression of radicalisation outwith the Party was the creation of

[9]See for example Šik's view in his influential work *Economics, Interests, Politics* (1962), that 'society is the assertion of interests of one social group against the interests of another' (quoted in Kusin 1971, p. 102).

[10]On the interpretation of these polls and their shortcomings, see Skilling (1976, pp. 528–32).

[11]This was the answer given by 88% of respondents in a poll in late March (Skilling 1976, p. 41).

organisations which were commonly referred to as parties but were never recognised by the state as such. One example was KAN, the 'Club of Committed Non-Party members' (*Klub angažovaných nestraníků*), which defined its aims in its manifesto of May 1968 in terms of 'contributing to a new political system, never realised so far, of democratic socialism' (Navrátil *et al.* 1988, pp. 156–58). It favoured a multiparty system and 'the defense of civil liberties' such as free speech. Its impact on public debate was reflected in the rapid growth of its membership, from 144 founding members to 3,000 on the eve of the invasion. KAN's founding manifesto offered elements for an investigation of the 'political, ethical and philosophical foundations' of the Czechoslovak nation and state. There were three such foundations, it was said, and they should form the basis of politics in Czechoslovakia because of their historical importance to its people. First, human and civil rights and civil equality (there was reference here to the United Nations as well as to the 'defence of these rights against the dehumanising forces of capitalism, fascism and Stalinism'). Secondly, the humanist tradition of Czechoslovak culture, 'which greatly inspired the advancement of our nations ... rather than on the battlefield ... or in multiplying material wellbeing'. The third principle was 'democratic socialism', which ought to be combined with 'the noble programme of individual freedom'. The Stalinist past was referred to as a 'violation in our national traditions of humanism, democracy and socialism' (Navrátil *et al.* 1988, pp. 156–58).

Tension between the Communist Party leadership and the intellectuals reached a boiling point at the time of the publication on 27 June 1968 of the 'Two Thousand Words Manifesto' by writer Ludvík Vaculík.[12] The text proposed a powerful re-interpretation of Czechoslovak post-war history, which diametrically opposed the official KSČ narrative and expressed what many had quietly known: 'The first threat to our national life was from the war; then came other evil days and events that endangered the nation's spiritual wellbeing and character. Most of the nation welcomed the socialist program with high hopes, but it fell into the hands of the wrong people' (Navrátil *et al.* 1988, p. 177). Vaculík voiced his anger at 20 years of (neo-)Stalinist rule in the most powerful way when he referred to the instrumentalisation of the notion of working class politics by the KSČ: 'The chief sin and deception of these rulers was to have explained their own whims as the "will of the workers". ... Every worker knows they had virtually no say in deciding anything' (Navrátil *et al.* 1988, p. 178). Vaculík proposed that beyond the disputes between writers and Party leaders, the key force of change was located at the grassroots, among the masses of workers and ordinary people. 'The everyday quality of our future democracy depends on what happens *in* the factories and on what happens *to* the factories' (Navrátil *et al.* 1988, p. 180). It is clear that even the most outspoken critics of Communist Party rule were unwilling to abandon the notion of a political legitimacy based on concern for social equality and on an investigation into the living and working conditions of ordinary people.

[12]The 2,000 words referred to 'Two Thousand Words that belong to Workers, Farmers, Officials, Scientists, Artists and Everybody'. The manifesto is reproduced in Navrátil *et al.* (1988, pp. 177–81).

'Everything remains to be imagined': interpretations on the French left

Viewed in a longer-term historical interpretation of European Marxism, the 1968 events in France, too, can be understood as the re-emergence of the question of liberty in relation to politics based on social justice. Yet, the differences between the ways in which some of these fundamental dilemmas of Marxism were articulated in France on the one hand and in Czechoslovakia on the other, and the very different political and socio-cultural contexts in which these debates were situated, gave rise to a number of misinterpretations. 'Socialism with a human face' as it was being debated in Prague, inspired the student radicals and small leftist parties ('*gauchistes*') only in a very limited way; and, as will be discussed below, Dubček's reform communism presented the *Parti communiste français* (PCF) with an embarrassment more than anything else. To the moderate socialist forces—the *Section française de l'internationale ouvrière* (SFIO) and the newly formed *Fédération de la gauche démocratique et socialiste* (FGDS)—the events in Czechoslovakia mattered only to the extent to which they impacted on their relations with the PCF. In sum, the French left understood little of the nature of the Prague Spring, projected its own conflicts and debates onto the events in Prague, and in some cases, although more so in the 1970s than in 1968, French responses to the Prague Spring were a matter of strategic appropriation.[13]

Political discourse in France in the context of the student and worker protests between March and June hinged on the dichotomy of revolution versus reform. Reform was fiercely and unambiguously rejected by student protesters and radical leftist groups; instead, it was revolution that needed to be re-invented, re-invested and re-created. The rejection of reformism—which in this context could be defined as an institutionally managed transformation to socialism, in which a key role was reserved for political parties and trade unions, social bargaining and parliamentary action—was based on an analysis of the situation in Western Europe, and what was seen as the integration of the working classes into the capitalist system. Related to this were fierce critiques of the strategies of the traditional left, the communist and socialist parties and the trade unions connected to them. In a discursive context where 'revolution' was the central object of both enquiry and desire, the KSČ reformers, unlike Ho Chi Minh or Che Guevara, did not satisfy the need for charismatic leaders; and neither did the critical intellectuals of the revival movement, who were often portrayed as bourgeois thinkers disconnected from the working classes and ordinary people. One of the influential Trotskyist groups, *Lutte ouvrière*, largely dismissed the KSČ's attempts at reform of the existing system, and its weekly paper stated that the Prague Spring was 'not likely to develop into a genuine situation of revolutionary socialism'. It qualified the Prague Spring as: 'limited by the popular strata it represents as well as by its political content', and as nationalist and chauvinist. The paper in early July still considered it very unlikely that the Soviet Union would put an end to the Prague Spring by military means, as there were 'no signs of popular revolt'.[14]

[13]I am here largely in agreement with the general argument in Grémion (1985).

[14]All quotes from 'Menaces soviétiques contre la Tchécoslovaquie', *Lutte ouvrière*, 3 July 1968, p. 1. All translations from French primary sources are the author's.

One issue which did receive attention in France during May and June 1968, was the factory councils. However, the fact that the council movement in Czechoslovakia—very differently to what had happened in Hungary in 1956—was largely a KSČ initiative, made it hard for the *gauchistes* to relate to it, and led once more to misunderstandings. The notion of factory councils was loaded with historical significance in the French left, related as it was to the Paris Commune of 1871. The Trotskyist groups specifically placed it at the centre of their political discourse in 1968, linking it to *autogestion* and the working classes' appropriation of full control over the production process, thus placing it in a revolutionary, workerist tradition. Quite distinctly, the 'new left', the *Parti socialiste unifié* (PSU) and the left-catholic trade union *Confédération française démocratique du travail* (CFDT), invented a new meaning for it, as part of what was presented as a new model of democratic socialism different to both Stalinism and social democracy. Here, factory councils were invoked as a crucial dimension of participatory democracy, and a necessary compensation for the limitations of representative parliamentarism. While the popular student leader Daniel Cohn-Bendit often referred to the revolutionary nature of factory councils, including also those in Czechoslovakia, other student leaders and intellectuals, such as Cornelius Castoriadis, noted the limited role played by the working classes in the Czechoslovak factory councils.[15] To all these groups, their support or lack thereof for the councils in Czechoslovakia was largely rhetorical and functional to their political legitimacy and symbolic battles at home, rather than an actual investigation of their nature.

It was sections of what is referred to here as the 'new left', which attempted to politically appropriate the Prague Spring, primarily in its dimension of cultural revival. The newspaper which identified most with the PSU and the new left, the daily *Le nouvel observateur,* noted and positively appreciated elements of a liberal-bourgeois democratic tradition in the Prague Spring.[16] It expected the emerging of this tradition to be the outcome of the debates between Dubček and the critical revival movement. *Le nouvel observateur's* analysis of harmonious relations between the reform communists and the critical intellectuals, against conservatives in the KSČ (Held 1968), was largely a mistaken one and the fruit of wishful thinking. It was motivated by a wish to have an impact on the situation of the French left and in the PCF more specifically, and implied a critique of the (neo-)Stalinists in the PCF and support for those who were seen as the Party's more progressive, moderate leaders, such as General Secretary Waldeck Rochet. The Prague Spring was seen by both the PSU and *Le nouvel observateur* as a model of democratic socialism, to be followed in France through the coming to power of a broad left-of-centre alliance, reformist but also modern and in touch with young people's critiques and movements. As the only ideological current in the French left, *Le nouvel observateur* perceived connections between the 1968 events in Western and Eastern Europe, and situated them in the global Cold War context. It wished to see the Prague Spring as the herald of a new international and European order that would help to undermine the existing 'social

[15]More details are given in Grémion (1985, pp. 110–16).

[16]Elements of this can be seen in Lentin (1968) and Held (1968).

and political status quo' in Europe and the static bipolar world, characterised by superpower hegemony over the old continent:

> They [the Prague Spring protagonists] resemble the French revolutionaries of May ... The Czechoslovak reformers know that they find themselves in *terra incognita*. Everything remains to be imagined and constructed ... The world divided between neo-capitalists and neo-Stalinists risks one day to be upset by this, and in a good way. (Held 1968)

Ironically, thus, both the 'far left' and the 'new left' interpreted the Prague Spring as a reformist movement that was moving towards the adoption of market-based social democracy—but did so with different degrees of enthusiasm. It was this discursive context which placed the leadership of the French Communist Party (PCF) in a position from which it was forced to defend the revolutionary (rather than reformist) nature of the Prague Spring, without, however, ever being convinced of this. The PCF was traditionally very loyal to the USSR although since 1964, under the leadership of Waldeck Rochet, it had given some proof of a cautious distancing from Moscow.[17] Now it experienced much difficulty in defining what the Prague Spring was and how it related to Soviet-style 'orthodoxy'. Thus, the PCF's responses to Dubček's changes between January and April shifted between lack of interest and tolerance *vis-à-vis* certain aspects of it, and a taboo on the questions it raised regarding de-Stalinisation. In so far as the PCF leadership did lend its support to the Prague Spring, it was formalistic rather than substantial, that is to say, motivated by a willingness to defend the formal principles of party autonomy and state sovereignty. At no point did the PCF take the Prague Spring as an example for its own policies, and the Party refused to allow the changes in Czechoslovakia to lead to a wider debate on socialism and democracy, in contrast to, for example, currents within the Italian Communist Party (*Partita Comunista Italiano*, PCI) (Bracke 2007, pp. 167–75).

While the PCF's daily paper *Humanité* did carefully hint at some of the structural problems of the Czechoslovak communist system which had provoked the leadership change in the KSČ (economic recession, the Slovak question and need for a separation of party and state institutions), the fundamentally new character of Dubček's policies was consciously ignored.[18] One reason why the PCF needed to emphasise the continuum between Soviet-style communism and Dubček's 'socialism with a human face' was the taboo on Stalinism. For a party which itself had failed to carry out a consistent de-Stalinisation, either organisationally or ideologically, it was impossible to discuss the rejection of Stalinism as a key motive behind Dubček's reforms. In early April the PCF *Secrétariat* dryly noted that the KSČ's April Programme 'ought to be considered positive'; not, however, for the innovations it was expected to bring about, but because it allegedly showed Dubček's readiness to combat 'certain attempts to threaten socialism'.[19] Indeed, if support for Dubček was never more than lukewarm, the PCF leadership had little or no confidence in the socialist credentials of the

[17]For more detail see Bracke (2007, pp. 117–20).

[18]See for example Acquaviva (1968, p. 3). On PCF coverage of the Prague Spring, see also Daix (1980, p. 242).

[19]Archives Parti communiste français (Place Colonel Fabien, Paris), box *Secrétariat* (agenda and conclusions), 2 April 1968.

intellectuals of the revival movement. As of April, the 'danger of the rightist forces' was increasingly stressed. For example, *Humanité* referred to instances of criticism of Prime Minister Černík which had appeared in *Rudé právo*, as a dangerous case of 'the political debate becoming personal' (Acquaviva 1968, p. 3). The 'Two Thousand Words Manifesto' was largely ignored by the PCF press, thus indicating the Party's disagreement with it (Deli 1981, p. 94).

As the intellectuals' criticisms of Dubček mounted towards the summer, so did the PCF's attempts at discrediting them, and their veiled yet clear warnings to the KSČ to regain control over civil society. In old-fashioned Leninist style, the PCF press reminded the Czechoslovak communists of the 'leading role of the Communist Party' when reporting the developments in Prague (Hentgès 1968b, p. 3). Internally, the PCF leadership was, in fact, even more preoccupied with the 'rightist' dimensions of the Prague Spring than it would seem from its public statements. In an elaborate *Bureau politique* report, for internal discussion only, PCF envoy to Prague, Philippa Hentgès, emphasised the country's economic problems, as well as its request for a loan from West Germany. According to this analysis, there were further negative points also: the increasing influence of the 'petty bourgeoisie'; the 'fascination with the West in certain layers of the population'; disagreements in the leading organs of the KSČ on issues such as the economic programme; and political opposition ('problems created by the adversary').[20] Thus, when General Secretary Waldeck Rochet went to speak to Dubček in Prague on 19 July, following his meeting with Soviet leaders in Moscow, he did so not because he wished to 'save' the Prague Spring, as some of the literature has argued, but with an urgent request to undo the Prague Spring reforms and re-establish full Communist Party control, as the only way to avoid a now near-certain invasion.[21]

While the Party line was one which at all times abstained from genuine support for the experiment in 'socialism with a human face', a number of intellectuals connected to the PCF appropriated the project, invoking it as a useful example for the development of democratic socialism. In doing so, their aim was to provoke debate and changes within the PCF. Philosopher Roger Garaudy saw connections between the intellectual revival in Czechoslovakia and his own exploration of the humanistic and democratic character of Marxism. The Action Programme seemed to confirm his view that both the notion of class and the leading role of the Communist Party needed to be reconsidered (Grémion 1985; Streiff 2001, p. 500). The intellectuals connected to the journal *Les lettres francaises*, Pierre Daix and Louis Aragon in particular, granted extensive attention to the cultural revival—although they too abstained from publishing the 'Two Thousand Words Manifesto'. Their points of reference in Czechoslovakia were not the Party leaders but rather the critical writers and the journal *Literární listy*. Daix in his *Journal de Prague* discussed the problems of the Novotný regime (which he labelled as 'absolute monarchy centralism') and the ways in which it was criticised in the liberalised political climate. He wrote at length on the issue of the Stalinist trials, and denounced the 'demagogic workerism' of pre 1968 Czechoslovakia, which, according to him, 'did not correspond to the ideal of

[20]See Hentgès (1968b); Archives PCF, box 'Tchécoslovaquie—Plissonnier', folder III, file 2.

[21]More detail in Bracke (2007, pp. 162–65). I disagree here with Vigreux (2000), who sees Rochet's 'parallel diplomacy' as illustrative of his support for Dubček.

socialism'.[22] All this sounded like criticism of the PCF itself, motivated by the hope to see a change from within its structures, as seemed to have occurred in the KSČ.

The Prague Spring and its contested memory

The above analysis does not explain why the Prague Spring, and particularly certain aspects of it such as the factory councils, acquired the status of myth on the left in France and elsewhere in Western Europe. In fact, it was only after the Soviet-led invasion of August 1968 that the Prague Spring, misrepresented if represented at all before August, was appropriated by the various sections of the French left, which thus also backdated their own support for it. The Prague Spring became in the 1970s a standard weapon in the historical and political arsenal of the communist, socialist and intellectual left in France. While the factory councils started to receive much more attention among French intellectuals, such as André Gorz, in 1969, it was only in the mid-1970s that the two major parties of the left, the PCF and the Nouveau PS led by François Mitterrand, rediscovered the Prague Spring and invested it with symbolic and identitarian meaning. This, as analysed by Grémion, took place in the context of their bid for governmental power through the *Union de la gauche*, and the urgent need for a shared model or point of reference that could clarify what the two parties meant by 'democratic socialism' (Grémion 1985, pp. 199–234). Internationally, the re-appropriation took place in the context of the rise and fall of Eurocommunism in 1974–1977, during which the Spanish and Italian Communist Party leaderships often referred to the Prague Spring as their preferred model for socialism—in a way that was significantly more genuine than was the case for the PCF leadership of George Marchais.

This belated identification with the Prague Spring took place in the wider context of discrediting of the most radical political agendas of *Mai '68*—by a conservative backlash, by the PCF and PS, and by some former *soixante-huitards* themselves. As a result, the Prague Spring now needed to be presented as a fully social democratic and reformist project, a perspective that has remained the predominant one in Europe generally, particularly since the collapse of Soviet-style communism between 1989 and 1991. Current academic and public debate on the history of Central and East Europe under communism seems to be dominated largely by a grand narrative according to which all dissident and even reform movements expressed the wish to adopt liberal-democratic and free-market values. The history of political conflict in CEE is thus reduced to a teleologically inspired story of these societies' inevitable adoption of a 'West European' political and socio-economic model, through what has been called a 'rectifying revolution' (Habermas 1990). While this interpretation holds for some of the dissident movements in CEE, the history of opposition movements to Soviet-style communism is, as it is argued here in relation to the Prague Spring, far more complex. Investigations of reform as well as dissident movements in CEE during communism can only benefit from an understanding of how they related to the traditions of European Marxism.

University of Glasgow

[22]See Daix (2001 p. 438); see also the articles in the *Journal de Prague* series: Daix (1968a, 1968b, 1968c).

References

Acquaviva (1968) 'Le CC du Parti communiste tchèque ouvre ce matin une importante session', *Humanité*, 1 April.

Bracke, M. (2007) *Which Socialism, Whose Détente? West European Communism and the 1968 Czechoslovak Crisis* (Budapest, CEU Press).

Daix, P. (1968a) 'Notes pour comprendre les écrivains tchécoslovaques', *Les lettres francaises*, 3 April.

Daix, P. (1968b) 'Ce Printemps de Prague—I', *Les lettres françaises*, 10 April.

Daix, P. (1968c) 'Ce Printemps de Prague—II', *Les lettres francaises*, 17 April.

Daix, P. (1980) *Les hérétiques du PCF* (Paris, R. Laffont).

Daix, P. (2001) *Tout mon temps. Révisions de ma mémoire* (Paris, Fayard).

Deli, P. (1981) *De Budapest à Prague. Les sursauts de la gauche française* (Paris, Anthropos).

Grémion, P. (1985) *Paris/Prague. La gauche face au renouveau et à la régression tchécoslovaques 1968–1978* (Paris, Julliard).

Habermas, J. (1990) 'What Does Socialism Mean Today? The Rectifying Revolution and the Need for New Thinking on the Left', *New Left Review*, I/183, September–October.

Held, J.-F. (1968) 'Le face à face de Prague', *Le nouvel observateur*, 29 July.

Hentgès, P. (1968a) 'Note sur les circonstances qui amenèrent des changements in Tchécoslovaquie', *Humanite*, 19 January.

Hentgès, P. (1968b) 'La Tchécoslovaquie a toujours considéré ses liens politiques et militaires avec les pays socialistes comme la garantie de son indépendance', *Humanité*, 17 July.

Keane, J. (1985) *The Power of the Powerless* (London, Sharpe).

Keane, J. (1999) *Václav Havel. A Political Tragedy in Six Acts* (London, Bloomsbury).

Kosík, K. (1968) 'Naše nynější krize', in Liehm, A. J. (ed.) (1988) *Jaro 1968: Čítanka pro děti a mládež, 150 000 slov* (Cologne, Index), pp. 128–38, available at: http://www.blisty.cz/files/knihy/liehm/1968/059.pdf, accessed 21 August 2008.

Kramer, M. (1998) 'The Czechoslovak Crisis and the Brezhnev Doctrine', in Fink, C., Gassert, P. & Junker, D. (eds) (1998) *1968: The World Transformed* (Cambridge, Cambridge University Press).

Kusin, V. V. (1971) *The Intellectual Origins of the Prague Spring. The Development of Reformist Ideas in Czechoslovakia 1956–1967* (Cambridge, Cambridge University Press).

Lentin, A.-P. (1968) 'Lénine revu par Montesquieu', *Le nouvel observateur*, 3 April.

Navrátil, J., Bencík, A., Kural, V., Kramer, M., Moss, J. & Tosek, R. (eds) (1988) *Prague Spring 1968. A National Security Archive Documents Reader* (Budapest, CEU Press).

Satterwhite, J. (1992) 'Marxist Critique and Czechoslovak Reform', in Tarrat, R. (ed.) (1992) *The Road to Disillusion. From Critical Marxism to Postcommunism in Eastern Europe* (London, Sharpe Publishers).

Schildt, A. & Siegfried, D. (eds) (2006) *Between Marx and Coca-Cola: Youth Cultures in Changing European Societies, 1960–1980* (New York, Berghahn).

Šik, O. (1962) *Ekonomika zájmy, politika: jejich vzájemné vztahy do socialismu* (Prague, Nakl. Politicke literatury).

Skilling, H. G. (1976) *Czechoslovakia's Interrupted Revolution* (Princeton, Princeton University Press).

Streiff, G. (2001) *Jean Kanapa, une singulière histoire du Pcf* (Paris, L'Harmattan).

Tucker, A. (2000) *The Philosophy and Politics of Czech Dissidence from Patocka to Havel* (Pittsburgh, University of Pittsburgh Press).

Vigreux, J. (2000) *Waldeck Rochet, une biographie politique* (Paris, La Dispute).

Williams, K. (1997) *The Prague Spring and its Aftermath: Czechoslovak Politics, 1968–1970* (Cambridge, Cambridge University Press).

The Prague Spring of Science: Czechoslovak Natural Scientists Reconsidering the Iron Curtain

RIIKKA NISONEN-TRNKA

SCIENTIFIC COOPERATION WITH THE WEST FORMED ONE OF the most important embodiments and yet one of the greatest paradoxes of the Czechoslovak liberalisation process in the 1960s. This essay explores the agency of natural scientists in the developments. I argue that they served as instruments and catalysers of change in the attempts of the Czechoslovak state to modernise and integrate internationally. The scientific–technical revolution was seen as creating the framework for increasing contacts with the West: scientists' inventions brought economic value to the state; this, in turn, allowed scientists to make use of their political bargaining powers to ensure the continuity of their research and enhance their material conditions.

Echoing the prevailing sentiment following the August invasion of 1968, the president of the Czechoslovak Academy of Sciences (*Československá akademie věd*, ČSAV) František Šorm stated that:

> The character of science is international; the results of research are in essence a synthesis of the work of scientists from all over the whole world, resulting from their close mutual cooperation or exchange of experiences. For that reason we stand for completely free contacts of scientists in all countries and of course also that all the scientific works would be published and be public. Science is the property of the whole of humanity.[1]

His statement exemplifies the ideas guiding the developments in science in the preceding decade. Accordingly, the mid-1960s have even been called the 'new coming of Czechoslovak science' (Mišková *et al.* 1998, p. 17). The growth of international scientific exchanges was closely linked to the notion that successful economic reform required trading with the West. Despite the existence of the Iron Curtain, Czechoslovakia began to establish scientific contacts with the West on an unparalleled scale.

Scientific cooperation with the West formed one of the most important embodiments and yet one of the greatest paradoxes of the Czechoslovak liberalisation

[1]Archiv akademie věd ČR (A AV ČR)—Fond Františka Šorma (FŠ) (unarranged), *Reportér* interview with František Šorm, 23 October 1968. Further archival references will use the same abbreviations. Translations from Czech sources are by the author.

process. For the Czechoslovak state, Western cooperation was both a necessity and an ideological threat. On the one hand, the building of a socialist society—a process which was declared to have reached its goal in 1960—and the race between East and West for world supremacy created pressure to accelerate progress in the fields of science and technology. Achieving these goals necessitated scientific exchange with the West. In the words of Nils Roll-Hansen, 'even under tyrannical regimes, reason is a feature of human nature' (Roll-Hansen 2005, p. 14). On the other hand, science was one of the figureheads to strengthen the ideological hegemony of the socialist bloc. In a similar fashion to top sportsmen and women, or cosmonauts, prominent scientists were important propaganda tools of the Cold War. However, it was impossible for the state to control their motives, perceptions, contacts and even the impact of their actions. Western cooperation, or 'dealing with the devil', was therefore one of the most difficult issues challenging the coherence of the Eastern bloc.

To understand the grounds for different individual motivations and to examine the actions 'behind the scenes', this essay discusses the examples of two prominent Czech chemists. The first, František Šorm (1913–1980), was the president of the Academy of Sciences and a world-class biochemist. He governed the Academy from 1962 to 1969 and was also a member of the Central Committee of the Communist Party (*Komunistická strana Československa*) and the Ideological Commission (*Ideologická komise*).[2] He thus had a direct channel of communication to the top levels of the Party. What makes the example of Šorm particularly interesting are his two roles. Borrowing the notions of Slava Gerovitch and Vladimir Shlapentokh, we can describe Šorm both as a de-ideologiser (Gerovitch 2001, p. 259) and as a technocrat (Shlapentokh 1990, pp. 153–54). For him, communism did not mean the blind adoption of Soviet theories. He adapted to the changing requirements of the times and was able to distinguish them from ideology. Nevertheless, he did cultivate contacts with the leadership and wanted to reach the higher echelons of power. For a technocrat, the most necessary ingredient for the progress of society was science.

The second example is Otto Wichterle (1913–1998), another prominent chemist and the inventor of the soft contact lens.[3] He lost his university post in the purge of 1958, but almost immediately found asylum in the Academy of Sciences where he became the director of the Institute of Macromolecular Chemistry. Wichterle was never a member of the Communist Party, but at the height of the Prague Spring in 1968 he actively participated in the reform movement. In 1964, the licence of his contact lens patent was sold to the USA. Both at the time and in retrospect the licensing agreement has been considered as one of the most significant East–West transfers of technology.[4]

Prior research dealing with the period of the Prague Spring has rarely examined the role of natural sciences in the Czechoslovak liberalisation process.[5] A possible

[2]A AV ČR—FŠ, Životopisy.

[3]Otto Wichterle and his colleague Drahoslav Lím developed the polymer hydroxyethylmetacrylate (HEMA) in the 1950s—a material out of which the soft contact lens was made. Wichterle further developed a method for producing lenses (McMahon & Zadnik 2000, p. 730).

[4]*Science*, new series, 1966, 153, 3736, pp. 620–22; 'Picking Ivan's Brains', *The Economist*, 15 May 1982.

[5]An exception is the conference proceeding by Zilynská and Svobodný (2001).

reason for this could be the fact that the natural sciences have been classified as apolitical and therefore not essential for the reforms of the 1960s. In contrast to this assumption however, the hypothesis of this essay is that natural scientists were better able to prove the importance of their work to the state than were social scientists or scholars in the humanities. The time focus of this essay is exclusively the late 1950s and the 1960s. This leaves the so-called 'Normalisation' period to one side but enables us to see the reform period in question more clearly within its particular dimensions.[6]

The first part of this essay will show that the grounds for the relatively good position of natural sciences were created in the 1950s and the limits of 'ideologisation' or 'Sovietisation' of science in Czechoslovakia will also be discussed. The second part demonstrates that in the mid-1960s the notion of scientific–technical revolution worked as a stimulus for science and scientists to advance their goals, with a special focus on scientific cooperation with the West. In the final part of the essay, the example of Otto Wichterle is used to connect the activity of the individual to the broader context.

The era of optimism

The foundations for advancements in the natural sciences in the 1960s had already been prepared from the 1950s onwards. For many contemporaries, communism as the 'scientific world ideology'[7] had been the key to solving the problems of scientific work. In this vein, Czech communists claimed that the 'bourgeois society' of the First Republic (1918–1938) had undervalued its natural scientists (Winters 1994, pp. 275, 281) and in communist ideology they saw a chance to strengthen the position of science in society. The establishment of the Czechoslovak Academy of Sciences in 1952 was therefore a project that the Communist Party eagerly advocated. The Soviet Union had been the first country with a government policy and public support for science (Graham 1993; Roll-Hansen 2005) and it offered an attractive model for those who wished for a more efficient science policy. Against this background, it is understandable that it was not only communist natural scientists who welcomed the organisational changes (Kiser 1989, p. 94). The goal of the newly established Czechoslovak Academy of Sciences to combine research and industrial applications furthered the strengthening of physical, chemical and technical research. The Academy of Sciences grew rapidly as did the number of its institutions. One of its greatest international victories in the 1950s was the award of the Nobel Prize in chemistry in 1959 to Jaroslav Heyrovský, who was the first Czechoslovak to win the Nobel Prize (Winters 1994, p. 281).

[6]The essay is based on my ongoing PhD project *Scientific Relations between Czechoslovakia and the West during the Cold War*.

[7]The 1960 Constitution of the Czechoslovak Socialist Republic (Ústava ČSSR, Art. 18, Par. 2) stated: 'In accord with the scientific world ideology, the society of working people fully utilises the results of science for the management of society and in planning future development'. The Constitution of the Czechoslovak Socialist Republic as promulgated on 11 July 1960 as the constitutional law 100/1960 Sb (cited in Slamecka 1963, p. 7).

However, rebuilding the scholarly community and setting up a 'socialist' framework for research in the 1950s proved difficult, and the politically motivated character of the changes made them largely inconsistent. Efforts included various measures which affected organisations, disciplines and individual scientists. However, diverging rules in different institutions and perhaps even within them led to some paradoxical outcomes. This is seen most clearly in attempts to secure the ideological purity of the scholarly community by carrying out political purges at the universities and high schools. Although the Czech universities were purged soon after the communist takeover in 1948, at first the measures hardly touched the natural sciences at the level of professors (Connelly 2000, p. 132) and dependence on the intellectual capital of natural scientists formed an everlasting dilemma for the state. One concrete and radical attempt to resolve this dilemma took place in the aftermath of the Hungarian Revolution of 1956 when the Party attempted to reassert control and carried out a purge in the universities in 1958. However, in a number of cases the purges did not remove their targets from the scientific community. Significantly, the Academy leadership was able to offer professional asylum to many scientists who were thrown out of universities in the political purges of 1958. Paradoxically, as noted above, some of them, including Otto Wichterle, were even offered the opportunity to establish completely new institutions (Kostlán 2001, p. 96).

Part of the 'Sovietisation' of Czechoslovak science in the 1950s was the categorisation of some existing theories as 'capitalist' or 'imperialist' and suggestions to replace them with 'socialist' ones. It is not surprising that in the branch of natural sciences, Sovietisation in Czechoslovakia had its strongest impact on biology: the influence of Trofim Lysenko was not limited to the Soviet Union (Jindra 2003, pp. 49–51). However, the rhetoric on science was ambivalent. In this respect, Slava Gerovitch's remark concerning Soviet science in the late Stalinist era shows parallels to the Czechoslovak situation in the 1950s:

> The question of how to treat science produced by a Cold War enemy—as a value-neutral body of knowledge or as an ideological Trojan horse—acquired central importance in Soviet public discourse on American science in the early years of the Cold War. (Gerovitch 2001, pp. 253–54, 2002, p. 15)

In this process, Cold War propaganda played a visible role. As Gerovitch noted, the concept of 'two worlds—two ideologies in science' had become relevant (Gerovitch 2001, p. 259, 2002, p. 15). This is also the reason why scientists in the Czechoslovak Academy of Sciences were able to resist some serious Sovietisation attempts and how they managed to create a relatively wide space for free research. In chemistry, the most eminent example of an attempt to ideologise the discipline was the critique of the theory of resonance. The theory became an example of 'bourgeois Anglo–American trends'. The critique of resonance was, however, rejected by Otto Wichterle, Jaroslav Heyrovský and František Šorm, among others. According to the Czech historian Jiří Jindra it was to the credit of these leading chemists that Czechoslovak chemistry withstood ideological pressures and retained its place on the world stage (Jindra 2003, pp. 52–53).

In spite of attempts to bring science in line with ideology, the importance of continuity in scientific work had to be recognised. Language represented an important issue in this context. In the frozen phase of the Cold War the English language, the *lingua franca* of natural sciences, together with Western journals represented a tool to transfer Western ideas to the socialist bloc. As a backlash, Soviet scientific books started to be translated into Czech and lectures were organised to propagate Soviet theories. For example, the Czechoslovak chemical journal *Collection of Czechoslovak Chemical Communications*, published in English, had been discontinued and replaced by a Russian language version. However, thanks to František Šorm the *Collection* was soon brought back in its original form and language. In addition, Šorm managed to maintain subscriptions to Western journals in the library of his institution (Turková 2000, p. 228). Thus, already in the 1950s the 'communist manager of science' made concrete steps to secure the continuity of his field.

In the period 1956–1957, the relative isolation caused by the autarkic policy on the one hand, and the Western embargo on the other, finally gave way to new forms of cooperation. After Josef Stalin's death and Nikita Khrushchev's famous speech at the 20th Party Congress of the Communist Party of the Soviet Union (CPSU), Czechoslovakia gradually softened its attitude towards Western cooperation. Czechoslovakia adapted to these events more slowly than most other countries in the Eastern bloc, but there were concrete signs of changing policies in science in the late 1950s (Mišková 1986, p. 194). Already in the late 1950s, Šorm's Institute of Organic Chemistry and Biochemistry of the Czechoslovak Academy of Sciences (*Ústav organické chemie a biochemie*) became internationally recognised and its work highly esteemed. One of Šorm's best-known partners was Carl Djerassi, known for the invention of the contraceptive pill. He and Šorm initiated a collaborative project between the American firm *Zoecon* and the Czechoslovak Academy of Sciences on insect hormones. This was, as Djerassi writes in his autobiography, the first such formal arrangement between an American corporation and the Academy. Djerassi and Šorm exchanged reprints of their respective publications in the fields of common interests: steroids and terpenoids. In 1956, shortly after the events in Hungary, Djerassi gave lectures in Prague for the first time. According to him:

> Šorm was personally charming and scientifically open, but when it came to Hungarian events, he mouthed the party line—in keeping with the distracting picture of Stalin (his cunning eyes seemed to follow me whichever way I sat during our conversation) that hung on the wall behind his desk. (Djerassi 1992, p. 192)

Although Šorm saw international cooperation as an integral part of science, he was not a supporter of longer stays abroad for study purposes. This may reflect his acceptance of the prevailing policy but also the fact that he was outstandingly efficient and expected the same from others. According to his student and later colleague Antonín Holý, Šorm associated foreign trips with the objective to gain the required information as quickly and effectively as possible without wasting valuable time from the laboratory work back home (Holý 2004, pp. 27–28).

Before 1956, contacts with foreign countries were reduced to a minimum, even with other countries within the Soviet bloc (Havránek 2005, p. 176). However, in the late 1950s, the state had begun to reconsider some of the imposed travel restrictions in individual cases. For example, as early as 1956, Otto Wichterle, who was not a Party member, was allowed to travel to an IUPAC (The International Union of Pure and Applied Chemistry) conference in Israel, where he was asked to organise the next meeting in Prague. Both personal networks and economic reasons played their role. Wichterle's research on polyamids had begun to generate interest at the state level. František Šorm, Wichterle's former fellow student, interceded on Wichterle's behalf. The idea of an international macromolecular conference was ultimately approved by the government and the organisation of the conference began immediately after Wichterle's return to Prague. The symposium was the first of its kind in the whole of the socialist bloc. Organising a conference on such a scale required extensive arrangements, not least because it was supposed to act as an example for similar arrangements in the future. The conference was successful in achieving its aims. On the one hand, it worked as a platform for Czechoslovak science and especially for young Czechoslovak chemists at the beginning of their careers in the field of macromolecular chemistry. On the other hand, the decision-makers welcomed the financial profit the conference brought. Significantly, the conference had probably impressed the Soviet authorities as well, because the next conference was organised in Moscow (Míšková 1986, pp. 195–97; Wichterle 1992, pp. 63–64). Although the conference may have worked as an example of how to quietly change policy, the contradictory attitude of the state was demonstrated by the presence of the '*estébáky*', the men of the state security StB (*Státní bezbečnost*) who kept the conference under observation (Wichterle 1992, p. 64).

The wave of the scientific and technical revolution

Even though the 1950s witnessed significant growth and the establishment of many scientific disciplines and institutions, by the beginning of the 1960s scientists began to be more aware of the disadvantages of the state's overall science policy. The social and economic factors of the 1960s had a strong impact on the Academy of Sciences. The deep economic crisis that reached its peak in 1961 forced the Czechoslovak decision-makers to look for solutions. The Communist Party admitted that it needed experts (Williams 1997, p. 4). The development of science was understood officially in terms of the concept of the scientific–technical revolution.[8] This was seen as a global process that was going on both in the East and the West (Rindzeviciute 2008, p. 193). It was one of the factors that forced leaders to reconsider their attitude toward intellectuals. The intellectual capital of scientists was becoming increasingly important, which in turn improved their status and prestige. Two main principles legitimised changes in science: the first was the endeavour to make the economy more efficient and competitive and thus, to increase trade with the West. The second was the abolition of the personality cult (Skilling 1976, p. 132; Kaplan 2002a, pp. 16–17).

From the beginning of the 1960s, the main concern of the Academy of Sciences was the inadequate application of scientific research in practice. From the point of view of

[8]The notion of scientific–technical revolution is originally a Western concept. The origin of the concept seems to be uncertain. In some sources J. D. Bernal has been mentioned as the father of the concept (Richta 1969, p. 16), whereas in others the credit has been given to Bertrand Russell (Wilczynski 1974, p. 6).

chemists, for example, this meant there was a weak interaction between industry and research. In the estimation of many scientists, the real issue was excessively centralised planning and the Academy's lack of independence in any decision-making.[9] Some attempts to resolve the problems were carried out in 1962 and 1963. A new organisational model and new legislation gave the ČSAV more freedom than before. According to Czech historians of the Academy of Sciences, during the administration of František Šorm, from 1962 onwards, nominations to the board of the Academy were increasingly based on scientific rather than political criteria (Mišková *et al.* 1998, pp. 14–15).

Although relations with the socialist countries, and particularly with the Soviet Union, were always formally prioritised, problems of intra-bloc cooperation accelerated the process of the re-orientation of Czechoslovakia away from being a most loyal ally of the Soviet Union and towards Western cooperation. The members of the Council for Mutual Economic Assistance (CMEA) had serious difficulty finding common prospects and this was quite a significant factor in pushing Czechoslovakia to strengthen its Western contacts. For example, the practice of the CMEA to circulate research results free of charge was disadvantageous for Czechoslovakia, because it had to provide the less developed countries of the bloc with information it had developed without receiving compensation that would have profited its own economy (Kaplan 2002b, pp. 188–89). Both at the state level and in the discussions of the Academy of Sciences, references to the problems of cooperation with the CMEA countries became more common. Cooperation within the bloc was too formal and inefficient.[10]

In 1963, Cold War rhetoric still dominated the discourse on science. Accordingly, growing cooperation with the West was defined as part of the 'ideological battle' or 'psychological war' initiated by the West. The Party focused attention on cooperation inside the Eastern bloc—it had become aware that personal contacts had a great impact on the intensive development of cultural, artistic and scientific relations. The state was ready to remove formalities and the development of contacts was left more and more to the scientific community itself. The Central Committee wished to improve bilateral cooperation between the socialist academies and also to increase the exchange of information.[11] In the beginning the increase in Western contacts was depicted rather as a by-product of the overall improvement of international scientific cooperation. However, loosening up of formalities and strengthening the role of individual scientists in establishing and maintaining contacts worked as a stimulus to establishing contacts with academic institutions in the West.

Accordingly, by 1964 a new landmark had been reached and the quality of academic cooperation with the West reached its highest level in the post-war period.[12] In the Academy, the growth of foreign exchanges was dramatic. In 1964 contacts with the capitalist states, in particular in natural sciences, clearly increased and the overall amount of cooperation doubled in comparison with the previous year. Czechoslovakia began negotiations with many important Western scientific institutions. Furthermore,

[9]A AV ČR—Fond FŠ, Lidé—život—doba. Československý rozhlas, Praha. Vysílání, 3 May 1968.
[10]Národní archiv (NA)—Fond KSČ-ÚV 02/1, 107, 110, item 6.
[11]NA—Fond KSČ-ÚV 02/1, 37, 41, item 3.
[12]NA—Fond KSČ-ÚV-KI (ideologická komise) 58–68, 8, 32, item 2.

the country hosted the Pugwash Conference in Karlovy Vary. The Central Committee acknowledged that the economic benefit the state had gained in 1964 proved that the aim of increasing cultural relations through commercial channels, in particular by supporting Western cooperation, had been successful. In 1965 Czechoslovakia had more extensive scientific cooperation with many Western countries than other communist countries. Following the ideologically correct rhetoric, this was presented as a propagandist victory for the whole socialist bloc.[13]

It had become clear by the mid-1960s that trading within the CMEA would not be sufficient to fulfil the number one goal of Czechoslovakia, which was to restructure its economy in such a way that it would enable the country to take advantage of the 'wave of scientific–technical revolution' (Kaplan 2002b, p. 209). In 1965, the Central Committee openly stated that developments in the fields of science, education and culture were crucial for the national economy. Improvement of the economy would, however, require 'perfect knowledge of Western technology'.[14] The goal was echoed in the Academy. The leadership highlighted the point that Czechoslovakia, as a small country, did not have sufficient resources to succeed in the scientific–technical revolution without the use of Western technology. These statements were without doubt directed at the ears of the Soviet leadership, to justify Czechoslovakia's increasingly intensive Western cooperation.[15]

In the estimation of the Academy, international cooperation further improved, intensified, and even more importantly, stabilised in 1966 and 1967. The Academy was pleased with the primarily positive development, but pointed out that the current situation was only the beginning of a long process. It was remarked that resources given to international cooperation had not been used in a completely satisfactory way and the institutes had not yet taken enough initiative.[16] As a result of the loosening of visa requirements, a number of foreign scholars had attended conferences in Czechoslovakia. The Czechoslovak state saw organising conferences in Czechoslovakia as profitable because they brought money to the state.[17] Following the state policy to normalise relations with some capitalist states, the Czechoslovak Academy of Sciences established relations with a number of important scientific institutions in the West, including the National Academy of Sciences in the USA, the National Research Council of Canada and the British Royal Society. Even though cooperation was not allowed to collide with foreign policy principles, the authority of science was now gaining more importance. Accordingly, in 1967, the presidium of the ČSAV stated that in individual cases, scientific reasons could have more weight in decisions concerning Western cooperation than those relating to foreign policy (Brádlerová & Kmochová 2001, p. 112). This was the first time this already existing practice was pronounced publicly.

[13]NA—Fond KSČ–ÚV 02/1, 107, 110, item 6.

[14]NA—Fond KSČ–ÚV 02/1, 113, 116, item 16.

[15]A AV ČR—Fond Prezídium ČSAV, 25. Prezídium ČSAV (18 May 1967). Postavení vědy nastupující vědeckotechnické revoluci.

[16]A AV ČR—Fond Prezídium ČSAV, 21. Prezídium ČSAV (23 February 1967). Zpráva a průbehu a výsledcích vědeckých styků ČSAV se zahr. za rok 1966.

[17]NA—Fond KSČ–ÚV 02/1, 15, 17, item 8, p. 11.

The Party approved of the promotion of Czechoslovak science abroad and the ensuing economic advantages. Yet, from the Party's perspective the phenomenon remained a dilemma. Also the situation was not completely satisfactory for the Academy of Sciences: at least in the official rhetoric the ideological problems linked to cooperation had to be highlighted and concrete evidence of the benefit of cooperation to the Czechoslovak economy and Czechoslovak science had to be presented.[18] By 1966 West Germany, the number one enemy of Czechoslovakia, had become its most significant partner in trade and science. This is the best evidence of the fact that economic reasons had truly increased in importance. According to the Academy of Sciences, several factors had engendered the situation, including the poor financial situation of the Academy. Czechoslovak science was said to be 'exploited' by West Germany, which offensively and purposely attracted Czechoslovak scientists with money and research possibilities. The study trips of the Czechoslovaks were mostly paid for by the inviting party which was economically profitable but politically questionable because it gave the host more authority. The Czechoslovaks believed that long-term scholarships of the DAAD (*Deutscher Akademischer Austausch Dienst*) and *Humbold Stiftung* were motivated not merely by the scientific, but also by the political interests of West Germany, which was trying to normalise scientific, cultural and trade relations with Czechoslovakia. Earlier measures to prevent problems were not considered to be sufficient.[19] However, far-reaching concrete measures to improve the situation do not emerge from the documents, and in reality, cooperation did not slow down.

After West Germany another Cold War enemy of Czechoslovakia, the USA, became an important scientific partner. The Politburo of the Communist Party justified the contacts by citing the scientific–technical revolution—a factor that had been once again highlighted at the 13th Party Congress in 1966. It admitted that the efficient growth of the national economy needed more intensive scientific cooperation also with capitalist states. The high standards of American and German scientific institutions were acknowledged by the Party. It is not surprising that in the estimation of the Party, the motives of the USA were primarily self-interested—the Czechoslovaks believed on the one hand that the USA wanted to speed up its own development and on the other hand, that cooperation had an ideological mission. The Czechoslovaks considered the encouragement of foreign scientists to emigrate to be one of the most efficient but silent elements of American foreign policy.[20] However, the Americans did not only draw the Czechoslovak scientists to their country; as a matter of fact, Americans formed the second largest group of Western scientists working in Czechoslovakia.[21] The problems related to Western cooperation, such as the brain drain in the form of emigration, remained a constant concern. Due to lack of finances, Czechoslovakia was far too dependent on host countries, which naturally increased the threat of emigration. Despite the caution, the view was that the

[18]NA—Fond KSČ-ÚV 02/1, 15, 17, item 8, p. 11.

[19]A AV ČR—Fond Prezídium ČSAV, 21. Prezídium ČSAV (23 February 1967). Zpráva o průběhu a výsledcích vědeckých styků ČSAV se zahraničním za rok 1966.

[20]NA—Fond KSČ-ÚV 02/1, 27, 29, item 8.

[21]A AV ČR—Fond Prezídium ČSAV, 21. Prezídium ČSAV (23 February 1967). Zpráva o průběhu a výsledcích vědeckých styků ČSAV se zahraničním za rok 1966.

cooperation would increase and widen, and in the prevailing political situation the advantages of cooperation outweighed the concerns.[22]

A significant change in the discourse on science policy and planning took place in 1967. It was now characterised by the concept of integration which had been attached to the scientific–technical revolution. These concepts were replacing the Cold War rhetoric. The aim of Czechoslovakia was now to participate in the integration process of world science. Significantly, the West had become the yardstick for the comparison of research standards at the international level. Echoing the aims of the Communist Party highlighted at the 13th Party Congress, the scientific–technical revolution was at the top of the agenda of the Academy of Sciences. Accordingly, in the May session of the Academy the position of science in the impending scientific–technical revolution was extensively discussed. The message of the Academy was that Czechoslovakia was a small country, which, despite the best efforts of the Academy of Sciences, lacked the resources to keep track of the developments of modern science. The current 'integration process of world science'[23] was based on large research teams and finances which were based on the needs of superpowers and which bolstered their position in science.

However, the Academy did not give up on the hope that smaller developed countries, especially the ones with 'developed culture and intellectual and scientific traditions', could still preserve 'superiority or at least a place in the forefront of world science'.[24] As a solution, the Academy identified the aims of specialisation and prioritisation of disciplines as best serving their interests. However, more important was the plan to start from the basis: a well functioning system of scientific and technical information would be the first step to improve the current situation. Another step would be increased mobility, including interaction between disciplines, the mobility of scientists nationally and internationally as well as from one institution to another. The importance of transferring scientific know-how, as well as people, was an important part of the process.

The integration process of world science enabled the Academy to enter into a critical evaluation of the past. The Academy pointed out that Czechoslovak research had not profited from the economic, social and cultural life of Czechoslovak society because the scientific framework had been built up in ignorance of the real needs of life. The restructuring of the Czechoslovak economy in the late 1940s and the 1950s had not worked as a stimulus for Research and Development (R&D) and, in turn had led to the situation in which research had not actively taken part in technological progress. The message of the Academy was clear: Czechoslovakia should concentrate on asserting itself as a developer of advanced intellectual products.[25]

[22]A AV ČR—Fond Prezídium ČSAV, 21. Prezídium ČSAV (23 February 1967). Zpráva o průběhu a výsledcích vědeckých styků ČSAV se zahraničním za rok 1966.

[23]A AV ČR—Fond Prezídium ČSAV, 25. Prezídium ČSAV (18 May 1967). Postavení vědy v nastupující vědeckotechnické revoluci.

[24]A AV ČR—Fond Prezídium ČSAV, 25. Prezídium ČSAV (18 May 1967). Postavení vědy v nastupující vědeckotechnické revoluci.

[25]A AV ČR—Fond Prezídium ČSAV, 25. Prezídium ČSAV (18 May 1967). Postavení vědy v nastupující vědeckotechnické revoluci.

Otto Wichterle—'scientific currency' as a weapon

Although the best-known critics of the liberalisation process did not come from the ranks of natural scientists, Wichterle—the most successful of them—was one of the first natural scientists who actively and often daringly reminded the decision-makers of problems in scientific research. In his memoirs, published in 1992, Wichterle offers an explanation as to why he and his colleagues did not engage in the reform movement in its embryonic phase. According to Wichterle, there was almost no political life in his institute and the scientists there were well-off in 'every way'; they received recognition both inside and outside the country. Thanks to licence agreements the institute was able to equip itself with valuable new devices. Furthermore, in the estimation of Wichterle, he and his colleagues were not aware of the decreasing living standards in the country and assumed problems had been ameliorated by technological progress (Wichterle 1992, p. 162). When compared to social scientists, natural scientists are commonly perceived as apolitical, and they often tended to define themselves as such as well.

Although declaring oneself apolitical was perceived as a suspicious act, natural scientists had a choice to remain outside of the most delicate discussions. It had not been the principal duty of natural scientists to participate in the issues of society.[26] The transformation (*proměna*) of thinking, a process many communist intellectuals went through, was more underlined at the level of scholars in social sciences and humanities, whose world view was inseparable from their actual research. Although it is not the purpose of the essay to offer comparison between natural sciences and social sciences, it is yet necessary to note that natural scientists mostly saw continuity in their discipline: reforming science was directed towards the practicalities of their work such as financing research, equipping laboratories, travelling, publishing and trading with licences.

However, Wichterle's scientific achievements formed an important contextual background for his political activities in the late 1960s. When Wichterle made the first samples of lenses in 1961 he had begun to anticipate the economic potential of the production of the lens in the USA, and the way this could profit the ČSAV and Wichterle's institute (Wichterle 1992, p. 145). Even before the licence for his contact lens was actually sold in 1965,[27] Wichterle used his invention as a tool for putting pressure on the state. In 1964, he reminded the decision-makers that the production of the lens did not actually belong to the tasks of the Academy because it was not basic research. The head of the Institute of Macromolecular Chemistry worked as an 'engineer-technologist' and a craftsman—time for 'real' scientific work, such as publishing papers, was therefore extremely limited. In January 1964, he estimated that it was a 'question of days'; if the lens were not sold soon as 'a great export', Czechoslovakia would lose the competition over production of the soft contact lens to the West. According to Wichterle, this would be a great loss to the Institute of Macromolecular Chemistry because only a stable flow of currency would ensure its

[26] A AV ČR—Fond FŠ, *Reportér* interview with František Šorm, 23 October 1968.

[27] A AV ČR—Fond OW, Soudy, Rozsudek (10 c 431/80), Obvodní soud pro Prahu 1, 23 October 1981.

positive future.[28] Wichterle was constantly concerned about the financing of research: to maintain the world-class level of the institute demanded financing that would come from outside the ČSAV. This was not merely the conclusion of Wichterle, but the state too supported the increasing efficiency of research. The way Wichterle gained state support for his project is not only a proof of his skills in negotiating with the decision-makers but it also indicates that the invention was regarded as highly important by the state (Wichterle 1992, pp. 146–47).

With the sale of the licence to produce the soft contact lens in 1965, Czechoslovakia perhaps made its most successful East to West transfer of technology. The licence was sold to the small American company National Patent Development Corporation (NPDC) which hitherto had been focusing its attention on technology in the Soviet Union. In 1966, NPDC sublicensed to Bausch and Lomb the rights to hydrogels and to the manufacturing of the lens (Wichterle 1992, p. 159). Ironically, the invention made by a 'socialist scientist' became a pawn of the capitalist market economy. The transfer of the soft contact lens technology to the United States initiated intense interest in hydrophilic materials so that hydrogel studies were transformed into a totally new field (Kopeček 1998). The advance of the new invention proved to be significant. The soft lenses were soon prescribed more often than hard lenses, mainly because they were comfortable to wear. In 1966, *Science* noted that the method of using hydrophilic polymers for contact lenses is a 'notable early entry into East–West technological trade' (McElheny 1966, p. 621). The ČSAV was pleased with the trade: by the end of 1966 the American firm was supposed to pay the ČSAV $105,000. The licence agreement with the USA led to a significant improvement in the development and production of the contact lens. From the perspective of the ČSAV, the experience of the soft contact lens was evidence that the chosen policy was correct. The transfer of the lens was taken as a pioneering example of how to sell licences to the West. For the state, the case also offered answers as to how obstacles could be overcome.[29]

After the selling of the lens, Wichterle wrote a critical report about the state of science to the president of the ČSAV.[30] In his report entitled the 'Era of economic threat to the Republic' ('*Doba hospodářského ohrožení republiky*') Wichterle wrote that the optimism of the 1950s had been a manifestation of 'self-delusion' (*sebeklam*) which had now led into a deep depression. He urged the ČSAV to adapt to these problems. By using the West as a positive example Wichterle stated that Czechoslovak economic decision-makers did not understand that science as such, at least in the fields of natural and technical sciences, is a 'profitable form of trade'. Wichterle believed that the organisational middle-level had not been as active as it could have been. The state was not solely to blame because, he claimed, the ČSAV could have learned to sell its products in a more efficient way. Although he did not speak for a broad commercialisation of science, which in Wichterle's opinion could have risked its most important aims, he questioned the meaning of science to the state, which was not

[28]A AV ČR—Osobní fond Otto Wichterle (OW), Zpráva o činnosti akademika O.Wichterla za rok 1963.

[29]A AV ČR—Fond Presidium ČSAV, 6, zasedání (17 March 1966). Zpráva o stavu výroby a exportu kontaktních čoček za rok 1965.

[30]A AV ČR—Fond OW, Úloha Akademie v době hospodářského ohrození republiky (Koncept pro akad, *Šorma* 23 November 1965).

sufficiently interested in competing with the Western world. For Wichterle the problem lay in the Czechoslovak economy, which did not have to compete with the rest of the world, and therefore did not need science. As a solution, he suggested open-door tactics and more licence agreements in foreign scientific trade. He hoped for the creation of favourable conditions for scientific–technical cooperation, which would assist deliberations on the issuing of licences. Significantly, Wichterle stated that the positive feedback from the first licence agreements proved that by breaking down the licence barriers, the Czechoslovaks could become attractive partners in the world.[31]

The economic problems in Czechoslovakia had a strong impact on Wichterle who, in 1967, wrote a cautionary essay addressed to the ČSAV, entitled 'The pessimistic alternative' ('*Pesimistická alternativa*') on the possible problems of the future.[32] Wichterle pointed out concrete problems which the organisational model of science had created. Rather than suggesting the replacement of the existing system with a capitalist one, he offered possible solutions to increase the efficiency of science. In this respect his statements were in line with the scientific–technical revolution. Wichterle's interest focused mainly on the ČSAV and his own field of research. He belonged to a group of employees of the ČSAV who were given the task of preparing the Action Programme of the ČSAV (*Akční program ČSAV*) in line with the concepts formulated in the Action Programme of the Communist Party (Mišková *et al.* 1998, pp. 19–20, 78).

Wichterle openly promoted the widening of international cooperation. In his opinion the main problem hindering the development of research was the conflict between the high production capacity of science and the low demand for research results. As a solution, he suggested cooperation with the developed countries and the creation of more favourable conditions for making use of scientists and the fruits of their research. He also suggested that the state should create 'bridges' that would enable more effective international cooperation. He suggested the revision of the directives, which regulated and limited scientific exchanges and stressed the importance of long-term or even permanent stays of Czechoslovak scientists in foreign scientific institutions at least in the 'most important fields'. The loss to the work force in Czechoslovakia would be compensated for by increased income from royalties.[33]

The culmination of changes in 1968

The change in the political course in January 1968 was a necessary precondition for concrete reforms in the field of science. In March 1968 the ČSAV suggested new science policy measures which highlighted the importance of foreign contacts. One of the first measures was the cancellation of the regulation of scientific relations with West Germany and the USA. Altogether, the ČSAV suggested the preparation of new,

[31] A AV ČR—Fond OW, Úloha Akademie v době hospodářského ohrození republiky (Koncept pro akad, *Šorma* 23 November 1965).

[32] A AV ČR—Fond OW, Studie o rozvoji makromolekulární chemie a technologie do roku 1980, 16 January 1967.

[33] A AV ČR—Fond OW, Ke kádrové politice v oboru vědy, 1967.

simpler rules for foreign scientific relations.[34] The General Assembly of the ČSAV in April 1968 marked an important event in the reform course of the Academy. The institution declared full autonomy and freedom of research. It decided that cooperation with foreign scientific institutions would be carried out according to scientific needs rather than be determined by foreign policy concerns (Mišková *et al.* 1998, p. 19). In the 'Action Programme' of the Academy, contacts with foreign scientific institutions were strongly emphasised. It went so far as to state that: 'the integration of the world has moved so far forward that it is not possible to hamper the development of many sectors with regional and other borders' (Mišková *et al.* 1998, p. 79).

Unlike the Party leadership, the directors of the Academy had not been replaced in 1968. The most enthusiastic reformers inside the Academy did not seem to believe that the leadership was genuinely advocating the reforms. Amongst the issues raised was the accusation that the leadership had ignored the social sciences. As president of the organisation, František Šorm had to react to the criticisms. He admitted that social sciences had suffered from dogmatism in the past. However, he tried to lessen the alleged impact of the failures of past policies by stating that the ČSAV had nevertheless managed to create a relatively wide space for free research in the natural and technical sciences. In them, dogmatic theories had been mostly rejected at an early stage. Šorm admitted that he had made mistakes but pointed out that the real problem was the over-centralised management of the Academy. Because of this, the power of the Academy and his own influence was very limited or even weak.[35] František Šorm was cautious in his statements before the invasion. His careful attitude can be illustrated by the fact that in the preparation process of the Action Programme he had suggested avoiding the use of the concept of a 'new model of socialist democracy' because it could irritate the 'fraternal countries' (Jindra 2001, pp. 137–38).

In 1968, Wichterle was elected to the National Assembly. He was also a member of the planning committee for the organisation for scientific workers (*Český svaz vědeckých pracovníků*), a group of scientists who were worried about the 'political handicap' of scientists compared to other intellectuals and who wished to establish an independent organisation of scientists. They felt that the Academy of Sciences was not capable of this function because of its dependence on the Party. The ideas of Wichterle reflect an era characterised by strong faith in scientism. Wichterle defined himself primarily as a scientist, who acted as a spokesman for science even in the political arena. For him politics represented a way to rationalise the society in which science had to operate. According to Wichterle, scientists should take care not to end up being the victims of changing political trends; they should correct the decisions made by politicians (Wichterle 1992, pp. 172–73; Schwippel 2001, pp. 167–71).

In the summer of 1968, the 'Two Thousand Words Manifesto' was published as the culmination of the democratisation process (Navrátil 2006, pp. 177–81). Otto Wichterle participated in the planning of the manifesto as a member of a small hard-core, which was unanimous that scientists and scholars should express their

[34]A AV ČR—Fond FŠ, Podklad k vystoupení předsedy ČSAV akademika F. Šorma na aktivu komunistů z ústavů ČSAV, pořádném MěV KSČ v Praze dne, 26 March 1968.

[35]A AV ČR—Fond FŠ.

opinion openly. The manifesto became one of the decisive elements that provoked the Soviet Union and its allies to use stronger measures against Czechoslovakia's liberation process. A radio interview in April 1968[36] offers one possible answer as to how Wichterle saw the process around him. In his opinion, people in Czechoslovakia were able to speak relatively freely, but without authority. The real issue was whether those with authority would be liberal enough to respect the will of the people.

Wichterle's hopes did not come to pass: Czechoslovakia was invaded in August 1968. However, the reforms of the Academy of Sciences continued even after the invasion while the leadership remained unchanged. The Action Programme of the Academy of Sciences was accepted in October 1968. It gave the authority on questions of science to scientists themselves and stressed the democratic principles governing science. It stated that political and economic pressures should be removed. Perhaps the most radical point in the Action Programme was in relation to the freedom and autonomy of research. The legislative changes that the Action Programme would have required were planned during autumn 1968 and spring 1969. The changes would have made the Academy of Sciences an autonomous, though state financed, institution and the plan was to establish two independent academies, one in the Czech lands and one in Slovakia (Mišková *et al.* 1998, pp. 19–27).

After the invasion, František Šorm tried to persuade the directorate of the ČSAV to further promote the reforms. As late as September 1969 the Academy sent a letter to the academies of the Soviet Union and other occupying Warsaw Pact countries, in which it expressed regret at the invasion and declared that it would stand behind the reforms. Pressures from outside grew rapidly however, and in its October 1969 meeting the members of the Academy voted for the removal of František Šorm, who had refused to vote in parliament for the right of the Soviet troops to stay on Czechoslovak soil. A new era began as the new president Jaroslav Kožešník took over the Academy and the Normalisation measures extended to a growing number of workers of the ČSAV (Otáhal *et al.* 1993, p. 48). The legal measures directed against the individuals who had participated in the scientific reforms of the Prague Spring were implemented in March 1970, when the new legislation ensured direct control of the government over the Academy of Sciences.

In the estimation of František Šorm, the development of Czechoslovak society differed from most countries in the East and West because the participation of scientists was fully 'programmed' and in many cases scientists had had real opportunities to influence things.[37] This was also one of the reasons why the process had to end. The impact of the invasion led to a limitation of the space of activity of scientists in the whole socialist bloc. As Vladimir Shlapentokh (1990, p. 173) has noted, for the Soviet Union the developments in Czechoslovakia acted as a final warning that the intelligentsia had been provided with too much freedom. The practical policy of the state, which had valued the competence of scientists over their political orientation, changed. Accordingly, one of the best-known scientists in the country, Otto Wichterle, was removed from his position as the head of the Institute of

[36]A AV ČR—Fond OW, Československý rozhlas, Praha, 23 April 1968.

[37]A AV ČR—Fond FŠ, *Reportér* interview with František Šorm, 23 October 1968.

Macromolecular Chemistry of the Czechoslovak Academy of Sciences. Both Otto Wichterle and František Šorm became *personae non gratae* of the Normalisation period.[38]

Conclusion

One of the elements of the liberalisation process of Czechoslovakia was the state's rapprochement towards the West. The phenomenon was accelerated by economic necessities. Thus, cooperation with the West was an economically pragmatic approach, seen as the last opportunity to catch up with the West and to restore Czechoslovakia's lost glory as one of the most industrialised countries of the world. As cooperation within the Soviet bloc did not help in fulfilling this goal, Czechoslovak attention was diverted towards partners in the West. However, the state's dependence on technological and economic progress was realised before the actual Prague Spring of 1968, which was the culmination of the attempts to realise and openly express ideas that had developed over a long period.

In the advent of the scientific–technical revolution in the first half of the 1960s, dependence on technological advancement had amplified the need to remove obstacles to international cooperation. Natural scientists within the Academy of Sciences saw in the scientific–technical revolution the possibility to improve research conditions in Czechoslovakia. Furthermore, the idea of integrating with world science legitimated more extensive contacts with Western scientists. Natural scientists were unquestionable actors in the process 'heading toward a better future' because of the economic benefit and intellectual capital they brought to the state. An illustrative example of the predominance of natural sciences is the leadership of the Academy of Sciences. Significantly, all successors of František Šorm to the post of the president of the Academy have been natural scientists.

However, cooperation with the West was politically and ideologically risky. There were many factors that slowed the process down, including ideological considerations, the threat of emigration and the lack of hard currency. Despite the difficulties, contacts with the West increased throughout the 1960s. By revoking travel restrictions and supporting international cooperation, the state managed to advance Czechoslovak research in many disciplines, and the country gained acknowledgment in the West. The liberalisation process created favourable conditions for innovative research, which led to successful transfers of technology. The example of Wichterle shows that the profit was mutual. Wichterle's innovation suggested that changes in practices were needed; and for Wichterle the successful trade with the contact lens gave him more

[38]Wichterle did not only lose his position in the Institute. He was not allowed to travel until 1976 and he furthermore became a target of vilification in newspaper articles that concentrated mainly on the counter-revolutionary character of the 'Two Thousand Words'. The discussion with its pro and contra arguments extended to a foreign readership in the pages of the *New Scientist* (A AV ČR—OW. Letter of Otto Wichterle to the *New Scientist*, 2 November 1970). To some extent, Wichterle was, however, able to continue working. Following the Velvet Revolution, he was chosen as the president of the Academy of Sciences in 1990. František Šorm lost his position as the head of the Institute and president of the Academy. Although he remained a scientist in his Institute, research conditions were very limited and he was not allowed to travel abroad. He died of a heart attack in 1980.

room for manoeuvre. The 'scientific currency' Wichterle brought to the state coffers increased his authority and led to his involvement in actual politics during the Prague Spring. Even though natural scientists have not been the most visible political actors of societal critique, and have been perceived as apolitical, they certainly had an influence on politics through their work and bargaining skills. Advocating more effective trade with the West and more intensive contacts with Western scientists can hardly be considered as apolitical aims.

University of Helsinki

References

Brádlerová, D. & Kmochová, N. (2001) 'Nástin zahraničních styků ČSAV 1962–1970', in Zilynská, B. & Svobodný, P. (eds) (2001).

Connelly, J. (2000) *Captive University. The Sovietization of East German, Czech and Polish Higher Education 1945–1956* (Chapel Hill, The University of North Carolina Press).

Djerassi, C. (1992) *The Pill, Pygmy Chimps, and Degas' Horse* (New York, Basic Books).

Gerovitch, S. (2001) '"Mathematical Machines" of the Cold War: Soviet Computing, American Cybernetics and Ideological Disputes in the Early 1950s', *Social Studies of Science*, 31, 2, April.

Gerovitch, S. (2002) *From Newspeak to Cyberspeak. A History of Soviet Cybernetics* (Cambridge, MA, The MIT Press).

Graham, L. (1993) *Science in Russia and the Soviet Union. A Short History* (New York, Cambridge University Press).

Havránek, J. (2005) 'Czech Universities under Communism', in Connelly, J. & Grüttner, M. (eds) (2005) *Universities under Dictatorship* (University Park, Pennsylvania State University Press).

Holý, A. (2004) 'Organický chemik František Šorm', in Šmahel, F. (ed.) (2004) *Učení očima kolegů a žáků* (Prague, Academia).

Jindra, J. (2001) 'František Šorm—závěr politické kariery', in Zilynská, B. & Svobodný, P. (eds) (2001).

Jindra, J. (2003) 'The Sovietization of Natural Sciences in Czechoslovakia (1945–1960)', in Zub, A. & Solomon, F. (eds) (2003) *Sovietization in Romania and Czechoslovakia. History, Analogies, Consequences* (Bucharest, 'A.D. Xenopol' Institute of History—Romanian Academy).

Kaplan, K. (2002a) *Kořeny československé reformy 1968* (Brno, Doplněk).

Kaplan, K. (2002b) *Rada vzájemné hospodářské pomoci a Československo 1957–1967* (Prague, Karolinum).

Kiser, J. (1989) *Communist Entrepreneurs. Unknown Innovators in the Global Economy* (New York and Toronto, Franklin Watts).

Kopeček, J. (1998) 'Obituary Otto Wichterle (1913–98)', *Nature*, 24 September, available at: http://www.nature.com/nature/journal/v395/n6700/full/395332a0.html, accessed 12 June 2007.

Kostlán, A. (2001) 'Československá akademie věd v letech 1952–1970', in Zilynská, B. & Svobodný, P. (eds) (2001).

McElheny, V. K. (1966) 'Research and Industry in Czechoslovakia', *Science*, 153, 3726, August.

McMahon, T. & Zadnik, K. (2000) 'Twenty-five Years of Contact Lenses. The Impact of the Cornea and Ophthalmic Practise', *Cornea*, 19, 5.

Metcalf, L. K. (1993) 'The Impact of Foreign Trade on the Czechoslovak Economic Reforms of the 1960s', *Europe-Asia Studies*, 45, 6, September.

Mišková, A. (1986) 'Vytváření mezinárodní vědecké spolupráce ČSAV v letech 1952–1961', in *Práce z dějin Československé akademie věd Studia Historiae acedemiae scientiarium bohemoslovacae Fasc. 1* (Prague, Ústřední archiv ČSAV).

Mišková, A., Barvíková, H. & Šmidák, M. (1998) *Československá akademie věd 1969–1972. Restaurace komunistické moci ve vědě* (Prague, Ústav pro soudobé dějiny AV ČR).

Navrátil, J. (ed.) (2006) *The Prague Spring 1968. A National Security Archive Document Reader* (Budapest, Central European University Press).

Otáhal, M., Nosková, A. & Bolomský, K. (1993) *Svědectví o duchovním útlaku 1969–1970. Normalizace v kultuře, umění, vědě, školství a masových sdělovácích prostředcích* (Prague, Ústav pro soudobé dějiny AV ČR).

Richta, R. (1969) *Civilization at the Crossroads. Social and Human Implications of the Scientific Technological Revolution* (Prague, International Arts and Sciences Press).

Rindzeviciute, E. (2008) *Constructing Soviet Cultural Policy. Cybernetics and Governance in Lithuania after World War II* (Linköping University).

Roll-Hansen, N. (2005) *The Lysenko Effect. The Politics of Science* (Amherst, Humanity Books).

Schwippel, J. (2001) 'Otto Wichterle a Český svaz vědeckých pracovníků', in Zilynská, B. & Svobodný, P. (eds) (2001).

Shlapentokh, V. (1990) *Soviet Intellectuals and Political Power. The Post-Stalin Era* (Princeton, Princeton University Press).

Skilling, G. H. (1976) *Czechoslovakia's Interrupted Revolution* (Princeton, Princeton University Press).

Slamecka, V. (1963) *Science in Czechoslovakia* (New York, Columbia University Press).

Turková, J. (2000) 'Vědecká aspirantura v ústavu organické chemie a biochemie ČSAV v letech 1959–1962', in Barvíková, H (ed.) (2000) *Věda v Československu v letech 1953–1963. Sborník z konference* (Prague, Archiv Akademie věd České republiky).

Wichterle, O. (1992) *Vzpomínky* (Prague, Evropský kulturní klub) [published in English as *Recollections* (Prague, Ideu Repro)].

Wilczynski, J. (1974) *Technology in Comecon. Acceleration of Technological Progress through Economic Planning and the Market* (London, Macmillan).

Williams, K. (1997) *The Prague Spring and its Aftermath. Czechoslovak Politics 1968–1970* (Cambridge, Cambridge University Press).

Winters, S. B. (1994) 'Science and Politics: The Rise and Fall of the Czechoslovak Academy of Sciences', *Bohemia*, 35, 2.

Zilynská, B. & Svobodný, P. (eds) (2001) *Česká věda a Pražské jaro (1963–1970). Sborník z konference* (Prague, Ústav dějin—Archiv UK).

The Limits of Thought?: The Regulatory Framework of Social Sciences and Humanities in Czechoslovakia (1968–1989)

LIBORA OATES-INDRUCHOVÁ

IN THE CZECHOSLOVAK CONTEXT, IT IS RELATIVELY UNSURPRISING that humanities and social sciences became a primary focus of the ideological pressure in the aftermath of the Soviet-led invasion of Czechoslovakia in 1968. The mobilising power of Czech and Slovak intellectuals has been noted by scholars (Pynsent 1994; Hroch 1999) as being a political force at least since the nineteenth-century national movement. Therefore, after the communists came to power in 1948, intellectuals and their work had to be harnessed so that they would be effective for and not against the ruling ideology. In this context, the humanities and social sciences were seen as politically important, because they provided interpretations of social (and hence also political) reality that were seen as having the potential to influence public opinion. Sociology—seen as a 'bourgeois pseudo-science'—was considered especially dangerous and thus was abolished as a university discipline in 1950. It was re-established in 1965, as part of the political thaw of the 1960s (Petrusek 2004, pp. 598–601), when critical inquiry in other humanities and social sciences began to develop once again, but was then suppressed once more after 1968.

The severity of repressions among academic staff at universities and in the research institutes of the Academy of Sciences provided a telling testimony to the process of heightened ideological surveillance of the time;[1] yet, research interest among Czechoslovak scholars in academic life during the whole period of Normalisation between 1969 and 1989[2] has only developed significantly in recent years.[3]

The writing of this article was facilitated by a Marie Curie Intra-European Fellowship within the 7th European Community Framework Programme and held at the Collegium Budapest Institute for Advanced Study.

[1]For quantifiable aspects of the repressions, see for example, Tůma (2002), Urbášek (2002) and Mišková (2002).

[2]Milan Otáhal explains the history and usage of the term 'Normalisation' as follows: 'The term "normalisation" was introduced by the Communists, but they related it primarily to the beginnings of the period, for which one of the leading dissidents, Milan Šimečka, coined the term "the restoration of order". Post-1989 historians have adopted the term and use it usually to denote the whole period up to 1989 instead of the perhaps more fitting term "real-existing socialism" in its second, "static" phase' (Otáhal 2002, p. 6).

[3]See, for example, the comprehensive collection edited by Antonín Kostlán, covering the years from 1970 to 1975 (Kostlán 2002), and the special issue of *Sociologický časopis/Czech Sociological Review* on Normalisation sociology published in 2004 (volume 40, issue 5). Apart from these more comprehensive

This essay examines the institutional framework of ideological regulations that set the limits for academia in the humanities and social sciences within which research, publishing and university teaching had to manoeuvre. I use the English term 'academia' for brevity and convenience to include institutions, individuals and activities involved in both social science and humanities research (whether in the institutes of the Czechoslovak Academy of Sciences, applied research institutions outside the Academy, or at universities) and university education; in other words, any academic/research institutions and their employees, and activities that were subject to state control and funding. In practice, and in the absence of a private or non-governmental sector, that meant everything and everybody in social science and humanities research and tertiary education. The essays limits itself only to the realm of officially documented instruments of control, the regulatory documents and measures used by the governing institutions.[4]

While the scope of Normalisation in relation to academia was all-encompassing, its pace was uneven. The Communist Party asserted its influence by means of a top-down process: it started with the top layers of institutional hierarchy and gradually spread its controlling directives further down the ladder of academic institutions, from the academic 'centre' to its 'significant periphery' by various repressive, preventive, and structural means. The main parts of the process were completed within a year from the beginning of Normalisation in academia (between May 1969 and June 1970) and further substantial measures had followed by the mid-1970s. After that, and until the demise of state socialism in 1989, however, the speed and force of ideological control seemed to have slackened. I will propose that this slowing down of Normalisation was a manifestation of a shift in the Party focus from an emphasis on ideologically correct *content* of research (including its theoretical and methodological grounding) to ideologically correct *form*; that is, a shift from concern about the real convictions of academics as demonstrated by their creative approach to Marxist–Leninist theory and method, to a concern with the appearance of ideological loyalty, as demonstrated by academics keeping within set doctrinaire boundaries. The essay will further propose that the centralised system of power over academia was inherently inefficient in

works, several earlier memoirs by significant researchers address the issues (Komárek 1992; Machonin 1993; Potůček 1995), as well as bibliographic and documentation publications (most significantly, Otáhal *et al.* 1993; Otáhal 2002), and studies on specific research areas (Prečan 1994b; Šámal 2002). Perhaps the most thorough contemporary analysis of the general aspects of Normalisation and its underlying social psychology is Šimečka's *The Restoration of Order* (Šimečka 1985), originally published in *samizdat* in 1978. Another contemporary testimony of academic life in normalised Czechoslovakia is an account of the development in Czech philosophy '*Čeští filosofové po 30 letech: Současný stav "normalisované" filosofie*' ('Czech Philosophers after 30 Years: The Current State of "Normalised" Philosophy'), published in the exile journal *Studie* under the pseudonym XYZ [XYZ (Praha) 1977]. A unique contribution to the methodology of research on Normalisation in academia is *Our Lives as Database—Doing a Sociology of Ourselves: Czech Social Transitions in Autobiographical Research Dialogues* (Konopásek 2000).

[4]This leaves aside the so far little researched and complex areas of institutional and personal agency and power within the regulatory structure, including the generational issue (how the actual working conditions differed between the contemporaries of 1968 and those who entered academia after that date), as that would require drawing on empirical data, which are not available in the scope needed to cover adequately the entire institutional range over the whole period.

communicating the Party directives and supervising their implementation in all academic institutions by all their employees.

Published works and documentation resources are particularly useful for an outline of the regulative measures during the first years after the 1968 invasion. The further we move from this landmark date, however, the less systematic research there is. This study cannot lay claim to a comprehensive and exhaustive account of all institutional prescriptions and proscriptions. Such a study would require the processing of a vast amount of material that is not yet available from the various relevant archives because it has not been catalogued. Instead, with regard to the later years of Normalisation, I would like to propose to look for traces of the extent, magnitude and pivotal points of the regulation of academic life by the state and the Communist Party marked in the discourse of official documents, regulative measures and propaganda texts pertaining to the social sciences and humanities.

For the later years of Normalisation, the collections of Radio Free Europe/Radio Liberty Research Institute (RFE/RL) are, arguably, the most comprehensive, if ideologically driven, source of materials documenting this discourse. The RFE/RL needed official propaganda and other published material from Czechoslovakia for its own analyses and critical commentaries on the situation in various areas of life under state socialism in order to counter the dominant communist ideology.[5] Thus, it conducted comprehensive media monitoring of, among other things, the developments in social sciences, education and cultural policy. It amassed a wide range of materials: primarily, official Communist Party documents regulating the development of social sciences and universities, commentaries by politicians, Normalisation enforcers or sympathisers from among academics on these documents, and news-wire reports and newspaper articles on the various regulatory measures of academic research and teaching. It is possible to identify from among the mass of assorted materials the key regulatory documents and strategies and organise those into a chronological overview, illustrating the logic of the process of Normalisation that was to lead to hegemonic power of the Party over academic life.[6] This endeavour cannot provide an exact and detailed historical record. What it can do, however, is outline the main tendencies in the Party's efforts to control academic research in social sciences and humanities.

[5]The RFE/RL archives, housed in the Open Society Archives in Budapest, have significant limitations, and not only those stemming from the ideological purpose of their collection. Changes in RFE/RL's policies or the quality of the archivists also affected what was collected. (I am grateful for this comment to one of the reviewers of this article.) However, any archival source would have similar limitations and I took them into consideration in the selection of the documents I consulted for the argument presented in this article: I focused solely on substantial regulative decrees and measures issued during the period 1969–1989, while leaving aside RFE/RL's own Situation Reports of events and processes in individual institutions. (If I mention a particular case, it is merely for illustration of what forms a concrete measure or strategy could take.)

[6]A similar approach has been taken by others: Vilém Prečan, who documents in detail the period between 1968 and 1972 in Czechoslovak social sciences in general (Prečan 1994b); Alena Míšková, who gives an account of the Czechoslovak Academy of Sciences between 1970 and 1975 (Míšková 2002); and Pavel Urbášek, who outlines the situation at Czech universities between 1970 and 1975 (Urbášek 2002).

The intellectual community in 1968: an irritant in the eye of Normalisation

The Soviet-led invasion in August 1968 opened the way for the anti-reformist forces in the Communist Party to reclaim the power positions they had lost and to introduce measures to regain control of all spheres of life. A document issued following the plenary session of the Central Committee of the Party of Czechoslovakia (*Ústřední výbor Komunistické strany Československa, ÚV KSČ*) in May 1969 identified the priority areas for renewing their influence.[7] According to the summary in a further Progress Report ['Progress Report on the Executive Directions and Further Tasks of the Ideological Activities of the Party' (*Zpráva o plnění Realizační směrnice a další úkoly ideologické činnosti strany*) available in Otáhal *et al.* (1993, p. 119)] these included the following goals: 'to renew the unity of the Party on the principles of teachings of Marxism–Leninism', 'to increase the operational ability and fitness for revolutionary action of the whole party', and 'to renew the leading role of the Communist Party in society'. In relation to social sciences, these relatively vague statements began to take a concrete shape in a confidential document of the Ideological Committee of the Party Central Committee (*Ideologická komise ÚV KSČ*) discussed at the meeting of the committee in June 1970. The document outlined the main tasks for the whole area of academic research. Primary importance was given to 'the completion of the cleansing of the top executive bodies of the Czechoslovak Academy of Sciences and academic institutions of right-wing opportunist and anti-socialist elements'. Two further tasks were the 'drafting of an Act stipulating a unified control over and coordination of the development of academic research, technology and investments' and 'calling a plenary session of the ÚV KSČ on the further development of academic research and technology' ('Progress Report', available in Otáhal *et al.* 1993, p. 49).

According to Otáhal and his colleagues, social sciences and intellectuals in general became prominent targets of the propagators of 'consolidation' and later 'Normalisation' because, first of all, of the involvement of intellectuals in the reform process of the Prague Spring (Otáhal *et al.* 1993). The political activism of university students during that time and of Czech writers at the Writers' Union Congress in June 1967 and after is well documented.[8] Researchers at universities and in institutes of the Czechoslovak Academy of Sciences had expressed their political views, for example, by signing the declaration 'Two Thousand Words Manifesto' formulated by Czech writers, which expressed support for Dubček's government, but also called for civic initiatives independent of the directives of the Party and the government.

However, it was not just political activism that was held against intellectuals at the onset of Normalisation, but also their research, if it was perceived as having

[7] *Realizační směrnice květnového pléna ÚV KSČ pro další postup strany v příštím období* ('The Executive Directions of the May Plenary of the ÚV KSČ toward Further Party Actions in the Upcoming Period').

[8] For contemporary documentation, see, for example, 'Proceedings of the 4th Czechoslovak Writers' Congress, June 27–29, 1967, and a Follow-up Resolution by the CPCz CZ Plenum September 1967 (Excerpts)', in Navrátil (1998). Otáhal expanded his research over the following years in several publications. The most relevant for the issue at hand is Otáhal (1999), and a useful bibliographic source is Otáhal (2002).

negative political implications. Foremost among these research initiatives was the collection of documents concerning the first week of the occupation published by the Institute of History of the Czechoslovak Academy of Sciences under the title *Sedm pražských dnů* (*Seven Prague Days*) (Sedm prazských dnů 1968). Other works that were labelled as 'opportunist' or 'revisionist' included work on the economic theories of Ota Šik conducted at the Economic Institute of the Czechoslovak Academy of Sciences, work of the research team working on the project 'Czechoslovak Society' led by Pavel Machonin at the Institute of Sociology, and works on non-Marxist philosophy conducted either at the Institute of Philosophy or at universities.

Thus, on the one hand, the social sciences were seen as 'a tool from the realm of ideology for acquiring knowledge of social reality and for the class struggle',[9] but on the other hand they embodied the potential for independent thought and action among intellectuals, an area which became a prime focus of the normalising forces as they attempted to reassert their power.[10] With reference to a 1970 Party analysis, Oldřich Tůma has noted that the ÚV KSČ considered researchers 'less reliable, because a lot of them were insufficiently tempered "in terms of class and of their politics" and participated in the preparations and incitement of the Party and overall social crisis' (Tůma 2002, p. 22). University lecturers were then often viewed as 'ideological conspirators and organisers of anti-socialist and anti-Soviet demonstrations' (Tůma 2002, p. 22).

The 'normalising executive' in the Party leadership assessed fairly correctly the level of influence social sciences could have on public opinion, education and the political consciousness of citizens. It was therefore necessary to subjugate them and prevent potential disobedience by academics in these fields, and then to use the social sciences and humanities for the promotion of the ideology of Normalisation. The first step in the renewal of the 'unity of the Party' was a thorough vetting of all Party members ('*prověrky*') between 1969 and 1970. This was carried out through 'the replacement of Party ID cards' following a formal interview in front of a committee at one's workplace. Its goal was the elimination of politically unacceptable Party members—those who actively participated in the reform process or did not express their full support for the normalising developments. In a purely technical respect, the process meant issuing new Party ID cards to members; however, being or not being issued the new ID card carried enormous consequences for every individual member. Thus Vilém Prečan characterises the implications of being placed into one of the three

[9]A. Dolina, 'Fakta k zamyšlení', Radio Praha programme (Prague, Czech Republic), 4 January 1972. Radio programme. OSA 300-30-6, box 44.

[10]When referring to those who constructed and perpetuated the machinery of Normalisation, I deliberately avoid naming concrete individuals in executive positions or political authorities because although the overall directions came from the top of the Party hierarchy, their implementation within particular institutions was influenced by personnel politics within the concrete institution/workplace. Anecdotal evidence in published literature (Potůček 1995; Prokůpek 2002) and my own yet unpublished research suggests that ideological unsuitability was frequently merely a cover for venting professional rivalry, personal grudges, and sometimes gender discrimination. By 'normalising forces' I mean the complex power dynamics of the political directives, the individuals appointed to executive posts, and personal motivations.

categories—'expulsion, membership cancellation and positive vetting result'—for an individual's career prospects:

> They were dealt with accordingly at their workplaces: contract termination, transfer to a less qualified job at the workplace, transfer to a less ideologically 'demanding' workplace but still being able to use one's qualifications; or, on the other hand, transfer to a higher post, a cushy seat on a gravy train. (Prečan 1994b, p. 298)

According to Tůma (2002, p. 21) the Party removed a total of 28% or almost half a million of its members in this vetting process. He further argues that academics were affected by the vetting more than other professions: 'Academics were represented among those expelled from the Party two-and-a-half times more than would correspond to their ratio in the overall membership before the vetting' (Tůma 2002, p. 22). Alena Míšková has confirmed this finding and concluded that the Czechoslovak Academy of Sciences showed a 61.5% decrease in its Party membership (Míšková 2002, p. 164).[11] The blacklisting of people from jobs, professions and publishing had gradually subsided by 1973 or 1974, when it became possible even for those who had been dismissed as politically undesirable to find some form of professional existence, but any formalised rehabilitation was not possible until after the fall of the regime in 1989.

The first year of Normalisation: in sweeping strides or faltering steps?

Reading through Party documents one cannot help but admire the ingenuity of the normalising forces and the thoroughness of the whole process of power centralisation. In addition to the readiness with which they realised the threatening potential of social science for their power system, the normalising forces also knew that in 1968 they had been in the minority, hence the intention, first to cleanse the Party, and then to encroach on the minds and freedoms of 'the masses'. They employed a strict top-down approach. The 'Progress Report' from June 1970 stated plainly that 'right-wing opportunist elements still prevail' among the intelligentsia and that they exerted an influence over the majority of 'our academic and intellectual front' (Otáhal *et al.* 1993, p. 4). The orchestrators of Normalisation knew only too well that if, in this situation, they tried to assert their influence in every research institute, university classroom or on every piece of published research from the start, they would encounter massive resistance. Thus it was necessary to weave a web of hegemonic power from the centre, because the centre was easier to subsume under control.[12] After that, they could gradually co-opt wider and wider circles, all the way through the hierarchy of intellectual institutions and their staff. The operational ability of the Party would thus

[11]František Morkeš (2002) has described the form of the vetting at universities and provides details of some of the questions asked at the interviews. Ladislav Prokůpek (2002) has detailed the Normalisation process in the Institute of Philosophy and Sociology of the Czechoslovak Academy of Sciences and outlined also the process of similar interviews with non-Party members at the Institute from autumn 1970.

[12]Alena Míšková also arrived at this conclusion in her case study of the Czechoslovak Academy of Sciences (Míšková 2002, p. 164).

increase and the leading role of the Communist Party in society would be renewed and secured.

The 'Progress Report' summarised the accomplishments of the Party over the first year after the issuance of 'The Executive Directions' and these accomplishments were certainly impressive.[13] The Party managed among other things: to conduct most of the vetting; to draft and pass the amendment to the Bill on the Czechoslovak Academy of Sciences, which 'fully respected the demands of the Party' (Otáhal *et al.* 1993, p. 86); to assemble a new leadership of the Academy of Sciences; to close down, merge (in the case of the Institutes of Philosophy and Sociology) or re-structure institutes of the Academy of Sciences and to dismiss their directors if they were deemed to have a blot on their political history; to deprive politically compromised researchers of their membership of the Academy or dismiss them from their jobs there; to do the same with university professors; to re-structure the teaching of Marxism–Leninism at universities through newly established institutes of Marxism–Leninism;[14] to sign new contracts for research visits to socialist countries, with an emphasis on the Soviet Union, in order to replace similar contracts with capitalist countries signed during the reform process; and to draft the state plan of research for 1971–1975 with three telling thematic areas for social sciences—'the social and human context of the scientific and technological revolution in the CSSR; the critique of the ideology of contemporary anti-Communism; and the Communist education of the population of the CSSR' (Otáhal *et al.* 1993, p. 88).

This process gave the Party control over the upper layers of the intellectual hierarchy and direction over all research in the social sciences, as well as over professional communication. New directors of research institutes and heads of university departments would now make sure that their institutions and staff followed Party directives; Party-defined research themes determined what research would be funded, and the new agreements about research visits would orient academic professionals toward the socialist countries and away from the West.[15]

At least that is how it was supposed to work in theory. In practice, the Party lost crucial time in spreading its 'normalising' influence between the invasion in August 1968 and the beginning of actual vetting in mid-1969. It admitted as much in the 'Progress Report': 'The situation in social sciences remained practically unchanged until the end of 1969. The process of differentiation between social science professionals was virtually impossible as long as the leading positions in the institutes

[13]The list of measures implemented by June 1970 in the whole field of 'ideology', as it was officially termed, and which included academic research, education, mass media, culture and art, and the measures planned for the next year are all listed and commented on in the 'Progress Report on the Executive Directions'. The document is reprinted in full in Otáhal *et al.* (1993, pp. 35–105).

[14]Apart from 'The Executive Directions' and the amendment to the Bill on the Czechoslovak Academy of Sciences, Vilém Prečan lists also the amendment to the Bill on universities as the third key document from the early stages of Normalisation. The Bill gave the Minister of Education the power to found and abolish university departments, and to conclude and terminate employment contracts with academic employees (Prečan 1994b). This amendment, nevertheless, came into force in August 1970, that is, after the 'Progress Report', which is discussed here.

[15]Prokůpek has written about the isolation and Sovietisation of Czech science from the onset of Normalisation giving the re-orienting of professional travel toward the East as an example of the process (Prokůpek 2002, p. 215).

were held by the right-wing powers' (Otáhal *et al.* 1993, p. 84). During this period, 'endangered' academics had time to close ranks in solidarity, prepare themselves for sanctions and perhaps even organise some minor, but important acts of resistance.[16]

Once the vetting process was underway, it was possible to implement Normalisation more fully. Once the *leadership* of the academic community was consolidated according to the new ideology of the Party, *all* researchers in the Academy of Sciences were put on probation: in June 1970 editorial boards of all academic journals were disbanded and editors-in-chief fired, to be replaced by those the Party now trusted. Furthermore, the new law on the Czechoslovak Academy of Sciences enabled the newly appointed directors of research institutes to sign new contracts with all academic employees—the main feature being that these were of a maximum four-year duration. Also in the spring of 1970, the main supervisory body of the Party for the whole sphere of education, academic research and culture, the Ideological Committee of the ÚV KSČ, began its activities. The committee had been established in May 1969, but its members never convened until a new committee was appointed in 1970 and met for the first time in March.[17] The committee worked in cooperation with the Department of the ÚV KSČ for Education, Academic Research and Culture. Their joint responsibilities were to put Party directives into practice, to oversee their fulfilment and to report their findings to the Central Committee. An important structural feature of the committee was that its chairman was a secretary of the Central Committee and its members included other members of the Central Committee and top executives of the media and research institutes of the Czechoslovak Academy of Sciences. As the committee reported directly and exclusively to the ÚV KSČ, it became the main means of bringing Party directives to research and educational institutions and, conversely, of reporting on these institutions to the Party itself.

The last thing that remained to be done in this initial stage of Normalisation was to codify the supervisory structure in legislation: the Party prepared a law on 'The Unified Management and Coordination of the Development of Academic Research, Technology and Investments' ('*Zákon o jednotném řízení a koordinaci rozvoje vědy, techniky a investic*') (Otáhal *et al.* 1993, p. 91). The Party, although it was the 'leading force in society', was not a legislative body, but in this way it ensured that its recommendations on the directions of academic research would now find support in law.

[16]In this context, it is interesting to note the analogous view of Vilém Prečan on the inner strategies of the Party: 'The intelligentsia could be attacked only after it was deprived of its public tribune and its connections to the wider public had been severed. To form consolidation groups and factions within the various areas of culture and its institutions including the educational system also required time' (Prečan 1994b, p. 283). Prečan wrote his article as a direct participant and a person persecuted in the vetting process; however, it has to be noted that he wrote it in 1973, that is at the time when the disastrous curtailment of Czech academic life was acutely felt, but when he could not have access to the text of the 'Progress Report', which was a confidential Party document, so he could not have known that the Party leadership was itself dissatisfied with the progress of Normalisation.

[17]See Otáhal *et al.* (1993, pp. 20–21 and 131), respectively, for a detailed account of the activities of the committee, and for a description of the general scope of responsibilities of all committees of the ÚV KSČ.

Advanced Normalisation: reaching further into the rank and file

Throughout Normalisation, the Party carried out the institutional and structural management of social sciences through the following sequence: it raised its concerns and demands at Party Congresses and plenary sessions of the Central Committee and worked these into guiding and binding documents; the appointed executives in the research institutes and Party media then wrote up these guidelines in the form of articles published in the appropriate journals and newspapers as guidelines for the academic community; at the same time, the Ideological Committee of the ÚV KSČ made other practical suggestions to influence the institutional process. The first key document after those mentioned above was a manifesto called 'The Lessons Learned from the Crisis Development in the Party and Society since the 13th Congress' (*Poučení z krizového vývoje ve straně a společnosti od XIII. sjezdu*). According to a secretary of the Central Committee, Jan Fojtík, 'this document is a foundation for critical analyses of individual academic areas, and it provides a clear orientation for the evaluation of the situation in institutional social-science units, as well as for identifying and setting the tasks of these units' (Fojtík 1972a, p. 147). The critical analysis of social sciences as a whole was published in an internal Party document in May 1971.[18] The Central Committee then formed committees which were to work from this overall analysis and produce 'critical analyses' for each discipline.[19] From then on the Party produced key documents periodically, evaluating social sciences in terms of their adherence to the Party priorities and setting research agendas for them. The titles of these documents are self-explanatory: 'The Development, Current State and the Tasks of Social Sciences', produced in 1974;[20] 'The Unified Program of Social Sciences after the 15th Congress of the CPCS' (*Jednotný program společenských věd po XV. sjezdu KSČ*) released in 1977 (Pecen 1977); and 'Partisan Work at the Czechoslovak Academy of Sciences and Slovak Academy of Sciences' (*Stranická práce v ČSAV a SAV*) issued in 1978 (Kubánek & Lacina 1980).[21] The document 'Further Development of the Czechoslovak Educational System' (*Další rozvoj československé výchovně vzdělávací soustavy*) published in 1976 focused on ideological work and the social science content of education (Janovský 1979).

[18]'*Nástin kritické analýzy společenských věd zejména v ČSAV*', published by the ÚV KSČ in May 1971 and comprising 167 pages. These data are cited in XYZ (Praha) (1977).

[19]The process of producing 'critical analyses' is described in XYZ (Praha) (1977).

[20]'Vývoj, současný stav a úkoly společenských věd: z materiálu předsednictva Ústředního výboru KSČ', *Rudé právo*, 20 June 1974. OSA 300-30-6, box 44.

[21]Bibliographic references to these documents may seem random as they include a range of media sources collected in the Open Society Archives, and thus raise questions as to the nature of the sources and credibility of information contained within them. To avoid the complex area of media representation as much as possible, I do not analyse any media commentaries on the Party documents and decisions, but use the sources only to record the publication and distribution of these documents and decisions. Thus the relevance of from what source I cite a particular document lies only in that it helps give an idea about the communication channels for Party directives. Similarly, if I quote from any media, it is a quotation of a quotation from a high Party and/or academic official, not the medium's own commentary.

Interestingly, there do not seem to be any similar key documents in the collections of the Open Society Archives after 1978.[22] While umbrella research themes continued to be set down in each Five-Year State Research Plan, the discontinuation of the accompanying key documents outlining the ideological foundations of all research can be explained by the change in the direction of the Party's ideological focus from the content of academic research to its form. If, in the 1972 document the plenary set out as the primary task of social science 'the principled criticism of inimical ideology with simultaneous creative development of Marxism–Leninism and positive solutions to theoretical problems' (Hrzal & Matouš 1972), by 1977 the Party, in a similar document, declared: 'we will gradually increase the extent of the Party influence in the social science area' (Majcharčík 1977, p. 9). In other words, the aim was no longer even to maintain the appearance of developing a theoretical foundation of Party-directed sciences, and hence, still adhering to the principles of scientific inquiry, but to exert unbridled ideological influence. We can also see this as a development from a dynamic to a static approach to ideological regulation of intellectual work: creativity and development of Marxist–Leninist theory and method were no longer required or needed, but only a preservation of the ideological status quo.

Several interpretations of this development are possible. First, as the years went by and the Party took control over the circles of hierarchies in social science institutions further and further from the centre, it could now be bolder in its goals and drop any remaining pretence of caring about the professional standards of social sciences and concern that their research be directed toward society's needs. Second, the emphasis on more widespread, insidious, ideological influence was propelled by the Charter 77 movement and the subsequent increase in dissident activities. Third, by the end of the 1970s the Party knew that it was not succeeding in its ideological persuasion and, therefore, its attempts at ideological control were more and more desperate manoeuvres to save face, while in fact, it was retreating from its positions in the actual management of research. In other words, the Party was now concentrating on the surface and was satisfied with keeping up the appearances of ideological compliance on the part of social science institutions and their researchers, instead of the incessant examination of their real commitment and convictions, for which it was aiming at the beginning of Normalisation.

The first interpretation was definitely the original goal of the normalising forces. As to the second, it is a well established fact that the Party was worried by the gradual increase in, as well as the domestic and foreign impact of, dissident activities. This is

[22] I am fairly confident in ruling out both my oversight and a change in archival policies as factors, because if such a document existed, there would have been at least traces of it in the form of references to it somewhere in the bulk of the variety of media, academic and propaganda materials, as there were in the case of the previous documents. (Each of those documents was circulated widely and was mentioned numerous times in the mass media, academic journals and the Party press.) In contrast, later general articles on the role of social sciences do not cite any key documents: for example, 'The Main Tasks of the Social Sciences', an article by Vladislav Mokošín, an employee of the ÚV KSČ, refers to the state plan of basic research, but not to any expressly ideological documents (Mokošín 1986, p. 17 and passim); or two articles on *perestroika* in social sciences refer to Gorbachev's speeches, but again not to any existing binding documents (Kunovjánek 1987; Bauer 1988).

documented, for example, by the various trials of dissidents from 1977 onwards.[23] The third explanation is suggested by commentaries in contemporary Party press by high ranking communist officials, suggesting that the Party was not satisfied with the overall implementation of Normalisation. In 1972 Fojtík expressed his satisfaction that 'the management of [social science research] was entrusted to people who have proved their loyalty to the Communist Party, the politics of the Party, and their creative Marxist–Leninist abilities to contribute to solving the need for understanding social practice' (Fojtík 1972a, p. 168). In contrast, commentaries on Party statistics in the 1980s expressed open dissatisfaction with the percentages of Party members at universities and in research institutes. One of the main Party mouthpieces, *Život strany*, stated in 1980 that the target numbers of membership were not met at universities and, even, that 'the representation of Communists in many departments does not guarantee the leading role of the Party at those workplaces' (Kašparová 1980). Similarly, in 1986 *Život strany* acknowledged failure in increasing the membership percentages in the Czechoslovak Academy of Sciences (Mokošín 1986). A conclusive answer to the question of which of these interpretations is the closest to the truth, or even how they could be combined, will probably remain a key issue for any research on social sciences and humanities during Normalisation for years to come. It will always depend on the focus of a given research project: whether it is the investigation of the hegemonic rule of the Party, the impact of the alternative spaces created by the dissident movement, or the processes and relations of everyday academic life.

The first focus, by definition, is the governing perspective of the investigation of Party regulations and directives, such as this one. It leads to the study of the mechanisms of communicating and implementing the directives expressed in the key documents to the lower echelons of academic hierarchy and to the public. The Party used a wide range of its media outlets as vehicles for delivering its messages, notably newspapers and ideological magazines, such as *Rudé právo*, *Tvorba*, *Život strany*, *Nová mysl*, or *Tribuna*, but also academic journals, such as, *Sociologický časopis*, *Filosofický časopis* and *Český časopis historický*.

The document of 1974, 'The Development, Current State and the Tasks of Social Sciences' (*Vývoj, současný stav a úkoly společenských věd*) serves as a typical example of how the whole process functioned. Its origins can be found in an article by Jan Fojtík on the 'tasks' of social sciences after the 14th Party Congress in *Nová mysl* in February 1972 (Fojtík 1972a). In March he addressed the General Meeting of the Czechoslovak Academy of Sciences with an overview of the contents of his article (Fojtík 1972b). This material then reappeared in an article published in *Tvorba* in November (Hrzal & Matouš 1972). Throughout 1973 the Party organised seminars, in which it consulted academics and teachers in the social sciences before formulating the final version of the document.[24] The document was then published whole or in part,

[23]For an overview of dissident initiatives and their repressions by the regime see Falk (2003, pp. 59–108).

[24]Fojtík had first announced the seminars in 1972 (Fojtík 1972a). Míšková's study of the Academy records seven such seminars for 'academic employees-Communists' also in 1972 and 1973. They were held following the 'recommendations of the Presidium of the ÚV KSČ on country-wide seminars for social scientists of 11 February 1972' (Míšková 2002, p. 165). According to Míšková the strategy was

for example, in *Rudé právo* and *Nová mysl*, on the Czech Press Agency wire service, and it was also broadcast on the radio.[25]

Further guidance was given by Ladislav Hrzal, the chairman of the Academic Board for Philosophy and Sociology of the Czechoslovak Academy of Sciences and a Vice-Rector of the School of Politics of the ÚV KSČ, in a prescriptive article on the tasks, supposedly, of philosophy and sociology, in the *Sociologický časopis* in September (Hrzal 1974). This essay is a prime example of the not merely authoritarian, but also uncreative approach of 'normalisers' in executive positions. Hrzal did not bother or was not able to elaborate on the Party document and come up with a research agenda specific to 'his' two disciplines. His article listed the tasks of philosophy and sociology, but these were merely a compilation of the tasks set out in the Party document for all social sciences as general guidelines. The Party document was formally introduced to the academic community in September 1974, again by Jan Fojtík, at an agitation seminar for social science employees in managerial positions in the Academy and at universities.[26] The aim of this thorough and lengthy process was to secure the transfer of the message about the Party's decisions from the 'centre' at the Central Committee of the Party to the 'significant periphery', that is, to the heads of research institutes and university departments, who where then personally responsible for ensuring that their employees did not, and effectively could not, step out of line.

The Party implemented numerous other practical measures, in addition to the seminars mentioned above, to gain maximum control over academic research and university education. The seminars were a regular activity, in which the Party members employed in academia had to participate and, in the 1980s, some non-Party members also took part. At the nationwide seminars the instruction was provided by members of the Central Committee. Other similar meetings and seminars included regular meetings with representatives of the Academies of Sciences of socialist countries, and meetings of social science publishing houses of socialist countries, which in 1974, for example, resulted in the project for the book series 'Criticism of the Bourgeois Ideology of Anti-Communism and Revisionism' (*Kritika buržoazní ideologie antikomunismu a revizionismu*), in which the Pravda publishing house participated.[27] The Party also strove to increase its influence by setting up more specialised units for asserting its directives and reinforcing its position in existing units. These included, among others, the so-called Socialist Society for Academic Research, Culture and Politics (*Socialistická společnost pro vědu, kulturu a politiku*), established in 1971 and later re-named the Socialist Academy (*Socialistická akademie*), which was a

an effort towards the re-education of the communist body in research and considers it as the second phase of Normalisation (Mišková 2002, p. 165).

[25]'Vývoj, současný stav a úkoly společenských věd: z materiálu předsednictva Ústředního výboru KSČ', *Rudé právo*, 20 June 1974. OSA 300-30-6, box 44; 'Social Sciences' (1974), CTK, 20 June 1974. Press release. OSA 300-30-6, box 44; Filipec and Rohan (1973); J. Závada and M. Sulková-Zítková, 'Fakta k zamyšlení', Radio Praha programme (Prague, Czech Republic), 27 June 1974, OSA 300-30-6, box 44.

[26]'Celostátní aktiv pracovníků společenských věd', *Nová mysl*, 11 November 1974. OSA 300-30-6, box 44.

[27]'Politická aktualita' (Slovak Republic, Hviezda), 5 August 1974. Radio programme. OSA 300-30-6, box 39.

propaganda tool to organise lectures and courses on academic topics with a Party perspective for the wider public. In 1973 they also set up a Task Force for Multi-Lateral Academic Cooperation of Academies of Sciences of Socialist Countries on 'The Issues of Ideological Struggle in Relation to the Coexistence of the Two World Systems' (*Problémová komise mnohostranné vědecké spolupráce akademií věd socialistických zemí 'Otázky ideologického boje v souvislosti s koexistencí dvou světových soustav'*) (Filipec & Rohan 1973). Backing up these initiatives was a 1980 decision that local Party organisations in the 10 'most important' social science institutes of the Academy of Sciences would report directly to the Department of Education and Academic Research of the Central Committee of the Party.[28]

The Party also paid particular attention to universities. Already in 1974 it issued a request to the Czech and Slovak State Committee for Academic Degrees to oversee the selection of PhD candidates, 'so that they met the necessary moral, political and professional requirements, as well as had appropriate previous experience and the ability of creative thinking'.[29] In 1976 the Cabinet for Political Education and Agitation (*Kabinet politické výchovy a agitace*) was created at Charles University in Prague for ideological education of university teachers. This organised the Evening University of Marxism–Leninism (*Večerní univerzita marxismu–leninismu*, VUML) (Češka 1976) and in 1978 the party set down as a goal that every university teacher should complete VUML (Konicková 1978). Also in 1978, the Party units at universities were restructured to enable more flexible operations (Majcharčík 1979); and a year later, a new exchange of Party identity cards was carried out at universities based on an assessment of the teachers' attitudes to the project of the Further Development of the Czechoslovak Educational System (Bareš 1979, p. 24).

Apart from these structural and organisational measures, the Party implemented some conceptual and some blatantly restrictive mechanisms. Conceptually, for example, in 1972 it declared the need to narrow down the number of research topics in social sciences (Fojtík 1972a, p. 156), and throughout Normalisation it always set key research topics for each Five-Year Plan. These restrictive measures included the proscription of authors who did not pass the vetting procedures at the onset of Normalisation; an increase in the screening of translators and the imposition of quotas on paper consumption for publishing houses in 1970.[30] A later measure, in 1986, assigned to the directors of research institutes the unpleasant task of dismissing academics who did not have sufficient publication output (Mokošín 1986, p. 20). This

[28]The 10 institutes included: the Institute for Philosophy and Sociology, the Economic Institute, the Institute of Czechoslovak and World History, the Czechoslovak–Soviet Institute, the Institute of the State and Law, the Institute for Czech and World Literatures, the Institute of the Theory and History of Art, the Institute for the Czech Language, the Oriental Institute, and the Office of the Presidium (Kubánek & Lacina 1980).

[29]'Celostátní aktiv pracovníků společenských věd', *Nová mysl*, 11 November 1974. OSA 300-30-6, box 44. The term PhD refers to the postgraduate degree of CSc. (*candidatus scientarium*), as it was then called.

[30]V. Solecký, 'Komentář', Radio Praha programme (Prague, Czech Republic), 1 September 1972, OSA 300-30-6, box 38. For more details on the restrictions on publishing houses see Šmejkalová (2000) and Šmejkalová-Strickland (1994).

meant that people could be dismissed not only for their professional incompetance, but also for low levels of academic production due to their refusal to participate in fettered academic discussion out of a moral principle.

The above is not an exhaustive list of the steps taken by the Party towards gaining overall hegemony, but it gives an idea of the conditions in which academics whose loyalty was to their disciplines rather than to the Party had to conduct research, write and indeed survive professionally, and perhaps most importantly, teach further generations of university students. The alternative was to resign from their posts and vacate the field of intellectual instruction to Normalisation supporters and those academics who used politics primarily as a vehicle for their own career advancement. It also gives an idea of the conditions into which new generations—those without a 1968 political and academic past—entered when beginning their research and teaching careers.[31]

Conclusion

The complexity and thoroughness of the system of intellectual regulation created a highly restrictive framework for academic research, publishing and university teaching, but at the same time its emphasis on central control was just as cumbersome and, consequently, destructive to the system of management of social sciences as was central planning for economy.[32] The Party's attempt to control all aspects of the social sciences was inherently inflexible. It simply took far too long to send a message from the 'centre' to the 'periphery' and back with feedback. The Party leadership was hampered by its own procedures and could not respond to real-time developments, whether in order to increase its ideological influence, or to curb minor resistances among academics that may have been taking place.[33]

Of course, the picture assembled here from official decrees and directives can tell the story of only one element, even if it is the dominant element, in the complexity of discursive agents participating in the process of academic research, teaching and publishing. It should not be mistaken for a confirmation of the dichotomy of the oppressor and the oppressed, as the conditions of research under state socialism are often viewed in popular perception, for it cannot provide information on the actual

[31]However, further empirical research is needed to explore these generational issues.

[32]The following comment by the Hungarian economist, János Kornai, is appropriate here: '[Excessive centralization] seeks to regulate everything with instructions, a goal that is impossible. It sets out to centralize everything, an aim that is unattainable' (Kornai 2007, p. 90).

[33]Interestingly, John Connely arrives at a parallel conclusion concerning overcentralisation in his analysis of the Sovietisation of the Czech, Polish and German higher education systems between 1948 and 1954. He maintains that an emphasis on ideological micro-management on the part of both the Soviet and the East Central European decision-making bodies hampered the creation of Soviet-type models of higher education in East Central Europe. For example, each visit of a Soviet professor to another socialist country had to be approved at multiple levels by both sides; thus, it sometimes took several years before the visit took place. As a result, the tendencies towards overcentralisation were due more to 'self-Sovietisation' than to a coordinated and systematic effort by the Soviet Union (Connely 2000, p. 160).

practice of academic life and on issues of *agency* of its various participants.[34] Nevertheless, it is a picture necessary for providing a background for further study of the effects of the dominant agent's actions and of the negotiations conducted by the other agents within the given discursive limits.

The account of the relations between and the distribution of the relatively systematically collected Party documents and propaganda given above is a contribution to a more comprehensive understanding of the continuity of academic research conditions and strategies that were developed for the purpose of subjecting social sciences and humanities to communist power from 1968, throughout Normalisation, to the demise of state socialism. Even though the collections of the RFE/RL are not exhaustive, they are comprehensive and represent a systematic and consistent effort to follow the developments in Czechoslovak academic life and its institutions. Thus the framework constructed from these archival materials provides an illustration of the mechanisms of control the Party used toward social sciences and humanities and delineates the contours of the constraints placed on academic research.

Collegium Budapest Institute for Advanced Study

References

Bareš, I. (1979) 'Na naší nejstarší univerzitě: Výměny členských legitimací', *Život strany*, 24, November.

Bauer, J. (1988) 'Postavení a úloha společenských věd v přestavbě', *Rudé právo*, 4 August.

Češka, Z. (1976) 'Jaký učitel, takový student', *Rudé právo*, 16 June.

Connely, J. (2000) 'The Sovietization of Higher Education in the Czech Lands, East Germany, and Poland during the Stalinist Period, 1948–1954', in David-Fox, M. & Péteri, G. (eds) (2000) *Academia in Upheaval: Origins, Transfers, and Transformations of the Communist Academic Regime in Russia and East Central Europe* (Westport, CT, Bergin & Garvey).

Falk, B. J. (2003) *The Dilemmas of Dissidence in East-Central Europe: Citizen Intellectuals and Philosopher Kings* (Budapest, Central European University Press).

Filipec, J. & Rohan, R. (1973) 'Ideologický boj a společenské vědy', *Nová mysl*, 7, July.

Fojtík, J. (1972a) 'Situace na společenskovědním úseku a úkoly společenských věd po XIV. sjezdu KSČ', *Nová mysl*, 2, February.

Fojtík, J. (1972b) 'Věda a společnost', *Tvorba*, 15, April.

Hroch, M. (1999) *Na prahu národní existence: touha a skutečnost* (Prague, Mladá fronta).

Hrzal, L. (1974) 'Vývoj, současný stav a úkoly společenských věd v ČSSR', *Sociologický časopis*, 10, 5.

Hrzal, L. & Matouš, M. (1972) 'Společenské vědy po ideologickém plénu', *Tvorba*, 48, November.

Janovský, J. (1979) 'Poslání společenskovědního vzdělání v rozvinuté socialistické společnosti', *Společenské vědy ve škole*, 1, September.

Kašparová, S. (1980) 'Komunisté na vysokých školách', *Život strany*, 26, December.

Komárek, V. (1992) *Mé pády a vzestupy: Paměti ředitele prognostického ústavu za normalisace* (Prague, Nadas).

Konicková, M. (1978) 'Stranická práce na vysokých školách', *Život strany*, 5, February.

Konopásek, Z. (ed.) (2000) *Our Lives as Database—Doing a Sociology of Ourselves: Czech Social Transitions in Autobiographical Research Dialogues* (Prague, Karolinum).

Kornai, J. (2007) *By Force of Thought: Irregular Memoirs of an Intellectual Journey*, translated by B. McLean (Cambridge, MA, MIT Press).

[34]In the area of culture and everyday life, Alexei Yurchak has presented an excellent analysis of the layered discourse of official propaganda, ideology, resistance and discursive negotiation during late state socialism (Yurchak 2005).

Kostlán, A. (ed.) (2002) *Věda v Československu v období normalisace (1970–1975)*, Vol. 4, Práce z dějin vědy/Studies in the History of Sciences and Humanities (Prague, Výzkumné centrum pro dějiny vědy).

Kubánek, V. & Lacina, K. (1980) 'Stranická práce ve společenskovědních ústavech', *Život strany*, 17, August.

Kunovjánek, V. (1987) 'K otázkám přestavby ve společenských vědách', *Nová mysl*, 6, June.

Machonin, S. (1993) 'Deníkové záznamy z normalisačních časů', *Prostor*, 6, 24.

Majcharčík, J. (1977) 'Úkoly společenských věd po XV. Sjezdu', *Život strany*, 18, August.

Majcharčík, J. (1979) 'Stranická práce na vysokých školách', *Život strany*, 21, October.

Míšková, A. (2002) 'Proces tzv. normalisace v Československé akademii věd (1969–1974)', in Kostlán, A. (ed.) (2002).

Mokošín, V. (1986) 'Hlavní úkoly společenských věd', *Život strany*, 2, January.

Morkeš, F. (2002) 'Vysoké školy v letech normalisace', in Kostlán, A. (ed.) (2002).

Navrátil, J. (ed.) (1998) *The Prague Spring 1968: A National Security Archive Documents Reader* (Budapest, CEU Press).

Otáhal, M. (1999) *Podíl tvůrčí inteligence na pádu komunismu, Knihy/Dokumenty* (Brno, Doplněk).

Otáhal, M. (2002) *Normalizace 1969–1989: Příspěvek ke stavu bádání*, Vol. 36, Sešity Ústavu pro soudobé dějiny (Prague, Ústav pro soudobé dějiny).

Otáhal, M. Nosková, A. & Bolomský, K. (eds) (1993) *Svědectví o duchovním útlaku (1969–1970): Dokumenty* (Prague, Maxdorf and Ústav pro soudobé dějiny AV ČR).

Pecen, J. (1977) 'Jednotný program společenských věd po XV. sjezdu KSČ', *Tvorba*, 30, July.

Petrusek, M. (2004) 'Výuka sociologie v čase tání a v časech normalizace (1964–1989)', *Sociologický časopis/Czech Sociological Review*, 40, 5.

Potůček, M. (ed.) (1995) *Normalisace ve společenských vědách—Můj život v normalisaci* (Prague, ISS FSV UK).

Prečan, V. (1994a) *V kradeném čase: Výběr ze studií, článků a úvah z let 1973–1993* (Prague/Brno, Ústav pro soudobé dějiny/Doplněk).

Prečan, V. (1994b) 'Společenské vědy ve svěráku "konsolidace"', in Prečan, V. (ed.) (1994a).

Prokůpek, L. (2002) 'Normalisace v Ústavu pro filosofii a sociologii ČSAV', in Kostlán, A. (ed.) (2002).

Pynsent, R. B. (1994) *Questions of Identity: Czech and Slovak Ideas of Nationality and Personality* (Budapest, CEU Press and New York, Oxford University Press).

Šámal, P. (2002) '"Normalisace" literární vědy v zrcadle časopisu *Česká literatura*', *Česká literatura*, 50, 3.

Sedm pražských dnů (1968) *Sedm pražských dnů 21.-28. srpna 1968: Dokumentace (předmluva Josef Macek, doslov Vilém Prečan)*. (Reference is to the 1990 edition, Prague, Academia.)

Šimečka, M. (1985) *The Restoration of Order: The Normalisation of Czechoslovakia, 1969–1976*, translated by G. Turner (London, Verso).

Šmejkalová, J. (2000) *Kniha (k teorii a praxi knižní kultury)* (Brno, Host).

Šmejkalová-Strickland, J. (1994) 'Censoring Canons: Transitions and Prospects of Literary Institutions in Czechoslovakia', in Burt, R. (ed.) (1994) *The Administration of Aesthetics: Censorship, Political Criticism and the Public Sphere* (Minneapolis and London, University of Minnesota Press).

Snítil, Z. (1980) 'Úkoly společenských věd', *Život strany*, 20, September.

Tůma, O. (2002) 'Společenské a politické souvislosti termínu normalisace', in Kostlán, A. (ed.) (2002).

Urbášek, P. (2002) 'Diskontinuita jako určující faktor vývoje českých vysokých škol v letech 1970–1975', in Kostlán, A. (ed.) (2002).

XYZ (Praha) (1977) 'Čeští filosofové po 30 letech: Současný stav "normalisované" filosofie', *Studie (Roma)*, 49.

Yurchak, A. (2005) *Everything Was Forever Until It Was No More: The Last Soviet Generation* (Princeton, NJ, Princeton University Press).

Prelude to a Divorce? The Prague Spring as Dress Rehearsal for Czechoslovakia's 'Velvet Divorce'

SCOTT BROWN

ON 15 MARCH 1968, THE SLOVAK NATIONAL COUNCIL issued a proclamation calling for the federalisation of Czechoslovakia. Two weeks later, as public discussion of this and other reforms of the Prague Spring intensified, a Slovak, M. Javorský (1968), wrote to the daily *Rol'nícke noviny* on the meaning of 'equal with equal', the watchword in Slovak demands for a federation. 'It is necessary to think through and apply this "equal with equal" everywhere, really fraternally', Javorský argued.

> It is in the word 'Czechoslovak', and, so it is clear, the abbreviation is also 'CS'. But then why, to give an example, 'ČT'—Czechoslovak Television—'ČR'—Czechoslovak Radio—'Čedok'—Czechoslovak Travel Agency, and so on? It is high time to implement thoroughly the abbreviation 'CS'.

Javorský bemoaned the semantic confusion stemming from the use of 'Czech' or the single letter 'C' as shorthand for 'Czechoslovak'. This 'chaos in nomenclature' befuddled foreigners, he complained. But Javorský's lament also revealed how Slovaks perceived this linguistic convention as a slight to their position within the Czechoslovak state.

Twenty-two years later, another Slovak, Ján Klimko of Bratislava, echoed the rhetoric Slovak reformers had employed during the federalisation debate of 1968. At the outset of what became known as Czechoslovakia's 'hyphen war' in 1990, Klimko voiced his support for incorporating the hyphen into the official name of the state in a letter to the daily newspaper *Smena*: 'This hyphen does not divide but rather it binds us, and it is a symbol of the principle EQUAL WITH EQUAL'.[1]

From the perspective of Slovak elites, 'equal with equal' meant adjusting the Czech–Slovak relationship to provide institutional guarantees of the two nations' equal

My thanks go to James Felak and the anonymous referees for their feedback on this essay. Research for this was partially funded by a grant from the Fulbright–Hays Doctoral Dissertation Abroad (DDRA) programme.

[1]See Klimko's letter under the headline, 'Symboly', *Smena*, 8 February 1990. Emphasis in original.

standing within the state, along with the devolution of power from the centre in Prague to both republics. This objective remained largely unchanged from the reform movement of the late 1960s to the post-communist transition of the early 1990s. But as the complaints of Javorský and Klimko demonstrated, these seemingly trivial squabbles mattered to Slovaks at all levels. During both upheavals, Slovaks from the elite and the masses saw symbolic issues as symptomatic of deeper philosophical disputes that put strains on the Czech–Slovak union. At their core, these disagreements concerned divergent Slovak and Czech views of reform, democracy and the place of the nation in both.

Slovak and Czech approaches to federalisation during the Prague Spring proved a harbinger of their quarrels following the collapse of communism. As Rychlík (1998, p. 314) writes, 'in the years 1989–1992, nothing appeared in Czech–Slovak relations that had not already surfaced in the past, especially in 1968'. Comparisons between the federalisation debate during the Prague Spring and the disputes preceding the Velvet Divorce of the early 1990s offer insight into the divergent agendas that fuelled Czechoslovakia's dissolution in 1992.

In turn, a closer examination of these parallels shows how many interpretations of the Czech–Slovak split prove wanting. Rychlík (1998, pp. 360–61) attributes Czechoslovakia's disintegration to the different ways Czechs and Slovaks imagined a 'common state', as well as to the failure of the population to embrace a 'Czechoslovak' identity. However, Rychlík's argument suggests Slovaks were to blame for these shortcomings. He seems to imply Slovaks' interest in an 'association of states' or a 'co-state' was incompatible with a common state. Furthermore, in emphasising the weakness of 'Czechoslovak' identity, Rychlík (1998, p. 361) appears to suggest Slovaks were the 'citizens' who 'did not share an awareness that [Czechoslovakia] was their state' since Slovaks had long asserted a separate Slovak identity. True, in 1968 Slovak political and cultural elites called for a federation and symmetrical Slovak and Czech national organs to recognise their distinctly Slovak, rather than Czechoslovak, identity, an objective with broad support among Slovaks. But these demands also reflected a desire of many Slovaks to strengthen the country, a longing to feel Czechoslovakia really was 'their' state. In a similar way, both Slovak elites and masses in the 1990s expressed dissatisfaction with the federation, yet they also hoped reforms would give Slovaks their place within Czechoslovakia.

As seen in public opinion polling from the early 1990s, a majority of Slovaks still wanted a common state. Indeed, throughout the period from 1990 until the split and beyond, opinion polls consistently showed a clear Slovak preference for a reformed Czechoslovakia over an independent Slovak state, as seen in the survey data Hlavová and Žatkuliak have supplied for Slovakia (2002, pp. 325–28). Only 9.6% of respondents from Slovakia in October 1990 said the 'optimal' arrangement of the country would be two independent states, a figure that rose to 15% in January 1991, but stabilised near this level, with 13.4% of Slovaks supporting a Slovak state in May 1991 and 13% in January 1992. Even after the split, only 22% of Slovak respondents to a poll in December 1994 (Hlavová & Žatkuliak 2002, pp. 325–26) identified with the statement 'I was for the break-up of the CSFR from the beginning and I haven't changed my position', with a further 8% saying 'I was for the break-up of the CSFR, but today I think it was a mistake' (Hlavová & Žatkuliak 2002, p. 327). Thus, only

30% of Slovaks polled claimed to have supported the divorce when it happened, a figure consistent with a survey from September 1992, when 27% of Slovaks said they viewed the break-up 'only positively', compared with 36% who said 'only negatively', while another 22% expressed 'mixed' feelings (Hlavová & Žatkuliak 2002, p. 327). Clearly, most Slovaks either opposed or had strong reservations about Slovak independence, whatever their misgivings about the existing federation.

Comparisons of the Prague Spring with the Velvet Divorce also highlight the pre-existing points of disagreement between Slovaks and Czechs that made the dissolution of Czechoslovakia possible in the changed circumstances after 1989. While Leff (1996, p. 135) addresses historical factors, she cites the 'basically incompatible' Slovak and Czech ideas of a new constitutional settlement in the 1990s as the 'sticking point' that made the strains of transition fatal to the state. Similarly, Hilde (1999, p. 647) stresses the immediate pains of transition over more longstanding disagreements, claiming the restructuring of the Czech–Slovak relationship 'proved too heavy a burden' for the new regime to bear in conjunction with other reforms, especially economic reform.

Intentionally or not, interpretations of the Velvet Divorce that prioritise the pressures of the post-communist transition tend to treat the reworking of the Czech–Slovak relationship as a separate issue from the overhaul of the old communist order, a distinction Czech politicians like Václav Klaus often made, but one Slovak politicians such as Vladimír Mečiar and their supporters rejected. Slovak elites and the lower strata of Slovak society saw a reform of Czech–Slovak relations—federalisation—as an integral component of liberalisation in 1968, just as they regarded a reform of the federation as inseparable from processes of transition and economic restructuring after 1989. Though many scholars overlook this interrelationship in Slovak thinking, the connections between the two processes of reform—a critical parallel in both crises—are crucial for understanding the contrast in Slovak and Czech attitudes that facilitated the disintegration of Czechoslovakia.

While the strains of the transition were the proximate cause of Czechoslovakia's break-up, these deeper attitudinal differences to be proved the crucial underlying factor. Cataclysm, whether the upheaval of 1968 or the collapse of the communist regime in 1989, played an enabling role in both cases. Crisis brought to the surface more fundamental disagreements between Slovak and Czech leaders with the potential to split the state. Once sweeping reforms of society became open for discussion, Slovak and Czech politicians and cultural figures articulated different but not incompatible visions of the changes democratisation should bring to Czechoslovakia, diverging chiefly in the priority they ascribed to the nation within Czechoslovakia. Slovak elites also voiced a belief in the democratic rights of the citizen, but they consistently argued for Slovaks' special rights as one of the two 'state-forming' nations within Czechoslovakia, claiming this status conferred a 'democratic' right to national equality with the Czech nation. Understandably, Czechs at all levels exhibited less enthusiasm for this interpretation of Czechoslovak democracy, largely because they saw it as granting outsized importance to Slovaks, a numerical, if not (officially) national, minority.

The real culprit in the Velvet Divorce was not insufficient commitment to a common state, the weakness of 'Czechoslovak' identity or even the strains of the post-communist transition. Rather, as this essay argues, it was different understandings of democracy, and of the nation's place in democratisation, which caused Slovaks and Czechs to drift apart and eventually to accept the dissolution of the federation. These divergent ideas of democracy were not new in the early 1990s, but descended from the federalisation debate of the late 1960s, centring less on issues of multiparty elections than on balancing competing democratic impulses of regional autonomy and majority rule. During the Prague Spring, many reform-oriented Slovak political and cultural elites regarded the overhaul of the Czech–Slovak relationship, via a federation, as the foundation for more thoroughgoing liberalisation. They expressed their belief in the inseparability of federalisation and democratisation through calls for a symmetrical federation and the prohibition of *majorizácia* (Czech outvoting), which, they argued, would bring democratic principles to bear on Czech–Slovak relations. By contrast, most Czech elites did not place the same stress on the nation within Czechoslovakia, and they did not consider the nation a subject of Czechoslovak democracy on a par with the citizen. Czechs generally regarded federalisation as little more than an adjunct—and at times an obstacle—to democratisation, viewing reform of the Czech–Slovak relationship as less important than other aspects of liberalisation.

The premature demise of the Prague Spring in August 1968 rendered debates over democracy moot for the time being, yet the ensuing two decades of a 'normalised' federation provided fodder for renewed disputes between Slovaks and Czechs after 1989. As in the 1960s, Slovak politicians in the 1990s mined widespread support for federal reform, this time through the creation of an 'authentic federation' or confederation. Many Slovak elites played to a broader desire to see the democratic principles thwarted during Normalisation applied at last to national relations. Yet many Czechs, even those identified with the democratising movement of the Prague Spring like Ludvík Vaculík or Petr Pithart, saw the federation enacted in 1969 as an ill-gotten benefit Slovaks had extracted at the price of greater persecution for Czechs.[2] Consequently, many Czech elites had little patience after 1989 for Slovak demands for a new constitutional position, believing as in 1968 a reformed federalism should take a back seat to more pressing issues of political and economic transformation.

In hindsight, it seems obvious that Slovaks and Czechs had already rehearsed the disagreements preceding the Velvet Divorce during the earlier federalisation debate. It would be a mistake, however, to draw a straight line from the 'marital' discord of the late 1960s to the amicable 'break-up' of the early 1990s. The fall of communism in 1989 removed the limitations that had constrained arguments over Czech–Slovak relations in 1968, while mutual suspicion and mistrust between the two partners grew during two decades of communist federation. Nonetheless, the parallels between these two periods make clear that Slovaks and Czechs largely rehashed old disputes over the federation when a new opportunity emerged after 1989. And yet, these comparisons show 'divorce' was not inevitable, since both partners expressed interest in patching up

[2]Vaculík (1990) helped to stoke Czech–Slovak tensions when he flatly accused Slovaks of viewing democratisation as a Czech affair in 1968 and abandoning Czechs after the invasion in order to gain a federation and milder punishment. Reflecting on the break-up, Pithart (1995, p. 327) claimed 'Slovaks gave precedence to federalization over democratization' during the Prague Spring: 'That is why after August 1968, Slovakia was not punished so severely', which 'helps to explain why Slovaks looked upon the period preceding November, 1989 with a mixture of not only aversion and embarrassment, but also nostalgia'.

their differences. Despite their qualms, many Slovaks remained committed to Czechoslovakia, pending reforms to make the partnership more equitable. On the other side, several Czech elites recognised Slovaks' national accent on democratisation as an effort to strengthen the union. Differences of opinion in how Slovaks and Czechs approached democracy doomed the marriage only when opportunistic Czech and Slovak politicians painted these differences as irreconcilable, orchestrating a divorce in the summer of 1992.

The Prague Spring: federalisation or democratisation?

During the 1960s, national-minded Slovaks became increasingly frustrated with their position within Czechoslovakia. Key bodies of Slovak self-rule, such as the Slovak National Council (*Slovenská národná rada*, SNR), a legislative and governmental body founded by the wartime resistance, or the Board of Commissioners (*Zbor povereníkov*), a Slovak administrative organ founded in 1944, had lacked specifically Czech equivalents since the re-establishment of Czechoslovakia in 1945. Instead, state-wide Czechoslovak bodies based in Prague, such as the National Assembly (*Národní shromáždění*) and ministries of the government, doubled as Czech national organs, meaning Czech national organs enjoyed *de facto* legal supremacy over Slovak organs, an arrangement Slovak proponents of federalisation later criticised as 'asymmetrical'. More importantly, the Communist Party of Slovakia (*Komunistická strana Slovenska*, KSS), another Slovak body created during the Second World War, had no Czech counterpart and was subordinate to the state-wide Communist Party of Czechoslovakia (*Komunistická strana Československa*, KSČ), extending this asymmetry to the Party as well as the state. But the 'socialist' constitution introduced in 1960 took this *de facto* arrangement one step further, formalising the unequal and subordinate position of Slovakia by eliminating some Slovak bodies, like the Board of Commissioners, and officially reducing the competency of the SNR and other Slovak national organs that remained. The net effect was to intensify the feeling among many Slovaks that they lived under Czech rule.

Even before the new constitution's ratification, some Slovaks lashed out at it as a symbol of Czech domination. In April 1960, an anonymous Slovak sent a letter to L'udovít Benada, a member of the KSS Central Committee (*Ústredný výbor*, ÚV) complaining about the plight of Slovak national organs. The author questioned how 'Czechs like you'—expressing the view that leading 'Slovak' functionaries like Benada or KSS First Secretary Karol Bacílek were crypto-Czechs of dubious Slovak origin—could 'bargain so recklessly' with other Czechs over the fate of Slovak institutions. The letter conveys the Slovak sentiment that 'Prague', synonymous with 'Czechs' in the minds of many Slovaks, ruled Slovakia for its own benefit, without regard for Slovak interests and without meaningful participation from *bona fide* Slovaks. The author of the letter also claimed Antonín Novotný, the KSČ first secretary, 'stole like a Gypsy' the right to self-governance that belonged to Slovakia.[3] This unsigned letter revealed how, from the beginning of the 1960s, there was already considerable discontent with

[3] *Anoným zaslaný s. Benadovi*, 14 April 1960. Slovak National Archive (SNA), ÚV KSS, carton 2232.

the position of Slovakia, which Slovak elites later mined in claiming the Slovak nation enjoyed a special status within the Czechoslovak state that entitled it to national equality, though initially Slovak elites and the masses felt unable to voice this desire openly.

Slovak grievances slowly crystallised around transforming Czechoslovakia into a federation of two equal national states. This idea first emerged in a study the Slovak historian Miloš Gosiorovský drafted from 1960 to 1962 and submitted to leading functionaries in the KSČ and KSS Central Committees in March 1963. Gosiorovský criticised the constitution of 1960, remarking how the diminished position of Slovak national organs and the elimination of the Board of Commissioners consigned the Slovak nation to the position of being the only nation in the socialist camp that did not have its own ethnic territory and organs of socialist state power that were adequate for its existing development, its current level, its size, and especially its needs for a fully equal position as a nation in a multinational state (Gosiorovský 1968, p. 12).

In response, the KSČ Central Committee called Gosiorovský a 'political prostitute' who tried to exploit a sensitive issue for his own benefit, and it blocked publication of his study.[4] Despite the Party's rebuke however, Gosiorovský distributed his study to Slovak intellectuals. His insubordination earned him the Party discipline of 'censure with warning', but the dissemination of Gosiorovský's ideas helped the goal of a federation to penetrate the thinking of Slovaks.[5] In June 1963, a 'group of national and Party workers' in Slovakia sent a letter to the Soviet Consulate in Bratislava, in which they bemoaned the plight of Slovakia under the current constitutional settlement: 'Today's Slovak National Council and other Slovak national and central organs remain only symbols of national organs. The whole economic, political and cultural life of Slovakia is basically directed from Prague'.[6] The way to rectify this state of affairs and the solution for which its authors appealed to the Soviet comrades came straight from Gosiorovský's study: a federation of Slovakia and the Czech Lands.[7] Gosiorovský's study also prompted the KSS to take a closer look at the position of Slovak national organs in order to appear responsive to popular pressure, even though the KSS did not budge on its position.[8]

Nonetheless, Slovak proponents of a federation had to wait until the upheaval of 1968 to voice this desire publicly without fear of reprisal. In turn, the appearance of federalisation as a cardinal demand among the Slovak public during the Prague Spring revealed how individuals throughout Slovak society, not just at the elite level, linked reform of the national settlement to larger questions of liberalisation. In particular, the advocacy of symmetry by reform-oriented Slovaks—the establishment of parallel Slovak and Czech national organs subordinate to state-wide Czechoslovak bodies—as the institutional expression of 'equal with equal' showed how several Slovaks

[4]*Záznam o besede s. Dubčeka, prvého tajomníka ÚV KSS s predsedami ZO KSS SAV a funkcionármi CZV KSS pri SAV*, 6 March 1964. SNA, ÚV KSS Presidium (P-ÚV KSS), carton 1121.

[5]*Návrhy rehabilitačnej komisie ÚV KSS*, 17 May 1968. SNA, P-ÚV KSS, carton 1205.

[6]*Anonimný list zaslaný konzulom*, 19 June 1963. SNA, ÚV KSS Secretariat (S-ÚV KSS), carton 239.

[7]*Anonimný list zaslaný konzulom*, 19 June 1963. SNA, ÚV KSS Secretariat (S-ÚV KSS), carton 239.

[8]*Z referátu s. Dubčeka na zasadnutí ÚV KSS*, 6 June 1963. SNA, P-ÚV KSS, carton 1168.

understood federalisation as the application of democratic principles to national relations.

On the surface, symmetry offered a remedy to lingering Slovak perceptions of Czech domination. Július Strinka, a member of the commission that prepared the KSS Action Programme, explained in a *Pravda* interview in April 1968 what symmetry meant to Slovaks:

> We can speak about symmetry at that time when both state-forming nations are, in the full sense of the word, independent and able, this means that each nation is in and of itself master on its own territory, and in accord with this is, naturally, also fully equipped with appropriate power organs and institutions, legislative, administrative, judicial, cultural, etc. The organs of one nation are, simply put, the mirror image of organs of the second nation, in this they are in a relationship of symmetry. (Zajanová 1968, p. 5)

Like other Slovak advocates of symmetry, Strinka (1968, p. 1) envisioned a federation as its precondition. A symmetrical federation would be an 'enormous conquest', he argued, not just for fulfilling Slovak desires, 'but also from the standpoint of the democratic structure of the whole republic'. Symmetry would dispel Slovak notions of Czech rule while also enshrining the democratic right to national equality to which both Slovaks and Czechs were entitled within Czechoslovakia as state-forming nations.

Strinka and other pro-reform Slovaks connected federalisation to democratisation, viewing a federation as unthinkable without democracy. In their view, democracy did not mean free elections as much as giving both individuals and nations a greater say in matters directly affecting them, such as allowing Slovak bodies a greater role in managing Slovakia's economy rather than following the policy decreed from Prague. Though Slovak antagonists of liberalisation, mainly hardliners like the new KSS first secretary Vasil Bil'ak, tried to divorce federalisation from democratisation in an effort to sidetrack more thoroughgoing reforms, reform-minded Slovaks conceived the two processes as inseparable (Steiner 1973, p. 175). As Strinka explained to an interviewer in April 1968,

> it would be a fateful mistake if we divided a federation from democratisation, if we saw in it a self-contained goal, the achievement of which in and of itself would solve the problems of the nation and ensure its unhindered development. (Zajanová 1968, p. 5)

Federalisation was only part of the solution, Strinka argued, since the form of federation would do little to redress Slovak grievances without democratic content.

Calls for federalisation garnered an overwhelmingly favourable response from Slovaks. In a poll conducted in April 1968, 79% of Slovaks expressed full agreement with the federation proposed in the KSČ Action Programme, with another 15% voicing partial agreement; none of the Slovak respondents said they disagreed with federalisation (Piekalkiewicz 1972, p. 111).[9] Anecdotal evidence also supported claims

[9]Czechs exhibited less enthusiasm for federalisation, yet they still supported it in sizable numbers, with 52% of Czech respondents in the same poll agreeing fully with the proposed federation and another 31% agreeing in part, while just 10% of Czechs said they disagreed with this proposed adjustment to the Czech–Slovak relationship (Piekalkiewicz 1972, p. 111).

of virtually unanimous support among Slovaks for a federation. As of 31 May 1968, the SNR Presidium received 550 letters and resolutions regarding its proclamation of 15 March 1968, which called for a federation, and the KSČ Action Programme introduced in April 1968, which also endorsed federalisation. This response showed significant Slovak backing for federation. The Presidium reported 'unambiguous and unqualified support' for a federative arrangement, as 'a number of letters stress the need to expedite to the maximum degree the realisation of federalisation'.[10]

During the Prague Spring, as in the period following the collapse of communism, the response from the Czech public to Slovak calls for a reform of the national settlement was more tepid, but not wholly unfavourable. For example, in a roundtable discussion in March 1968, Bedřich Rattinger, who helped with the KSČ Action Programme, endorsed the view that nations also had democratic rights and regarded federalisation as part of democratisation:

> If, today, we speak about the application of democratic principles in our society, we must also apply them between both our nations. The absence of political democracy, which we felt here in the Czech Lands, is doubly felt in Slovakia. The problem appeared in Slovakia not only as an absence of democracy for the individual, but also as an absence of democracy in the application of national rights and interests.[11]

In the same conversation, the Czech legal expert Zdeněk Jičinský, who worked on the federalisation law, echoed Rattinger in pronouncing Czech–Slovak relations a vital question.[12]

Nonetheless, federalisation remained a lower priority for many Czechs. In June 1968, the Slovak historian Samo Falt'an (1968) expressed dismay that 'considerable silence endures' on federation among much of the Czech public, even though most Czechs agreed to this reform in principle. Falt'an was flabbergasted by the attitude he saw among most Czechs that 'federalisation was only the wish of Slovaks, and since they want it, they shouldn't have it'. 'The virtue of this calamity', he explained, 'is that it attests first of all to the misunderstanding of the principles of democratism in relations between two nations' (1968, p. 1). The root of the disagreement, as Falt'an perceived it, was not that Slovaks' emphasis on federalisation made them less committed to democratisation, as many Czechs claimed. Rather, he indentified Czechs' reservations regarding federation to their lacking a clear grasp of what democracy and 'democratism' meant in the national milieu of Czechoslovakia, where Slovaks and Czechs were recognised formally as state-forming nations. Falt'an implied the two nations were entitled to a voice in matters affecting them within Czechoslovakia, just the same as individual citizens.

As spring turned to summer in 1968, fault lines emerged in disagreements over the shape of the new federation. At the core of these conflicts lay the issue of how best to

[10] *Informácia o rezolúciach a listoch došlých Predsedníctvu Slovenskej národnej rady v súvislosti s Vyhlásením SNR z 15.3.1968 ako aj k Akčnému programu KSČ*, 10 June 1968. SNA, SNR Presidium (P-SNR), carton 167.

[11] 'Federácia klope na dvere', *Práca*, 23 March 1968, p. 6.

[12] 'Federácia klope na dvere', *Práca*, 23 March 1968, p. 6.

institute the formal equality (*rovnoprávnosť*) of both nations, and what mechanism, if any, should prevent *majorizácia*, the outvoting of Slovaks by the larger Czech nation. In contrast to the discord of the early 1990s, by July 1968 the committee preparing the law on federation had agreed that the Czechoslovak federation would be founded on parallel Slovak and Czech national-state entities, with sovereignty originating from the two national republics.[13]

Questions of parliamentary parity and the prohibition of *majorizácia* proved more difficult however. An SNR report on preparations for federalisation identified three main variants in proposals for expressing the equality of the two nations.[14] The first scheme, proposed by the SNR Presidium and associated with the Czech professor Jiří Boguszak, called for a unicameral Federal Assembly with deputies apportioned by national parity rather than proportionality. A second variant, introduced by the Czech legal scholars Jiří Grospič and Zdeněk Jičinský, inclined toward the opposite extreme. Grospič and Jičinský proposed a unicameral Federal Assembly with deputies allotted according to population. Their plan gave Slovaks an absolute veto over constitutional questions, but Czech representatives could still pass laws on crucial matters such as the state budget and economic planning without the support of a single deputy from Slovakia.

The third variant presented during the Prague Spring offered a hybrid of proportionality and parity. This plan, the SNR Presidium's second alternative, envisioned a bicameral Federal Assembly. The House of the People would base representation on population, upholding the principle of proportional representation, while the House of Nations would have national delegations of equal size. Both chambers would operate according to majority rule, but bills would require majority support in both houses, and from both halves of the House of Nations.[15] This third variant formed the basis of the law on federation signed in October 1968. As the new democratic order revealed after 1989, this mix of proportionality and parity gave Slovaks a *de facto* veto in the Federal Assembly, which forced Czech deputies to take Slovak interests into account as intended, but also allowed a small number of Slovak deputies to obstruct parliamentary business.

Disagreements over *majorizácia* in the Federal Assembly fuelled suspicions during the federalisation debate, but they also exemplified the underlying difference in the way Slovaks and Czechs conceived of democracy. The question of whether nations enjoyed democratic rights in the way that citizens did, and of how to reconcile the equality of the two nations with the equality of each individual citizen, laid bare disagreements on how members of both nations understood democracy. National equality seemed to matter less to Czechs in large part because they did not perceive the issue as a problem to them personally, since Czechs could not be outvoted on national lines, rendering the nation as a collective political actor less important than the aggregate force of individual (Czech) citizens.

[13]*Informácie o stave prípravných prác návrhu ústavného zákona o federálizácii ČSSR*, 22 July 1968. SNA, P-SNR, carton 170.

[14]Cartoons published in newspapers at the time indicate that these debates were of interest to the general population. See for example Figure 1 which was published in *Pravda*, 9 August 1968.

[15]*Informácie o stave prípravných prác návrhu ústavného zákona o federalizácii ČSSR*, 22 July 1968. SNA, P-SNR, carton 170.

FIGURE 1. 'Do It Yourself': Federation Coming between Democracy and Slovakia (Milan Stano, *Pravda*, 9 August 1968)

But the same numerical disparity that made national equality a non-starter for Czechs made the matter all the more important to Slovak elites, who sought to qualify majority rule in order to balance the democratic rights of individuals and (state-forming) nations. The writer Zora Jesenská saw protections for the smaller Slovak nation as consistent with a more broadly applicable democratic principle that majority rule should be balanced with protections for the minority, a principle that held for nations the same as individual citizens:

> This does not only mean minorities of nationalities ... since each of us can in some cases belong to the majority and in others to the minority. And only in the case of the weaker is it possible to say whether there is a democracy here. (Jesenská 1968, p. 1)

As Jesenská showed, one could defend the nation without being a nationalist or trampling the rights of the individual citizen. But Slovak reformers' insistence on prohibiting *majorizácia* followed in particular from their belief that Slovaks, like Czechs, enjoyed a democratic right to national equality within Czechoslovakia because they were a constitutionally recognised state-forming nation, unlike the Magyar and Rusyn minorities in Slovakia. At the same time, pro-reform Slovaks could leverage their standing as a state-forming nation to bring the will of individual Slovak citizens to bear on the Czechoslovak state, since the Slovak nation as a unified political subject was more powerful than the collective weight of individual Slovak citizens—a scenario many Czechs criticised because it made the political clout of the whole greater than the sum of its parts.

Whether Slovak elites thought the nation should have the same rights as the individual or their Czech counterparts believed nations did not possess democratic rights, their arguments during the federalisation debate amounted to differences in principle on the form—but not the content—of democracy in the Czechoslovak context. Yet many on both sides failed to draw this qualitative distinction between form and content, causing these philosophical differences to generate mutual mistrust.

A series of polemics erupted in July 1968, sparked by the contrasting Slovak and Czech attitudes regarding the role of the nation. Speaking in Bratislava on 5 July, Gustáv Husák warned the KSS city conference that federalisation had reached a critical juncture owing to the divergent conceptions of democracy: 'In Czech circles, a federation is being proposed according to the principle of "one citizen, one vote"'. In Husák's view, this approach would mean the preservation of the status quo: 'The equality of nations must be ensured so any sort of *majorizácia* of representatives of the smaller, that is, of the Slovak nation in federative organs is precluded'.[16] Husák endorsed an unarticulated principle of 'one nation, one vote', which appeared to place the nation above the individual, though this concept could also be interpreted as a way to protect the rights of individual Slovak citizens. But Husák exacerbated the conflict over the relationship of the nation to the individual by ascribing national attributes to mere differences of opinion, making it seem as if Czechs as a whole sought to wield their numerical superiority to dominate the Slovak nation.

On 10 July, Grospič and Jičinský responded to Husák in *Rudé právo*, arguing for the need to uphold the importance of majority rule, the principle underpinning their proposal for a unicameral Federal Assembly (Grospič & Jičinský 1968, p. 3). In turn, Grospič and Jičinský's reply to Husák elicited a new wave of critical responses in the Slovak press. On 11 July, E. R. Štefan attacked the two Czechs for failing to respect Husák's synthesis of democracy for nations as well as citizens. Štefan showed greater contempt for what he saw as Grospič and Jičinský's failure to understand Slovaks' insistence on prohibiting *majorizácia*:

> In relations between two nations there is not and cannot be such rhetoric about a majority and a minority. The ratio of votes in questions of national sovereignty, as well as in relations of Czechs and Slovaks, is and otherwise will always only be one to one. And only in respecting this ratio is it possible to fulfil democratically the principle equal with equal.... (Štefan 1968, p. 1)

Crucially, Štefan did not reject the concept of majority rule or the primacy of the individual citizen; he simply stressed that in specific scenarios—namely matters of Czech–Slovak relations—the nation was a more important political actor than the individual citizen. Two days later, the Slovak legal experts Vojtech Hatala and Karol Rebro (1968a) offered a more sympathetic view of Grospič and Jičinský's proposal, judging it well intentioned but wanting, since its insistence on majority decision-making would violate national equality, given the disparity in population between the two nations. Hatala and Rebro articulated an idea expressed by Jesenská and other Slovak elite members, arguing neither the nation nor the individual should take precedence over the other, because both entities had democratic rights. The best way to protect these rights, Hatala and Rebro (1968b) maintained, was a federation, which

[16] 'Federácia v krízovej situácii', *Práca*, 6 July 1968.

'should stand for democracy for the individual citizen, while it should also stand for a large community of individual citizens, as it is all one nation'.

These polemics inflamed passions on both sides, with arguments over the meaning of democratisation and the place of federalisation within it. As the Slovak historian Jaroslav Šolc commented in August 1968, Slovaks found Czechs' condescension on the national issue baffling, given the belief common among Slovaks that federalisation was a question of democracy:

> Democracy and national sovereignty, democratisation and federalisation are intimately connected for the majority of Slovaks, and therefore they have a hard time understanding the several months of constant tutelage from Czech intellectuals (and from several Slovak exponents) that first should come democratisation, then federalisation. In Slovakia we have a historically conditioned, unfailing reference to the fact that we cannot separate, prioritise and subordinate one to the other. (Šolc 1968, p. 5)

The experiences of the interwar period, Šolc explained, had already taught Slovaks that democracy could not survive without a solution to the Slovak question (a federation) and vice versa. Another Slovak legal scholar, Karol Laco, echoed this sentiment in terming the reform of Czech–Slovak relations an 'organic component of the democratisation process'. Laco (1968, p. 12) voiced a conviction shared by other reform-oriented Slovaks that 'without a democratic adjustment of the constitutional relationship of Czechs and Slovaks, thorough democracy is unthinkable'.

The Soviet-led invasion of Czechoslovakia in August 1968 brought an abrupt end to efforts at democratisation, but not to federalisation. Preparations continued up until the symbolic deadline set during the Prague Spring for 28 October 1968, Czechoslovakia's 50th anniversary. Yet federalisation in the absence of democratisation disappointed many pro-reform Slovaks when it failed to bring a symmetrical arrangement of national organs. Under Normalisation, Czechoslovak bodies continued to double as Czech national organs, keeping Slovak organs in a subordinate position. Plans to create separate Czech national organs were not carried forward in many cases, most critically with the KSČ, which never followed through on proposals to create a separate branch for the Czech Lands. For Slovak protagonists of the Prague Spring, without the symmetry needed to enshrine the democratic rights of the Slovak nation, the federation remained incomplete.

Marital difficulties after the fall of communism

Nonetheless, when Czech politicians and cultural figures looked back after 1989 on the federalisation of the Normalisation period, they often regarded it as a Slovak betrayal. Moreover, Slovaks' realisation of one of their principal aims with the Kremlin's apparent connivance encouraged post-communist Czech elites to think of themselves as selfless champions of the democracy that Slovaks had selfishly undermined. The Czech writer Ludvík Vaculík set off a new round of controversy during the 'hyphen war' when he suggested Czechs would be better off parting with their 'Slovak little brother'. One of the reasons Vaculík presented for ending the union was the ingratitude Slovaks had demonstrated for Czech sacrifices during the Prague Spring:

> When we tried to free ourselves from dictatorship in 1968, Slovaks regarded this as our concern and went for autonomy. When we were then punished for our revolt, they, seeing how they were not very committed to us, received milder punishment; and their autonomy, which they took advantage of our revolt to get, meant for us an aggravated punishment that did not fall on them. (Vaculík 1990, p. 1)

Slovaks may have gotten their federation, Vaculík and many other Czechs believed, but Czechs had paid the price for it, whether through the loss of jobs to Slovaks in the name of national equality or by heightened investment in Slovakia at the expense of the Czech economy.[17] This attitude made these Czechs less willing to tolerate renewed Slovak calls for a reform of the national settlement and the creation of an 'authentic federation'.

Naturally, their Slovak counterparts had a different opinion of the birth of the federation. In November 1990, the Slovak premier Vladimír Mečiar offered a rationale for why Slovaks had proceeded with federalisation after the invasion, claiming Slovaks had sought to rescue one of the key reforms of the Prague Spring. But Czechs had misread Slovaks' motives, he claimed, because they failed to grasp federalisation's democratic essence. Czechs wanted to postpone federalisation in order to try to protect what could still be salvaged from the reform movement, Mečiar explained, failing to understand 'the constitutional arrangement was also a component of the democratisation process. Thus, suspicions arose that Slovaks had other interests. They did not, they only wanted to gain what could still be gained in the given moment' (Mečiar 2002, p. 136). Slovaks did nothing wrong in proceeding with federalisation, Mečiar insisted. They simply sought to make the best of a difficult situation and meant Czechs no harm.

But what mattered after the collapse of the communist regime was not the reality of Slovak and Czech experiences with federalisation, but rather the way Slovaks and Czechs perceived the federation and blamed each other for its failings. The developing controversy in the spring of 1990 over the new name of the state reminded Petr Šabata (1990, p. 2) of the Slovak proverb, 'Under Novotný, the Czechs ruled us and it was bad', and the Czech retort, 'Under the federation, the Slovaks ruled us and it was even worse'. Many Czechs accused Slovaks of profiting from federalisation and Normalisation while Slovaks responded by accusing Czechs of not appreciating the need for a federation in spite of the invasion. After 1989 this mutual mistrust became a stumbling block to necessary processes of transition, especially economic reform.

Controversy over the Czech–Slovak relationship emerged in January 1990, when President Václav Havel proposed that the Federal Assembly delete the word 'socialist' from the name of the state, the Czechoslovak Socialist Republic, and adopt a new, non-communist coat of arms. To the surprise of Havel and other Czechs, this

[17]See, for instance, Pithart's claim (1995, p. 327) that the boost in Slovakia's standard of living under Normalisation inspired a certain 'nostalgia' for this period among Slovaks.

suggestion inflamed Slovak passions. According to Jičinský, Havel's proposed name change would have probably been approved by parliament without incident had he not connected it to the question of the state emblem. Instead, by suggesting the country create a new coat of arms, Havel touched an open wound for Slovaks (Rychlík 2002, p. 112).

The state emblem was a sensitive subject for Slovaks, especially those with longer historical memories, not because they hated to part with the communist coat of arms, but rather because the emblem was a reminder of what they believed was their subordinate position in the Czechoslovak state. Havel had tried to show concern for Slovak sensibilities in his speech to the Federal Assembly, urging it not to revert to the original coat of arms from 1920, 'because for us it is all inevitably joined historically with the idea of a single Czechoslovak nation' (Havel 2002a, p. 59). But Havel's rejection of both the 'Czechoslovakist' emblem of 1920 and the communist shield of 1960 required a new coat of arms, which led national-minded Slovaks to fixate on how best to represent symbolically the national equality they wanted.

There was a precedent from the 1960s for the Slovak complaints concerning the Czechoslovak coat of arms that resurfaced in the 1990s. In the communist emblem of 1960, adopted with the socialist constitution, the Czech lion occupied the dominant position, capped with a five-pointed communist star instead of the traditional Czech crown. The shield depicted Slovaks in a subordinate position, exchanging the traditional Slovak crest of a double-barred cross (representing St Cyril and St Methodius) atop three peaks (Tatra, Mátra and Fatra) with the flame of the Slovak National Uprising of 1944 burning on a generic mountaintop.[18] In 1968, Husák had suggested a change of emblem in conjunction with federalisation, since Slovaks and Czechs needed a coat of arms that 'speaks to them' as the traditional symbols of both nations had before.[19]

When Slovaks addressed the issue of a new emblem in 1968, they 'almost uniformly proposed to return to the traditional Slovak emblem', but their proposals also called for a coat of arms that 'should express symbolically the equal position of both our nations of Czechs and Slovaks'.[20] A Slovak expert in heraldry, Jozef Novák, proposed a new emblem in May 1968, a shield divided into equal halves with the Czech crest on the left side and the Slovak emblem on the right. Novák regarded his emblem as 'symmetrical', and believed this coat of arms would be adopted only when the 'real conditions' for it—a symmetrical federation—arose in Czechoslovakia (Novák 1968). The state emblem mattered to pro-reform Slovaks in the late 1960s, just as it did to Slovaks at all levels in the early 1990s, because it symbolised more than just the equal footing of the Slovak nation within the Czechoslovak state. For many Slovaks, the adoption of a new, symmetrical state shield represented a sign of good faith that

[18]'Návrh štátneho znaku Československej socialistickej republiky', *Smena*, 13 July 1960.

[19]'Slovo má dr. Husák', *Smena*, 14 April 1968.

[20]*Informácia o rezolúciach a listoch došlých Predsedníctvu Slovenskej národnej rady v súvislosti s Vyhlásením SNR z 15.3.1968 ako aj k Akčnému programu KSČ*, 10 June 1968. SNA, P-SNR, carton 167.

Czechs were willing to treat them as equal partners and apply the principles of democracy to relations between the two nations.

The continuity of this attitude among reform-oriented Slovaks became apparent early in the 'hyphen war', when several Slovak cultural figures published a statement on the emblem in *Smena*.[21] They criticised the interwar coat of arms some Czechs wanted to restore, because 'the Slovak emblem was placed on the breast of the Czech lion unequally and asymmetrically'. The statement claimed to speak for the Slovak public, which 'categorically rejects this as undemocratic, antifederative, ahistorical, and with a demagogic anti-Slovak subtext'. To make the emblem democratic, the signatories proposed adopting the emblem Novák had first proposed during the federalisation debate. The statement made explicit a view held by several Slovaks that accepting a symmetrical symbol of the state was a question of consistently respecting the democratic rights of the Slovak nation.

But the most visible and contested symbol of the Czech–Slovak disagreements to come was the hyphen proposed for the name of the state. A cross-section of Slovak society responded to Havel's call for a name change, with many arguing for the insertion of a hyphen in the word 'Czechoslovak', yielding the 'Czecho-Slovak Republic' (and other permutations), or 'Czecho-Slovakia' for short. For Milan Zemko, a Slovak historian, the adjective 'Czechoslovak' recalled the 'mistaken' thesis of a single Czechoslovak nation:

> The simplest and most logical solution is offered in the introduction of the perhaps still always feared (but why should we be afraid of it?) hyphen in the name of the whole republic, the Czecho-Slovak Republic and, needless to say, Czecho-Slovakia. (Zemko 1990, p. 1)

The hyphenated name made it clear the country comprised two distinct nations, Zemko believed, plus it corresponded to tradition, since the name of the state had been written as Czecho-Slovakia, with a hyphen, from 1918 to 1921.

But many Czechs resisted the hyphen because it recalled traditions less pleasant to them. 'Czecho-Slovakia' had also been the name of the short-lived Second Republic that existed from the Žilina Agreement of October 1938 to the Third Reich's annexation of the Czech Lands in March 1939. Czech representatives' refusal to adopt the hyphen and Slovak deputies' insistence on it forced an awkward resolution when the Federal Assembly first adopted a name change on 29 March 1990, with the country officially the (unhyphenated) 'Czechoslovak Federative Republic' in the Czech Lands and the 'Czecho-Slovak Federative Republic' in Slovakia (Act on Name Change 2002a, p. 73). This compromise satisfied no one. Though many Slovaks welcomed the new name used in Slovakia, most expressed unhappiness with the adoption of two names for the same state. Many regarded the law as a fiasco and thought Czechoslovakia would lose respect with two official names. Other Slovaks voiced displeasure that the hyphenated name was not applied uniformly, and they doubted

[21] The signatories included the cartoonist Milan Stano, writers Jozef Pavlovič and Štefan Moravčík, the journalist L'udmila Neamcová, Rudolf Demovič, the political writer Vladimír Daubner, the teacher Gabriela Gombošová, and 'many others' not named. 'Stanovisko k znaku a názvu našej republiky', *Smena*, 30 January 1990.

the outcome would have been the same had the country been called the 'Slovakoczech Republic', with a 'small c' used for the Czech nation.[22] Less than a month later, a second law provided a more workable compromise, renaming the country the 'Czech and Slovak Federative Republic' (CSFR) in both languages (Act on Name Change 2002b, p. 80).

For national-minded Slovaks, the hyphen was a symbol of their national identity. It both recognised them as a nation and expressed their equality with the Czech nation. These Slovaks felt their insistence on a hyphen was a justified call for applying democratic principles to national relations, which made it all the more puzzling when Czechs labelled such demands 'nationalistic' or 'separatist', reserving the 'patriotic' mantle for themselves. In April 1990, the Slovak Librarians Society warned of the disintegrative effects this one-sided tolerance would have on the state, since it would only play into the hands of actual (not imagined) Slovak separatists. Fair treatment by one side of the legitimate demands of the other was a precondition for a secure federation, the Slovak librarians argued:

> We think our common state can be a federation of two really equal nations only when all the laws, the legislative and economic decisions to approve the path [of transition] from below are mutually respected. The supreme and representative expression of this equality is also the uniform name of the federation.[23]

But mutual respect was in short supply during the 'hyphen war', with Czech public figures taking a dismissive attitude toward Slovak demands while some Slovaks viewed Czech criticism as hypocritical. In June 1990, Štefan Polakovič (1990) wondered 'why the advocacy of the political separation of Slovaks and Czechs in the spirit of a confederation should be a "criminal" political act', when it simply offered a way for Slovaks to fulfil their democratic rights as a nation, such as putting an end to the '*majorizácia* of Slovakia by Prague'. Slovaks' calls for a looser arrangement of the Czech–Slovak union were not nationalism, Polakovič maintained, since nationalism was characterised by 'snobbery, disrespect, impatience, truculence, force and cruelty toward other nations' (Polakovič 1990, p. 10). If anyone was guilty of nationalism, Polakovič contended, it was Czechs. Czech deputies had exhibited their contempt for Slovaks as a nation by demonstratively yawning and reading newspapers in parliament as Slovak representatives spoke out in favour of a hyphen. 'This Czech mannerism was a manifestation of disrespect and defiance toward the Slovak nation', Polakovič explained, 'the lowest level of nationalism' (Polakovič 1990, p. 10).[24]

The clash of attitudes: irreconcilable differences?

At stake during the 'hyphen war' and beyond was whose vision of democracy would prevail and what consequences it would have for the transition. Slovak political

[22]'K názvu republiky', *Práca*, 31 March 1990.

[23]'Chýba symbol národnej identity', *Pravda*, 2 April 1990.

[24]Polakovič, the chief ideologue of the wartime Slovak state who had outlived communism in exile, criticised Czechs' 'nationalism' without apparent irony, showing how some Slovaks played the democratic card opportunistically.

representatives entered discussions over the federation after 1989 with an agenda taken straight from the Prague Spring. When Mečiar arrived at Trenčianske Teplice for constitutional talks in August 1990, he brought the Slovak game plan of 1968, championing the principle that all federal powers derived from the republics as sovereign national states (Innes 2001, p. 101). As Mečiar explained at an SNR plenary session,

> we follow from the fact that the basis of the state is the free citizen, who joins into free communities, free communities into free republics, and republics as bearers of sovereignty [*suverenita*] pass along part of their own sovereignty to federal organs in that which is favourable to them. (Mečiar 2002, pp. 136–37)

Mečiar showed he could advocate the cause of the nation without coming across as a nationalist, since he placed the citizen above the nation, which nonetheless was a close second. Moreover, Mečiar's understanding of federalism, a view shared by many Slovaks, saw sovereignty originating from the bottom up. His notion of sovereignty also showed how nations and individuals had interrelated democratic rights. Implicit in Mečiar's vision of citizens forming 'free communities' was the idea that these communities of individuals were nations, which in turn stood as democratic subjects in the Czechoslovak context. Thus, Mečiar saw a relationship between the democratic rights of nations and individuals identical to the ideas prevalent in Slovak thinking during the federalisation debate of 1968.

By invoking the Slovak agenda from the Prague Spring, Mečiar appealed to many Slovaks who felt the goals of 1968 had not been realised. Whereas reform-minded Slovaks had called for a federation based on symmetry in the late 1960s, their successors in the early 1990s advocated an 'authentic federation' as the solution to the Slovak question. In June 1990, Dušan Nikodým (1990) explained that an 'authentic federation' meant the constitutions of the two republics determined the powers of the federal state and government, and not the other way around. This vision of an 'authentic federation' as a Czech–Slovak partnership in which power originated in the two republics was identical in its essence to Slovak demands for a 'loose federation' (*vol'ná federácia*) in 1968, when Slovak reformers had sought a union of national states with original sovereignty.[25] A 'loose federation' had confederative elements, since the federation existed at the pleasure of both national states, with the implication that either one could elect to dissolve the federation. Yet the citizen remained the foundation of an 'authentic federation', Mečiar explained, since 'every citizen is a citizen of the federation, but at the same time is a citizen of the republic'—a reaffirmation of his contention that nations were 'free communities' of 'free citizens' (Mečiar 2002, pp. 137–38).

Much as Slovak demands for rapid federalisation had seemed overzealous to pro-reform Czechs during the Prague Spring, calls for an authentic federation appeared just as bewildering to them after 1989. Mečiar noted how 'Czechs pose the question to us of why Slovaks are again raising the question of federation and why they are again beginning a public discussion of these questions. It is simple: because we still are not a

[25] 'Federácia v štádiu príprav zákona', *Práca*, 8 June 1968.

federative state' (Mečiar 2002, p. 136). Slovak and Czech differences over reform of the federation proved an obstacle to the post-communist transition, since their divergent attitudes on the question bogged down the new constitutional settlement.

In the same way some Slovak observers felt these federal issues detracted from more important reforms, a few prominent Czechs appreciated the need to be sensitive to Slovak grievances. The Czech premier Petr Pithart communicated his understanding of the Slovak position following the Trenčianske Teplice talks, remarking 'there is no other path to strengthening the federation than strengthening the competency of the republics'. Because the federation was a voluntary union based on the will of both nations, 'mutual trust, accommodation and then voluntarism' were essential (Pithart 2002, p. 108). Similarly, Havel expressed his empathy for Slovak frustrations following failed efforts to solve the Slovak question in 1918, 1945 and 1968:

> Is it any wonder Slovaks, after this third disappointment, do not want to be disappointed for a fourth time? Is it any wonder sometimes they are perhaps impatient and demand the rapid construction of an authentic federation more energetically than Czechs? (Havel 2002b, pp. 112–13)

Slovak demands for an authentic federation and the priority they placed on this reform were understandable, even justified, as Pithart and Havel acknowledged, demonstrating the willingness of at least some Czechs to comprehend the Slovak position. Yet Pithart's and Havel's empathy for the Slovak position did not amount to sympathy, since these two Czech leaders lacked the enthusiasm of Slovak politicians for federal reform.

Furthermore, the empathy of these two political leaders did not extend to all circles of the Czech public, creating disagreements that eroded the commitment of many Slovak and Czech politicians to preserve their union. Slovak leaders continued to insist on prohibiting *majorizácia*, which their belief in the democratic rights of both nations within Czechoslovakia required. Yet Czech politicians and commentators felt frustrated by what they perceived as Slovaks' determination to obstruct other reforms, especially economic liberalisation, until their demands for national equality were realised. As Vaculík explained to Soňa Čechová in April 1990, no constitutional provision could resolve this issue:

> Equality between Czechs and Slovaks—just as it concerns equality between men and women—cannot succeed in being directed by any institution, by any established relationship [that] there needs to be one to one or two to one. Real equality between people, let it be man–woman, Czech–Slovak, begins when the most capable people are chosen without regard to whether they are Czech or Slovak. (Čechová 1990, p. 4)

Vaculík hoped Slovaks and Czechs could finally transcend their mistrust and embrace an equality based on merit rather than proportion. He also implied Slovaks had failed to recognise that equality and democracy were a matter of mutual trust, not legislation, as the deficiencies of the communist federation had shown. In arguing against formal national equality, Vaculík revealed that insofar as he had given any thought to the democratic rights of the two nations within the Czechoslovak state, he considered these less important than the rights of the individual citizen, irrespective of nationality.

Similarly, Zdeněk Eis accused Slovaks of quashing the democratic rights of Czechs by subjecting them to a peculiar form of *majorizácia*. Eis (1990) acknowledged Slovaks were not homogeneous in their attitudes, and it would be 'the greatest mistake' for Czechs to judge all Slovaks by the opinions of a few. He even recognised the validity of Slovak concerns for their rights as a nation. But Eis's patience wore thin when it came to Slovak parties blocking progress on a constitutional settlement until they secured a confederative arrangement. As Eis wrote in August 1990, this obstructionism subverted the essence of democracy:

> We went through federalisation on national principles, and this led to the suppression of democratic principles. A democratic order recognises above all the relationship of the majority and the minority ... So there is no mistake: I am against the *majorizace* of Slovaks in all their national affairs. But I am also against the *majorizace* of Czechs by a numerical minority. (Eis 1990, p. 1)

Eis laid bare the conflict between majority rule and national equality that had created friction between Slovaks and Czechs during the federalisation debate in 1968 and threatened to drive the two nations apart in the early 1990s. The will to live in a common state was not lacking on either side, as Eis recognised for Slovaks and exemplified for Czechs. In spite of this shared desire, Slovak and Czech leaders had divergent ideas about the democratic rights of the nation and the urgency of federal reform in the context of the transition, differences that increasingly seemed incompatible. The two nations had drifted further apart following federalisation in 1969, a product in part of the dissatisfaction on both sides with the effects of Normalisation on the federation.

Moreover, even as Vaculík and Eis urged their compatriots to judge Slovaks on an individual, rather than collective, basis, they lapsed into generalisations in suggesting Slovaks had failed to appreciate the importance of mutual trust or majority rule, to the detriment of Czechs, which reinforced national binaries. In this way, political and cultural elites on both sides mapped differences of opinion onto the two nations, leading Slovaks and Czechs to view each other as uniformly minded nations rather than differentiated entities. The perception of a uniform 'Slovak' or 'Czech' view of the state and the federation fuelled a rising sense that disagreements over federal reform were part of a more intractable dispute between the two nations. Yet these same differences of opinion were not irreconcilable and did not doom Slovaks and Czechs to divorce. However, what became apparent from the outset of the 'hyphen war' was the perception gaining ground in both nations that their disagreements could not be resolved within Czechoslovakia.

An amicable break-up

The constitutional impasse persisted beyond the 'hyphen war', through the conflict over competency in 1991, and cast a pall over the elections of June 1992. When the parties of Vladimír Mečiar and Václav Klaus triumphed in their respective republics, the prospects for forming a governing coalition were not encouraging. However, the likelihood of a protracted, contentious process of coalition building brought an unpleasant surprise when Klaus almost immediately proposed the break-up of Czechoslovakia. Mečiar all but claimed Klaus had arrived for talks in Brno after the election intent on dissolving the federation, saying Klaus' delegation decided on ending the federation after 40 minutes of discussion.[26]

Klaus' unwillingness to indulge prolonged coalition talks made the disintegration of Czechoslovakia seem unavoidable. But when Klaus pronounced the death of the federation at Brno in June 1990, it proved a *fait accompli* only because Slovak and Czech elites both proved willing to accept it. The notion that the marriage was unworkable resonated among the population more widely because it squared with the attitudes of sizeable segments of both nations, even as majorities on both sides still openly opposed a split.

In particular, the speed with which segments of the Czech public accepted Klaus' assessment of the federation and its future made his pronouncement of its demise a self-fulfilling prophecy. Within two weeks of Klaus' declaration in Brno, several Czech cultural figures, including Vaculík, published a statement in *Literární noviny* expressing their opinion on the apparent end of Czechoslovakia. The preamble of the statement made it clear whom these Czechs blamed for the imminent divorce:

> Elections in the Czech Republic as well as the spectrum of opinions and forces from left to right affirmed the will of our nation for a free economy and political democracy. In Slovakia they point to a development toward a society directed by the state, with elements of national socialism, and these two tendencies cannot, in our opinion, be joined in a common will under a common government. It is startling to us.[27]

Pro-reform Slovaks at least must have been surprised at the assertion of a Slovak creep toward 'national socialism'. Though meant mainly in terms of state intervention in the economy (more popular in Slovakia than the rapid privatisation favoured in the Czech Lands), the term offered an unpleasant reminder of the wartime pro-Nazi Slovak state.

Even more telling, however, was the way the Czech supporters of the statement pinned blame for the current crisis on Slovak voters. A referendum on dissolution would be redundant, according to the statement, since elections in Slovakia had expressed the will of the Slovak nation to divorce. The break-up of Czechoslovakia was described as a welcome relief to these Czechs, who noted how the Slovak question 'got a different answer than we wished', but would be resolved at last.[28]

[26] 'O dezintegrácii federácie rozhodol Klaus', *Smena*, 8 July 1992.
[27] 'Úleva z rozhodnutí', *Literární noviny*, 18–24 June 1992, p. 1.
[28] 'Úleva z rozhodnutí', *Literární noviny*, 18–24 June 1992.

In a similar vein, a front-page editorial in *Mladá fronta Dnes* from June 1992 promoted the idea that Czechs had tried hard to save the federation, but now had to yield to Slovaks' separatist desires:

> We fully understand the legitimacy of the emancipatory efforts of the Slovak nation. But we will not abandon the idea that the terrain of a federal Czechoslovakia could be secure and broad enough for the solution of all conflicts and the realisation of these efforts ... It seems the Slovak nation wants and must have its own statehood, though this experience will be quite painful.[29]

Even though he was a Czech politician, Klaus took the decisive step to press for divorce, just like another Czech, Vaculík, first broke the taboo on a break-up during the 'hyphen war'. Many Czech elite members embraced the suggestion that Slovaks were to blame. They offered little resistance when Klaus proclaimed the end of Czechoslovakia because the notion of Slovak guilt seemed to fit with their pre-existing attitude that not only had Slovaks hindered the post-communist transition in their stubborn insistence on a reformed federalism, but it was Slovaks who were responsible for the poor functioning of the federation in the first place.

Despite these disagreements, neither in the early 1990s nor during the late 1960s were Slovak and Czech differences of opinion beyond repair. Both during the Prague Spring and in the years leading to the Velvet Divorce, many Slovak and Czech elite members tried to reconcile their differences and reach an accord, since most members of both nations still exhibited the will to live together in Czechoslovakia. Yet disagreements over the meaning of democracy in a Czechoslovak context, and in particular over what democratic rights the two nations should possess and what priority these should have in democratisation, degenerated into mutual mistrust, even enmity. The sheer length of the squabbles over federalisation and a reformed federalism—a dispute many individuals on both sides dated to the Prague Spring—led members of both nations to become retrenched in their positions and question whether a breakthrough would ever happen. It was these lingering doubts, stemming from divergent but not incompatible Slovak and Czech attitudes toward the position of the nation within democracy, which led Slovaks and Czechs first to entertain the possibility of living without the other partner, and then helped them to accept the end of Czechoslovakia with relatively little resistance or remorse when word of its demise came in June 1992.

University of Washington

References

Act on Name Change (2002a) 'Ústavný zákon číslo 81 z 29 marca 1990 o zmene názvu Československej federatívnej republiky', in Hlavová, V. & Žatkuliak, J. (eds) (2002), pp. 72–73.

Act on Name Change (2002b) 'Ústavný zákon číslo 101 z 20. apríla 1990 o zmene názvu Československej federatívnej republiky', in Hlavová, V. & Žatkuliak, J. (eds) (2002), pp. 80–81.

[29] 'Poločas rozpadu', *Mladá fronta Dnes*, 19 June 1992.

Čechová, S. (1990) 'O pomlčke, vzájomnej zodpovednosti a iných ošemetných veciach', *Kultúrny život*, 18 April.

Eis, Z. (1990) 'Jací jsou Slováci?', *Lidové noviny*, 14 August.

Falt'an, S. (1968) 'Akú federáciu?', *Nové slovo*, 13 June.

Gosiorovský, M. (1968) 'Historické predpoklady česko-slovenskej federácie III', *Nové slovo*, 6 June.

Grospič, J. & Jičinský, Z. (1968) 'K projevu soudruha Husáka na konferenci v Bratislavě', *Rudé právo*, 10 July.

Hatala, V. & Rebro, K. (1968a) 'Invalidná symetria', *Práca*, 13 July.

Hatala, V. & Rebro, K. (1968b) 'Ide o obsah československej federácie', *Pravda*, 13 July.

Havel, V. (2002a) 'Výňatky z prejavu prezidenta Václava Havla o štátoprávnych otázkach—o názve spoločného štátu a republík, ako aj o ich štátnych znakoch vo Federálnom zhromaždení', in Hlavová, V. & Žatkuliak, J. (eds) (2002), pp. 57–62.

Havel, V. (2002b) 'Prejav prezidenta ČSFR Václava Havla vo Federálnom zhromaždení o rozdelení kompetencií', in Hlavová, V. & Žatkuliak, J. (eds) (2002), pp. 112–15.

Hilde, P. S. (1999) 'Slovak Nationalism and the Break-up of Czechoslovakia', *Europe-Asia Studies*, 51, 4, June.

Hlavová, V. & Žatkuliak, J. (eds) (2002) *Novembrová revolúcia a česko-slovenský rozchod: Od česko-slovenskej federácie k samostatnej demokratickej slovenskej štátnosti. Výber dokumentov a prejavov november 1989–december 1992* (Bratislava, Literárne informačné centrum).

Innes, A. (2001) *Czechoslovakia: The Short Goodbye* (New Haven, Yale University Press).

Javorský, M. (1968) 'Úvahy nad federáciou', *Rol'nícke noviny*, 1 April.

Jesenská, Z. (1968) 'Práva občana', *Kultúrny život*, 5 April.

Laco, K. (1968) 'Osobitosti našej federácie', *Nové slovo*, 1 August.

Leff, C. S. (1996) *The Czech and Slovak Republics: Nation versus State* (Boulder, Westview).

Mečiar, V. (2002) 'Časti vystúpenia slovenského premiéra Vladimíra Mečiara v pléne Slovenskej národnej rady k návrhu ústavného zákona, ktorým sa menili kompetencie podl'a ústavného zákona číslo 143/1968 Zb. o česko-slovenskej federácii', in Hlavová, V. & Žatkuliak, J. (eds) (2002), pp. 135–42.

Nikodým, D. (1990) 'Bez suverenity niet národa', *Verejnost'*, 2 June.

Novák, J. (1968) 'Nový štátny znak', *Pravda*, 31 May.

Piekalkiewicz, J. A. (1972) *Public Opinion Polling in Czechoslovakia, 1968–69: Results and Analysis of Surveys Conducted During the Dubcek Era* (New York, Prager).

Pithart, P. (1995) 'The Division of Czechoslovakia: A Preliminary Balance Sheet for the End of a Respectable Country', *Canadian Slavonic Papers*, 37, 3–4, September.

Pithart, P. (2002) 'Výňatky z vystúpenia českého premiéra Petra Pithart v pléne Českej národnej rady k rokovaniam v Trenčianskych Tepliciach a k česko-slovenským vzt'ahom', in Hlavová, V. & Žatkuliak, J. (eds) (2002), pp. 108–11.

Polakovič, Š. (1990) 'Čo je a nie je nacionalizmus', *Literárny týždenník*, 15 June.

Rychlík, J. (1998) *Češi a Slováci ve 20. století: Česko-slovenské vztahy 1945–1992*, Vol. 2 (Bratislava, Academic Electronic Press).

Rychlík, J. (2002) *Rozpad Československa: Česko-slovenské vztahy 1989–1992* (Bratislava, Academic Electronic Press).

Šabata, P. (1990) 'Češi a Slováci', *Mladá fronta*, 2 April.

Šolc, J. (1968) 'Jedno bez druhého nemôže obstát'', *Nové slovo*, 1 August.

Štefan, E. R. (1968) 'Rebelantská rovnoprávnost'', *Práca*, 11 July.

Steiner, E. (1973) *The Slovak Dilemma* (Cambridge, Cambridge University Press).

Strinka, J. (1968) 'Federalizácia a demokratizácia', *Kultúrny život*, 5 April.

Vaculík, L. (1990) 'Naše slovenská otázka', *Literární noviny*, 3 May.

Zajanová, V. (1968) 'Dôsledná rovnoprávnost'', *Pravda*, 2 April.

Zemko, M. (1990) 'Symboly a názov štátu', *Verejnost'*, 2 February.

The Normalisation Regime and its Impact on Slovak Domestic Policy after 1970

JURAJ MARUŠIAK

THE AIM OF THE ESSAY IS TO DISCUSS THE CHARACTER OF THE Normalisation regime in Slovakia and its impact on Slovak domestic policy after the political changes of 1989. The first part of the essay offers an analysis of Slovak society's adaptation to the 'new reality' after the Warsaw Pact occupation of Czechoslovakia in August 1968. It provides a discussion of the differences between the policies of the Communist Party of Czechoslovakia (*Komunistická strana Československa*—KSČ) in the Czech lands and in Slovakia, and an examination of the sources of stability and legitimacy of this version of 'real socialism' in the specific conditions of Slovakia. It also analyses the political, historical and socio-economic reasons for the weakness of the political opposition, represented mainly by the dissident movement around the civil initiative Charter 77, in Slovakia. The second part of the essay examines the effects of Normalisation on the development of Slovakia and its influence on Slovak domestic policy after 1989, asking in particular why anti-communism in Slovakia was so weak.[1]

This article was prepared in the framework of the VEGA grant 'The Communist Power in Slovakia – language and practice' nr. 2/6120/27.

[1]The documents of the leadership of the Communist Party of Czechoslovakia and the Communist Party of Slovakia, as well as the archives of the State Security (*Štátna bezpečnosť*, ŠtB) are already available, the latter concerning Slovakia in the archive of the Nation Memory Institute in Bratislava and in the two volumes of documents, focused on the period of the 1970s and 1980s (Žáček 2002; Sivoš 2008). However, so far there has been little research drawing on this material, and none on the economic, social or cultural context of the Normalisation regime, particularly in the case of Slovakia. Historiography has focused primarily on the Czechoslovak events of 1968 and their aftermath, including the opposition movement and the political persecutions in Czechoslovakia (*Słownik* 2007; Císařovská & Prečan 2007; Blažek & Pažout 2008); the development of the structures of communist power (Pešek 2003, 2006; Pešek & Letz 2004); and the history of the Catholic Church (Pešek & Barnovský 2004; Šimulčík 2003). Generally, research in the 1970s and 1980s (Kusin 1978; Mlynář 1987, 1990; Renner 1989), along with the majority of recent scholarly work, have focused on the Prague Spring and the subsequent Normalisation in the framework of Czechoslovakia as a whole (Kurlansky 2004; Doskočil 2006; Williams 1997; Ramet 1995). The majority of works by Slovak scholars have been concerned with specific aspects of how the Normalisation regime functioned in Slovakia (Blehová 2006; Kmeť & Marušiak 2003; Pekník 2002; Pešek & Szomolányi 2000; Žatkuliak 1999a, 1999b; Blehová 2006; Szomolányi 1999). Differences between Slovak and Czech versions of Normalisation are also analysed by Czech historians Petr Pithart (1990) and Jan Rychlík (1998, 2002). In recent English-language research the differences between Normalisation in Czech lands and in Slovakia have been examined by political scientists, most often in the context of the study of nationalism in Central Europe

In Czech and Slovak historical writing the concept of Normalisation has two meanings. First, following Soviet terminology, it is used to describe the process of restoring communist control over society and the return to a 'normal' Soviet-type system (Williams 1997, p. 40). In the context of Czechoslovak history, Normalisation covered the period between the Soviet invasion of Czechoslovakia on 21 August 1968 and the completion of the political purges in 1970. Secondly, the term Normalisation is used to describe the specific local variant of the regime of 'real socialism' in the conditions of post-invasion Czechoslovakia during the entire period of the 1970s and 1980s. In our essay we will use this second understanding of the term. In essence the post-1968 regime was based on the restoration and consolidation of full control over society by the Communist Party of Czechoslovakia, the elimination of any independent civic activities in public life and the restoration of Soviet supremacy over Czechoslovakia.

Slovak society and the introduction of the Normalisation regime

A particular feature of Slovak distinctiveness was the relatively high level of personal continuity of the Slovak communist elites before and after the Soviet occupation, caused by the relative homogeneity of Slovak politics. This was rooted in turn in the distinctive character of Slovak politics before 1968. Prior to January 1968, the Slovak faction within the Communist Party of Czechoslovakia was perceived as a monolithic group in the struggle with the previous First Secretary of the KSČ Antonín Novotný.[2] Thus the crucial integrating factor of the Slovak communists was loyalty to particular local Party leaders, not loyalty to a particular political programme. As a result, while at the level of the KSČ the events of January 1968 triggered the process of democratisation, in the Communist Party of Slovakia (*Komunistická strana Slovenska*, KSS) the election of Dubček's former ally Vasil Bil'ak as General Secretary of the KSS resulted in the consolidation of the position of the Slovak Party hard-liners.[3]

In this context a seemingly paradoxical feature of the Slovak version of communist Normalisation was that the specific individuals whose names were the symbols of the Prague Spring democratisation process were identical to those that later became symbols of Normalisation. While the extraordinary Congress of the KSS (26–27 August 1968) did decide on the removal from the Central Committee of the most prominent representatives of the hard-line wing, including its most active representative, Vasil Bil'ak, at the same time the Congress became the official forum for Party consolidation in Slovakia when, under the command of the new first secretary of the Slovak communists Gustáv Husák, its delegation prevented the legitimisation of the extraordinary party congress in Prague. The victory of the former reformist politician

and concerning the effects of the past on post-communist policy in this region (Auer 2004; Bugajski 1994; Cohen 1999).

[2]There were a few exceptions however, including Michal Chudík, then speaker of the Slovak National Council (*Slovenská národná rada*).

[3]This situation had not been resolved by the time of the Soviet-led invasion. Thus, one day before the Soviet occupation, the conditional leader of the Slovak reform communists Gustáv Husák, anticipating public discontent, was promising the resumption of the democratisation efforts of January 1968 (*Rudé Právo*, 21 August 1968).

Husák also meant the victory of conservative forces, although the delegates to the Congress were not aware of this transformation (Štefanský 1992a, p. 149). Overall, a large number of pro-reform politicians proceeded smoothly to the new era of Normalisation and in spite of their previous activities became active performers of the new hard-line course.[4]

Among the general population, the initial reactions of Slovaks to the Soviet invasion in August 1968 were similar to those of the Czech population, and the demonstrations in Slovakia and the Czech lands in the autumn of 1968 were similar in nature (Figures 1 and 2). According to recent research by the Institute of National Memory (*Ústav pamäti národa*, ÚPN), during the first days of the occupation 19 inhabitants of Slovakia were killed by Soviet troops and 130 were injured.[5] However, by the following year the mainstream of Slovak society was already gradually lapsing into passivity. While in the Czech lands people from different social strata, including activists of the nascent civil society, were actively involved in resistance against the

FIGURE 1. SMOKE FILLED STREETS IN BRATISLAVA. PHOTOGRAPH BY LADISLAV BIELIK, COPYRIGHT PERMISSION PETER BIELIK

[4]In 1969, a number of former representatives of the so-called reformist wing of the KSS shifted back to the camp of Party hard-liners relatively easily—as in the case of Štefan Sádovský (1923 1984), an official of the KSS and state administration. Although he condemned the Soviet invasion in August 1968, later (in 1969), as Prime Minister of Slovakia, Sádovský shifted to the group of the main executors of Normalisation. Despite this shift he was excluded from the KSS after the purges in 1970 due to his activities before August 1968. For further details see Pešek (2003).

[5]'Obete augusta 1968. Bratislava, Ústav pamäti národa', available at: http://www.upn.gov.sk/data/pdf/august_obete.pdf, accessed 30 April 2008.

FIGURE 2. SOLDIER CHALLENGED BY CITIZENS IN BRATISLAVA. PHOTOGRAPH BY LADISLAV BIELIK, COPYRIGHT PERMISSION PETER BIELIK

impending Normalisation, in Slovakia manifestations of dissent were limited to the younger generation. While in the Czech lands, in the summer of 1969 alone, as many as 46 persons were sentenced in political trials, in Slovakia very few individuals were persecuted (Kalinová 1991, p. 16). Only about 4% of all the workers' self-administration councils established in the whole territory of Czechoslovakia in the autumn of 1968 were established in Slovakia (Bárta & Mencl 1993, p. 22).

In fact, the Normalisation purges in 1969–1970 took place in Slovakia without any significant manifestation of resistance. The results of the purges within the Communist Party of Czechoslovakia are significant. While in the Czech lands 23% of Party members were expelled or deleted from the list of Party members, in Slovakia such measures were taken against only 17% of members (Maňák 1997, pp. 58, 117). While the majority of the victims of the 'Normalisation purges' in the Czech lands were completely excluded from official public life, were not allowed to practise their original professions and had their works banned, in Slovakia a model of differentiated, selective and directed persecutions was adopted.

Although many Slovak intellectuals, scientists and writers were expelled from their previous jobs after 1969, many of them, such as Milan Ferko, Peter Karvaš or Ladislav Ťažký, were allowed to return to official literary or academic life. This was the general rule, with only a few exceptions. Individuals such as Dominik Tatarka and Milan Šimečka who joined the opposition against the regime were isolated. Such isolation of non-conformist intellectuals was one of the tools of the communist regime in Slovakia in the struggle against the political opposition. Tatarka's isolation served as a preventive measure for those intellectuals who were considering resisting communist power. Another group of Slovak intellectuals were those who were not actively involved in the independent initiatives but refused to express their support for the Normalisation. They too were not allowed to return to public life. At the same time, for the majority of the victims of the purges, the situation was not as hopeless after 1970 as in the Czech lands. Unlike their Czech colleagues, they were not faced with unemployment or forced to take manual jobs.

There was differentiation among the community of loyal intellectuals in Slovakia, however. Alongside traditional followers of Stalinism, who openly supported the restoration of total control over society by the Communist Party (for example the poets Daniel Okáli and Milan Lajčiak), there was a group of so-called 'national-wing' Slovak communists, made up of Slovak writers who actively supported the movement for the federalisation of Czechoslovakia in the 1960s and were in those days Gustáv Husák's allies. In 1968 they to some extent spoke and acted in support of the democratisation process and condemned the Soviet occupation of the country. Their motivation for supporting Normalisation was diverse. Some of them supported Husák as a 'lesser evil'. Such a belief was widespread even among certain pro-reform intellectuals in the Czech lands and Slovakia. The best known of these in the Czech lands was the historian Milan Hübl; in Slovakia the theory of 'lesser evil' was supported mainly by allies of Husák, for example by Ladislav Novomeský (Doskočil 2006, pp. 251, 254). On the other hand, for many of them it was a matter of their personal career. Although they were aware of the character of the regime, they were ready to disclaim their pro-reform past and move to the hard-line wing of the Slovak cultural elites. Examples of this group included the writers Vladimír Mináč, Alexander Matuška and Michal Chorváth, the poets Miroslav Válek, Vojtech Mihálik and Pavol Horov, as well as social scientists including Ondrej Pavlík and Felix Vašečka. Some of them, particularly in the field of culture, had never been members of the Communist Party or supporters of communism and they had even been persecuted after 1948, yet they seized the opportunity of returning to high positions in cultural life. (The poet Emil Boleslav Lukáč is a good example.)

While in the Czech lands a critical mass of people were actually forced into open confrontation with the regime, in Slovakia such a conflict did not take place. There is even a Czech word '*osmašedesátník*' (sixty-eighter) referring to the generation of those persecuted after 1968; but there is no such word in Slovak. In the Czech case we can genuinely speak about a generation sharing certain sentiments and experiences, and preserving a common generational consciousness which, following the events of 1989, to a large extent subscribed to social-democratic values. On an organisational level, in the framework of the dissident movement, this part of the society was conspicuous in Charter 77 as a very significant wing, and later some of its members established the *Obroda* (Renaissance) club. In Slovakia, *Obroda* was established only after 1989, and although some of its representatives (Alexander Dubček, sociologist and historian Ivan Laluha and economist Hvezdoň Kočtúch) stood in the first free parliamentary elections in 1990 on the list of the civic anti-totalitarian movement Public Against Violence (*Verejnosť proti násiliu*—VPN), *Obroda* in Slovakia never delivered any political programme and its aims were confined to demands for rehabilitation.[6]

This differentiated approach has given rise to the widespread myth of the 'soft version' of Normalisation in Slovakia. However, although direct persecutions were not as numerous as in the Czech lands, some former active protagonists of the Prague Spring had to pay the price for their return to public life by openly expressing

[6]Personal archive of Ivan Laluha, 1990–1992 chairman of the *Obroda Slovenska*.

self-criticism, and others had to abandon all pro-reform activities. Thus the price for escaping persecution was unconditional loyalty. In the early 1980s the State Security (*Štátna bezpečnosť*, ŠtB) put pressure even on Dominik Tatarka to be more accommodating in order for his books to be published in Czechoslovakia.[7] Thus the Normalisation regime in Slovakia was not more moderate, as is asserted by some historians and political scientists (Škaloud 2003, p. 6), but more effective in integrating larger parts of society into official structures. The so-called 'soft Normalisation' was one of the sources of stability of the communist regime in Slovakia, not a manifestation of its liberalism or even weakness.

In the early 1970s only the underground movement of the Catholic 'Secret Church' remained immune to communist power.[8] This became the most influential form of independent civil initiative in Slovakia. Although only a few members were actively involved in political activities (for example Ján Čarnogurský and František Mikloško), the first *samizdat* journals were published in this environment.[9] On the other hand, while the movement for religious freedom in the Czech lands was led by the highest official representative of the Catholic Church, Cardinal František Tomášek, the official hierarchy of the Catholic Church in Slovakia provided only limited support to the initiatives of the 'Secret Church' and believers. The highest representatives of the 'official' Catholic Church in Slovakia maintained a reserved attitude towards this movement almost until November 1989 (Šimulčík 1999, pp. 20–21). Thus we can conclude that the Catholic Church in Slovakia, unlike in Poland, was unable to act either as an organiser of a wider parallel social life, involving the development of independent intellectual life or social networks, and protection of the victims of political persecutions, or as a negotiator between communist power and society, due to the lack of the engagement of the official Catholic hierarchy and strict state control over the churches.[10]

Slovakia's so-called 'civil dissent', which focused mainly on issues of human rights, was reduced to a relatively small group of intellectuals who were not able to develop their own political initiatives or to publish their own *samizdat* journal. Their close connections to the dissident environment in Prague, in particular Charter 77, contributed to their increasing importance, but also limited their potential for developing independent political activities in Slovak conditions. A large part of the independent initiatives in Slovakia were based on primarily non-political activities, such as environmental protection and 'alternative culture' (the cultural underground). A degree of political ambition was displayed at the end of the 1980s by the circle of collaborators linked to Alexander Dubček, the Christian Democratic intellectuals around Ján Čarnogurský and the unofficial journal *Bratislava Letters* (*Bratislavské*

[7]Archive of the Ministry of Interior of the Czech Republic, temporary archival unit No. 218.

[8]The 'Secret Church' was established by Pope Pius XII in 1949–1950 as a separate structure within the Catholic Church. In the period of the worst persecutions against the Church, the duties of Czechoslovak bishops were transferred to officials in the 'Secret Church'. This underground network functioned until state control over the Church ended in 1989. The Secret Church was an integral part of the Catholic Church, although in certain cases it was allowed to act independently from the 'official' episcopacy, which was controlled by the communist authorities (Kmet' 2000, pp. 266–67).

[9]For more about the history of Catholic *samizdat* in Slovakia see Lesňák (1998).

[10]For further information see Pešek and Barnovský (2004).

listy), but the search for a common political platform for the particular currents of Slovak political opposition began only in 1987.

The so-called 'soft version' of Normalisation not only integrated the victims of the political purges into the pro-regime mainstream of society but also limited the space for human rights, democratic socialist or liberal dissident movements. Therefore, the emancipation of civil society in Slovakia proceeded far more slowly than in the Czech lands. On the one hand it allowed the writer Hana Ponická to prepare an undelivered contribution condemning the persecution of independent writers for the 3rd Congress of Slovak Writers in 1977 (Skilling 1981, pp. 306–09), but at the same time it preserved the belief that the impulse for changes would arise from within the ruling establishment. Thus the decisive moment for independent actions which definitely disregarded the official institutions, came only in August 1989 in connection with the imprisonment and political trials of five dissidents from Bratislava: Ján Čarnogurský, Miroslav Kusý, Hana Ponická, Anton Selecký and Vladimír Maňák. As the prominent Slovak dissident, Milan Šimečka, expressed it, 'not with the Communists, now we have to go against the Communists' (Szomolányi 1999, p. 30). Yet only one day after the first declaration of VPN appeared, on 22 November 1989, the *Declaration of the Ordinary Communists* (Žatkuliak 1999c, p. 336) was issued by the Party to attract KSS members dissatisfied with the regime. There was no comparable declaration in the Czech lands and its appearance confirms the important role of the communists in the process of transition in Slovakia. Due to the weakness of the liberal dissident movement, dissidents could not become the dominant component of the anti-totalitarian movement VPN, unlike Civic Forum (*Občanské fórum*) in the Czech lands. (Later, during 1991 and 1992 its primarily non-political origin caused the failure of its attempt to transform itself into a stable political party.)

Why so easy?

An explanation of the unusual phenomenon of Slovak Normalisation must begin with the differing perceptions of the events of 1968 in Czech and Slovak society. At least until the occupation of August 1968, the most important issue in Slovak politics, both in the hard-line and pro-reform wings of society, was the issue of the emancipation of Slovakia within the framework of Czechoslovakia. The pro-reform intellectual discourse among Slovak intellectuals and in the Slovak press was in favour of the KSS leadership. This support was exploited by the Slovak communist elites in their power games with the central government and leadership of the KSČ in Prague (Rychlík 1998, pp. 191–99).

The liberal intellectuals, on the other hand, considered the restoration of the autonomy of Slovakia, abolished after the adoption of the new constitution in 1960, and the federalisation of Czechoslovakia to be part of the de-Stalinisation process. Thus there was no open conflict between the intellectuals and communist power in Slovakia comparable to that which emerged at the 4th Congress of the Union of Czechoslovak Writers in 1967. Indeed, the representatives of Slovak writers at the Congress were rather passive and they tried to avoid open confrontation with the establishment (Kaplan 1997). Due to the apparently liberal atmosphere in Slovakia, the pressure for political reforms, especially in the first months of 1968, was limited. As political developments in the first half of 1968 showed, the influence of the reform intellectuals and their concept of change did not present an immediate challenge to the ruling establishment.

The differences between public opinion in the Czech lands and in Slovakia emerged most noticeably in April and May 1968. While public opinion in the Czech lands indicated that the issue of federalisation was of interest to only 5% of citizens, in Slovakia it was a priority for 95% (Piekalkiewicz 1972, pp. 110–11). This resulted in part from the differing perceptions of their common history. The first Czechoslovak Republic was generally rejected both by the Slovak population as a whole and by Slovak intellectuals. In Slovakia, the most highly valued periods in Slovak history were the Slovak national renaissance in the nineteenth century and the Slovak National Uprising of 1944 (Pithart 1990, p. 117).

At the same time demands for political democratisation were not as strong in Slovakia as in the Czech lands. The abolition of censorship was viewed positively by 91% of Czechs, but by only 74% of Slovaks (Piekalkiewicz 1972, p. 82). The activities of the non-communist parties, support for the proclamation of the 'Two Thousand Words Manifesto' and pressure to establish independent non-governmental organisations beyond the control of the Communist Party were incomparably less than in the Czech lands. However, from June and July 1968 demands for political changes became the crucial priority for Slovak society too. What was also typical was the decline in popular support for Gustáv Husák. While in April 1968 he was in second place following Dubček in terms of popularity among Slovaks, in June 1968 President Svoboda was more popular than him and later, in March 1969, he was in fifth or sixth place (Piekalkiewicz 1972, p. 46). Based on the public opinion polls we can conclude that the Slovak population was much more loyal to the establishment, and discontent with the previous policies of the Communist Party during the era of Antonín Novotný was not as high as in the Czech lands.

Another characteristic phenomenon was that unlike the Czechs, many Slovak opinion poll respondents did not express any opinion on the vital questions of political life. In fact one of the reasons for the moderate support for political reforms in Slovakia was the lower degree of politicisation in Slovak society. Another example of the lower level of political participation in Slovakia was the perception of the so-called 'Moscow protocols'. Only a small number of Slovaks discussed them with their colleagues at work (Piekalkiewicz 1972, p. 28). Even earlier, at the beginning of the democratisation process in spring 1968, almost half of the Slovaks questioned stated that they lacked knowledge about the public discussions of the 'Action Programme of KSČ' (Piekalkiewicz 1972, pp. 70–73). Since the level of political participation in Slovakia was lower, after 1968 there was no need to perform such rigid purges as in the Czech case.

The social and demographic context of Normalisation

The differing perceptions of the 1968 reform process in Czech and Slovak societies, accompanied by the low level of public participation in politics in Slovakia, cannot be explained solely by personal factors, or by the lower level of identification with communism among the Slovaks compared with Czechs, or by the peripheral role of

Slovakia in Czechoslovakia. Explanations should also be sought in the broader social context.

Although the socialist and communist tradition in Slovak society before World War II was rather weak (Kopeček 2006, pp. 52–53), especially in terms of the tradition of political thinking, and although the KSS lost the 1946 elections, these weaknesses also became, paradoxically, a factor for stability of the regime. The Communist Party was forced to build its social and power base from the roots up and, therefore, Party membership was more easily available than in the Czech lands. In such conditions, after 1948, the Party leadership found it easier to transform the Slovak Communist Party from a political party with a totalitarian ideology, but operating under democratic conditions for a certain period, to the power base of the totalitarian regime in Slovakia. At the beginning of 1960 the average age of KSS members was 39. More than 55% of members and candidates had joined the Party after 1950. At the same time only 1.8% of members entered the KSS before 1945.[11] If the motivation for joining the Communist Party was not so much a matter of family tradition, political conviction or idealistic motivation, but rather a wish to change one's own social status, the ability to adapt to changes in Party policy was greater.

Moreover, although the Communist Party had lost in the last free elections in Slovakia in 1946, the advent of communism found Slovak civil society in only the early stages of consolidation. The establishment of total control over society both after 1948 and 1968 was facilitated by the totalitarian experience of Slovakia during World War II, under Hlinka's Slovak People's Party (*Hlinkova slovenská ľudová strana,* HSL'S) which had received some popular acceptance and was not considered to be a foreign imposition. At the same time the lack of a tradition of self-organisation in society was a stabilising factor for the communist regime. In spite of the high level of industrialisation and urbanisation that took place after 1948, Slovakia remained a predominantly rural country. Although the share of the urban population increased from 31.4% to 41.4% between 1961 and 1970, the majority of the new urban population had been born and educated in villages (Štefanský 1992b, p. 122). Thus the change of environment did not bring a change in social or political behaviour, particularly given the conditions of the totalitarian regime (Musil 1995, p. 84).

Due to the nature of social and economic changes after 1948, the proportion of the Slovak population benefiting from the communist regime was higher than in the Czech lands. Among the main beneficiaries were workers in heavy industry, constructed for the purposes of the Soviet bloc, as well as employees in the service sector, culture and education, who were more heavily represented in the Czech lands than in Slovakia. Although they did not have an adequate income and material living conditions were poor, they had a relatively high quality of life in terms of their lifestyle and self-awareness, as well as a high educational level.

[11]Slovak National Archive (SNA), collection Presidium of the Central Committee of KSS (fond PÚV KSS), file 1033, Session of the Bureau of the Central Committee of KSS, 29 April 1960. *Správa o vývoji v zložení a regulácii rastu strany na Slovensku k 1. januáru 1960.*

The phenomenon of the 'generation cork' ('*generační zátka*'), described by the Czech sociologist Pavel Machonin,[12] where an older established generation obstructed access to power by the younger generation and therefore caused conflict, was a much more pressing problem in the Czech lands than in Slovakia, where due to the 'younger' character of the Communist Party the road to joining the elites was easier. At the same time, however, in Slovakia there was significant public discontent arising from the under-representation of Slovaks in the central institutions. In fact, according to the 'stratification analysis' of Slovak society, the share of Slovaks in the two highest strata was only 6.1% of the population, whereas in the Czech lands the two highest strata included almost 13% of the population. The representation of the Slovaks in the central institutions and in top management was especially low (Sikora 1997, pp. 203–04).[13] Despite this, according to a public opinion poll conducted in October–November 1968, almost 87% of Slovaks stated that their lives had improved compared to the pre-war situation. Almost 94% of Slovaks expressed satisfaction with the material situation of their own family (Štefanský 1992c, p. 422). This could explain why, by the summer of 1969, protests against the Soviet occupation and Normalisation were reduced to members of the younger generation that was unburdened by the historical memory of the pre-communist past and who compared their way of life to that of their contemporaries in the West.

In these circumstances, after the federalisation of Czechoslovakia in 1969 and the new wave of industrialisation in the 1970s, and the new high-ranking political jobs that were created, the space for political discontent and the formation of a political alternative became narrower in Slovakia than in the Czech lands. At the same time access to Communist Party membership and to jobs in federal institutions, including the army, remained more open than in the Czech case. Thus in spite of the political purges, the level of employment in the legal system, education, science and the state administration was growing in Slovakia, as opposed to the decline in the Czech lands (Kaplan 1993, pp. 79–82). Therefore, many members of the younger generation, who had been actively involved in the protests in 1968, joined the communist establishment in order both to fill the gap left by the excluded generation of people aged 30 and over and to fill new jobs. Although aware of the need for reform and hindered by a new generation 'cork' in the 1980s, as part of the establishment they became unconditionally dependent on the existence of the Normalisation regime. Therefore, we can argue that due to the conditions of ideological rigidity of the regime, they could not have become the promoters of new ideas.

Measures taken by the Czechoslovak establishment in the field of social policy also had a positive impact on the perception of Normalisation in Slovak society, particularly due to the increased income of retired people and workers on collective farms, as well as the measures adopted for families with children; the population boom in the early 1970s was twice as high in Slovakia as in the Czech lands. These social and economic factors helped to stabilise the communist regime in the 1970s in the Czech

[12]For detailed information see P. Machonin, *Sociální situace v Československu před lednem 1968*, undated, Bratislava, Archive of the Institute of Political Science, Slovak Academy of Sciences.

[13]See also: R. Roško, *Dominantné charakteristiky sociálnej štruktúry Slovenhska v 60. rokoch*, Bratislava, undated, Archive of the Institute of Political Science, Slovak Academy of Sciences.

lands too, but due to the different demographic and economic development there were more beneficiaries of such a model of communism in Slovakia (Kalinová 1999; Kaplan 1993).

The fact that the social and economic changes brought about by the communists were perceived positively by the majority of the Slovak population can also be indirectly confirmed by a public opinion poll, focused on the historical consciousness of Slovak society, which the Institute of Political Science conducted in 2003. According to this poll, almost 55% of Slovaks considered that the communist coup in 1948 had brought an improvement in social and economic living conditions not only in the material sense, but also in terms of the development of education and culture. While 44% thought February 1948 was a positive milestone in the history of the Slovak nation, only 42% held the opposite view. In terms of economic development, the social situation of citizens and the development of culture and education, the Normalisation era was considered the most successful in the entire period of twentieth century Slovak history. Respondents evaluated the 1970–1989 period as the most successful in Slovak history in general. Even their perception of the collectivisation of agriculture was more positive than negative (Pekník 2006, pp. 37–46).

On the other hand, politicians representing the Normalisation era were perceived rather negatively. For example, 11% of respondents considered Vasil Bil'ak to be the personality with the most negative influence on Slovak history, whereas only 1.4% perceived him in a positive way; although he was a controversial figure, 11.4% of respondents felt Gustáv Husák was a positive influence on the development of Slovak society, while 9.4% had a negative view; whereas Alexander Dubček was definitely perceived positively (Pekník 2006, p. 46). Together with Milan Rastislav Štefánik, Dubček is a unique historical figure, eliciting unanimous consensus among the majority of the general population.[14]

The Normalisation era and the political development of Slovakia after 1989

The federal question

One of the most important results of the attempted democratisation of 1968–1970 was the federalisation of Czechoslovakia. The establishment of the Slovak Socialist Republic as one of the federal units led not only to a strengthening of the position of Slovakia within Czechoslovakia, but to an increased role in the everyday life of Slovak society and in Slovak politics for the Slovak national elites based in Bratislava. Although the previous high level of centralisation had been preserved and the national institutions—the Government of the Slovak Socialist Republic, the Central Committee of the Communist Party of Slovakia and the Slovak National Council—had only limited jurisdiction, the Slovak political class was ready to acquire more power at any

[14]The positive perception of communism in Slovak society was probably a consequence of the painful social costs of the economic transition process after 1989. In spite of their positive evaluation of the communist past, in February 1999 and in 2004 more than half of Slovaks surveyed expressed a critical attitude towards different aspects of KSČ policy (Gyárfášová & Velšic 2000, p. 153; Výskum 2004).

suitable moment. This was thus increasing quantitatively as well as qualitatively, because at least from the formal point of view, wide spheres of public life now came under the control of the national republics. For ambitious, educated Slovaks it was more acceptable to start their career in Bratislava than in Prague, both for social reasons such as access to housing and because Slovaks working in the federal institutions in Prague very often lost their political positions and authority at home. The latter was not only a problem for low ranking officials; Viliam Široký experienced this problem when he was Prime Minister of Czechoslovakia in the 1950s as did Gustáv Husák, after 1970, who eventually lost his direct support in the KSS leadership.

At the same time, the recentralisation introduced by the 1970 Constitutional Law No. 133/1970 Zb. limited the real sovereignty of the national republics. Instead of the primacy of the national (Czech or Slovak) citizenship, the primacy of federal (Czechoslovak) citizenship was introduced, and the national governments became subordinated to the federal one. National republics were not allowed to adopt national constitutions and national symbols, although this had been envisaged by the 1968 Constitutional Law on the Czechoslovak Federation No. 143/1968 Zb. At the same time the nomination of state and Party officials in Slovakia was strictly controlled by the Presidium of the Central Committee of the KSČ in Prague, and after 1975 Slovakia even lost its state holiday—29 August, which was the anniversary of the anti-fascist Slovak National Uprising in 1944 (Rychlík 1998, pp. 272–89). In fact, the Soviet model of federalism had been introduced in Czechoslovakia, where the core of the political system and power was the Communist Party with its highly centralised and hierarchical system. The project of federalising the KSČ was abandoned in autumn 1968 and the KSS remained a semi-autonomous regional organisation of the centralised KSČ.

Although the Slovak ruling political class did not risk openly criticising Slovakia's role in the federation during the rigid era of the Normalisation regime until 1989, it took the first available opportunity to manifest its discontent. This was during discussions on the preparation of the new Constitution of Czechoslovakia in autumn 1989, when some deputies of the Slovak National Council spoke out against the centralised constitution and demanded that constitutions for the national republics should be prepared first (Žatkuliak 2008, p. 205). As soon as it was announced that a new federal constitution was being prepared, a group of Slovak intellectuals, including the younger KSS members, demanded a separate constitution for Slovakia and the restoration of its national symbols. After 1989 individuals such as Ján Bobák, Pavol Kanis and Anton Hrnko were actively involved in the movement for Slovak independence along with other intellectuals associated with the newly-established weekly of the Slovak Union of Writers *Literárny týždenník* (Rychlík 1998, p. 301).

At the same time the Czechoslovak Party leadership at the federal level, including the General Secretary of the Central Committee of the KSČ, Miloš Jakeš, refused to discuss reforming the way the Czechoslovak federation functioned. It was the project to develop a new constitution which became the driving force behind independent Slovak initiatives to elaborate an alternative political programme in 1989 (Zala 1993, p. 10). Thus, in 1989, the Slovak communist elites were already prepared to respond to the forthcoming national emancipation process.

In spite of the high level of centralisation of decision making, a soft separation between Czech and Slovak society took place. A certain role in this process was played by the activities of the ŠtB, which aimed to hamper communication between Slovak and Czech dissidents. Due to the different character of the two societies and the differing political developments, two separate anti-totalitarian movements were established—Civic Forum in the Czech lands and Public against Violence (VPN) in Slovakia (Eyal 2003, p. 81).

The establishment of the Slovak Socialist Republic in 1968 contributed to the establishment of Slovak domestic business elites, although of course under the conditions of the communist planned economy. It was the business elites and officials of the state administration who were most actively involved in the movement for an independent Slovakia in 1990–1992. In spite of the fact that the management of culture had been controlled by the national republics after 1968, many of the liberal-oriented humanitarian intellectuals and artists often lobbied in favour of the preservation of Czechoslovakia. The reason for this was on one hand their fears that the 'national issue' would be misused for authoritarian purposes like in 1968, and on the other hand the fact that the liberal intellectual environment was much more powerful in Prague. Under such circumstances the liberal intellectual and anti-totalitarian movement VPN became heavily dependent on political support from the federal government, especially after the first dismissal of Vladimír Mečiar from the position of Prime Minister of Slovakia in 1991, notwithstanding the fact that its initial vision of the reform of the Czechoslovak federation was rather close to the model of confederation. Fears about the authoritarian style of Vladimír Mečiar were probably one of the factors why some Slovak 'pro-federal' politicians from VPN or the Christian Democratic Movement objected to Slovak separatism, although they were not fully convinced of the advantages of the continued existence of Czechoslovakia (Miklośko 1996, p. 188), and were often disappointed by the policies of their Czech counterparts, for example by the under-representation of Slovaks in the central political institutions in Prague (Eyal 2003, p. 81).

Relations with the Hungarian minority

Gustáv Husák together with Ladislav Novomeský, Daniel Okáli, Vladimír Mináč and other communist politicians and intellectuals that came to power in Slovakia after 1969, had been persecuted as 'Slovak bourgeois nationalists' to various degrees in the 1950s. This group had gained legitimacy by participating in the anti-fascist Slovak National Uprising of 1944 as well as through the struggle for greater autonomy for Slovakia within communist Czechoslovakia. They were also actively involved in the persecutions of the Hungarian minority in the years 1945–1948. Although the Minority Rights Constitutional Law No. 144/1968 Zb. was adopted together with the Constitutional Law on the Czechoslovak Federation on 28 October 1968 and representatives of the Hungarian minority organisation *Csemadok* were included in the communist nomenclature, Slovak–Hungarian political tensions from the first half of 1968 continued on the political level. The Slovak Party leadership tried several times (in 1979, 1981 and 1984) to transform schools where teaching was in Hungarian into 'bilingual' schools where the Slovak language would predominate. Although they failed, such attempts caused tensions in interethnic relations in Slovakia, even between Slovak dissidents and the dissident 'Committee for the Protection of the Rights of the

Hungarian Minority in Czechoslovakia' which operated in southern Slovakia and was led by Miklós Duray. Resentments from the 1970s and 1980s were one of the reasons for the tensions between Slovak and Hungarian politicians after the collapse of communism and the reserved attitude of ethnic Hungarians in Slovakia towards Slovak independence (Bugajski 1994, p. 324). At the same time the minority policy of the KSS before 1989 and persisting suspicion towards Hungarians among the centre-left parties, including the SDL', after the 'Velvet Revolution', meant that Hungarian minority politicians from southern Slovakia preferred to cooperate with the centre-right parties (Fisher 2002, p. 118).

The political landscape of Slovakia

The Slovak version of Normalisation contributed to the strengthening of the division of Slovak society into 'rulers' and 'ruled'. The KSS preserved its character as the 'party of power' and as discussed above, joining the KSS was a question of pragmatic choice rather than belief or conviction. The pragmatic dimension of the politics of the Normalisation regime is underlined by the fact that after the abolition of the 'Action Programme of KSČ' this party did not adopt any programmatic document until 1989. Thus the main political conflicts in Slovak society had a pragmatic rather than an ideological character. Even after 1989, the largest ruling political parties were, like the KSS in the previous era, built from above on the basis of personal loyalty and very often with the direct or indirect exploitation of administrative tools. The interconnections between political party structures, business–clientelist networks and state structures were typical phenomena of the largest ruling political parties, like Public against Violence, the dominant ruling party in 1990–1992, the Movement for Democratic Slovakia (*Hnutie za demokratické Slovensko,* HZDS), the dominant ruling party in 1992–1994 and 1994–1998, the Slovak Democratic and Christian Union–Democratic Party (*Slovenská demokratická a kresťanská únia–Demokratická strana,* SDKÚ–DS), the largest coalition party in the period 1998–2006, and Direction–Social Democracy (*Smer–sociálna demokracia*), at the time of writing, the dominant ruling party since 2006. Such a model of political culture was largely accepted by a society which had become accustomed to the blurring of state and party structures during the fascist and communist totalitarian regimes. At the same time programme-based political parties have not been particularly successful in Slovak political competition, like for example the Christian Democratic Movement (*Kresťanskodemokratické hnutie*, KDH), the neo-Stalinist Communist Party of Slovakia (*Komunistická strana Slovenska*) or the Party of the Democratic Left (*Strana demokratickej ľavice,* SDL') and the Social Democratic Alternative (*Sociálnodemokratická alternative*, SDA).

The pragmatic nature of politics is further exemplified by the fact that in spite of the absence of a 'reform wing' within the Party (which persisted in Poland and Hungary even after the purges) former communists preserved their influence on Slovak politics not only in the framework of the new political parties, but also as members of a 'transformed' Communist Party. In the majority of cases having a communist past was not a political obstacle for further involvement in politics after 1989. Communist politicians such as the Czechoslovak Prime Minister Marián Čalfa (1989–1992), the

Prime Minister of the Slovak Republic Milan Čič (1989–1990) or the Chair of the Slovak National Council Rudolf Schuster (1989–1990) played a very active role in the transfer of power from the Communist Party to democratic forces at the end of 1989 and the beginning of 1990, and these 'transition communists' (Szomolányi 1999, p. 41) very soon became the most popular politicians in Slovakia.

Later, in the first free parliamentary elections in June 1990, it was these politicians together with the 'reform communists' from 1968 (such as Alexander Dubček and Vladimír Mečiar) who became the leaders of the anti-totalitarian movement VPN, although they had nothing to do with its establishment in November 1989. As there had only been a limited need for the formation of a political alternative to the establishment in Slovak society before 1989, and the core of the first alternative movement, VPN, consisted of artists from the cultural underground, environmentalists and social scientists, the new democratic forces were only equipped to carry governmental responsibility to a limited extent. Thus former communists continued to play an important role in Slovak politics and business even after 1989. One of the most successful 'transition communists' was Rudolf Schuster, who later became President of the Slovak Republic (1999–2004). Not only was his involvement in the structures of the *ancien régime* not an obstacle to his success in the first direct presidential elections in 1999, but during the campaign he openly stated that he was proud of his work as a communist during the communist regime (Kotian & Matejčíková 1999). At the same time he identified himself as a staunch Catholic: 'Although I was a Communist, I remained Catholic'.[15]

At the same time, even some hard-line communist politicians continued in public and political life after 1989. The last communist Minister of Culture Pavol Koyš was actively involved in the restoration of the neo-Stalinist Communist Party of Slovakia in the period 1992–1993, and Bohuslav Chňoupek, one of the most active representatives of pro-Soviet journalism after the suppression of the Prague Spring, and later the Minister of Foreign Affairs of Czechoslovakia (1971–1988), was an active journalist and political writer almost until his death in 2004. He participated in the discussions organised by the Slovak Writers' Society (*Spolok slovenských spisovateľov*) focused on international relations, where he criticised the pro-Western orientation of Slovak foreign policy and the foreign policy of the USA. The Deputy Prime Minister of the last communist government of Slovakia, Štefan Murín, was chair of the Association of the Supporters of Neutrality in the second half of the 1990s, which campaigned against Slovakia's accession to NATO. This organisation gained an influential position in the media loyal to the government of Vladimír Mečiar (1994–1998).

Other politicians from the era of the *ancien régime*, like the former chair of the Slovak regional branch of the Union of Czechoslovak–Soviet friendship Jozef Mravík, were actively involved in organisations supporting Slavic solidarity. However, these initiatives only had a marginal character. On the other hand, after the death of the former Prime Minister of Slovakia, Pavol Hrivnák, who had been dismissed in November 1989 due to his hard-line convictions and his rejection of the 'Velvet Revolution', the then Minister of Economy Ján Ducký dedicated a bust in commemoration to him in the town of Svit, where he had worked in the top

[15] *Sme*, 5 September 1999.

management of the local chemical factory 'Chemosvit' in the 1950s and 1960s. Paradoxically Svit is a town with an old industrial tradition from the era of the first Czechoslovak Republic (1918–1938), and the bust of the communist director and politician is placed close to the statue of the capitalist businessman Tomáš Bat'a. The memorial to Hrivnák was justified by the local council and the management of 'Chemosvit' (already a commercial joint stock company) as recognition of his contribution to the development of the town, and not his ideological orientation.[16]

The pragmatic character of politics under the Normalisation regime also affected the process of the transformation of the KSS after 1989. In autumn 1990, the newly established SDL' adopted a social democratic programme very quickly, without major internal discussions or conflict. Although this was sometimes referred to as the 'success story' of the transformation of the former Communist Party (Kopeček 2002), after such an easy 'transformation' this party became, in 2002, the first post-communist party in the former Soviet block unable to manage the conflict between its own communist origins and its declared political orientation. It was only after the collapse of SDL' that a similar conflict took place in the Polish post-communist Union of Democratic Left (*Sojusz Lewicy Demokratycznej*, SLD). One reason which may explain the collapse of both former communist parties was the lack of commitment to social democratic values and the return to orthodox communist rhetoric that was supported by the majority of the party members. Thus the so-called 'transformation' of the communist parties in Central Europe was more the result of pragmatic choice than of ideological and programmatic debates within these parties. The post-communist parties of Central Europe could not be fully classified as programme-based parties, but rather more as parties based on personal loyalty, or as they are called by Polish sociologist Jacek Wódz, parties based on an 'apology for the biographies of their members' (Wódz 2004).

The long-term experience with the ideological indoctrination of society meant that the predominant Catholic Church, whose membership comprises 70% of the population,[17] demanded the institutionalisation of its influence (Weiss 2005, p. 73), although in the communist era the Church did not play the role of the moral authority as it did in Poland.

Slovak nationalism

The political atmosphere of the Normalisation era also influenced the character of Slovak nationalism. On the one hand, the communist regime fought against the revival of right-wing conservative nationalist projects based on the ideology of Hlinka's Slovak Peoples Party due to the Catholic character of the Slovak Republic (1939–1945). Yet, on the other hand, communist power perceived the October 1987 resolution of a group of Slovak intellectuals condemning the deportation of Jews during World War II to be a challenge to communism itself because the signatories stated that the principles for the future of Slovakia should be equality, tolerance,

[16] *Sme*, 2 May 2006.

[17] The Slovak Republic Government Office, available at: http://www-8.vlada.gov.sk/index.php?ID=1446, accessed 7 August 2008.

democracy and rule of law (Žatkuliak 1999c, pp. 171–72). Thus discussion of the real character of the regime of the 'Slovak state' 1939–1945 was forbidden during the era of communism. The Slovak nationalism that earlier, in the 1960s, had been a tool to legitimise Slovak communist politicians, was still in use, mainly in the late 1980s. Instead of a liberal and modern character, it adopted an isolationist form and it was rather suspicious of the West. To a certain extent it was focused on legitimising Soviet dominance through the idea of Slavic solidarity. At the same time, ideologists of this nationalism, such as the communist writer Vladimír Mináč, depicted the pre-communist Slovak elites as alien to Slovak society (Mináč 1970).

The Slovak nationalism that emerged in the Normalisation era was not conceptualised as a tool for the de-legitimisation of communism, as it was in Poland, or for other minority nations like Slovenians, Croatians, Ukrainians or the Baltic nations. On the contrary, in the case of Slovakia in the 1990s nationalism was used for the legitimisation of semi-authoritarian methods of government. Due to their suspicious attitude towards the West and liberalism, post-communist nationalists could find a common language with the representatives of right-wing nationalism appealing to the fascist Slovak Republic in 1939–1945 (Auer 2004, pp. 149, 353). A new, civic and pro-European Slovak nationalism has emerged only recently in the context of Slovakia's admission to the EU and NATO. The partially authoritarian character of Slovak nationalism caused the deep divisions within Slovak society that took place during the 1990s. Its consequence at the time was the ambivalent attitude of a large part of Slovak society towards independent Slovak statehood. Only the consolidation of democracy in Slovakia and its integration into the EU contributed to the positive acceptance of Slovak statehood by the majority of Slovak citizens. Whereas in 1993 almost 73% of Slovak citizens expressed a negative attitude to the division of Czechoslovakia and only 27% were in favour, by the end of 2004 61% supported and 39% opposed.[18]

However due to the lack of a free exchange of information and political freedoms, Slovak society was very fragmented even in 1989. The process of its integration into a 'national' society, where change in one segment of society will immediately lead to changes in all others (Bell 1990, pp. 228–29), was not yet complete in 1989. Before 1989, independent intellectuals from Košice had more intensive contacts with Prague dissident circles than with the intellectual underground in Bratislava. It is notable that in the first days of the Velvet Revolution cities in eastern Slovakia established local branches of the Czech-based Civic Forum instead of the Slovak Public against Violence. The level of support for an independent Slovakia was much lower in Košice and in eastern Slovakia than in Bratislava in 1992; Košice even had the rather curious 'Initiative for a Sovereign Košice', demanding a form of local city autonomy.

Civil society and power

The easy implementation of the Normalisation era in Slovakia was due to the low degree of self-organisation in society. The weakness of political parties, trade unions

[18] *Názory občanov SR a ČR na rozdelenie spoločného štátu sa zmenili v prospech samostatnosti*, Bratislava, IVO–Praha, STEM 2004.

and the non-governmental sector continued to be problematic for the consolidation of democracy throughout Slovakia in the 1990s. In certain periods, mainly during the third government of Vladimír Mečiar (1994–1998) and after the parliamentary elections of 2006, the 'third sector' was considered a potential risk to the stability of the government. Democratic governments after 1989 also took advantage of the weakness of civil society in order to enforce unpopular political or socio–economic measures. Thus not only the division of Czechoslovakia, but also unpopular social and economic reforms in the years 2002–2006 and the involvement of Slovakia in the Iraq War in 2003 were implemented without the approval of the majority of society. Even the accession of Slovakia to NATO did not enjoy the support of the majority of the population, although attempts to force a referendum on the issue failed. In fact, the single successful referendum in Slovakia was the referendum on EU-membership held in 2003, but even in this case the turnout was very low, only 52.15%.[19] No nationwide referendum initiated by a group of citizens or a political party has been successful to date. All failed because of low voter turnout.

The social structure of Slovakia

Rural and traditional stereotypes played an important role in political mobilisation even after 1989. The political consolidation of the urban population was a lengthy process; its first success was the result of the parliamentary elections in 1998, where a coalition of the forces supporting the liberal path of modernisation achieved a political majority (Krivý 1999, p. 249). The economic policies of political elites of the Normalisation era as well as after 1989 focused predominantly on the development of the industrial sector. Therefore, we can find a certain continuity between the communist propaganda focused on pride in the industrialisation of Slovakia in the 1950s and 1960s and the new slogan 'Slovakia—the largest producer of cars in the world per capita' introduced after huge investments in the automobile industry after 2002[20] as a source of national pride and an element of the modern Slovak identity.

Conclusion

Although in Slovakia as well as in the Czech lands the Normalisation regime's primary source of 'legitimacy' was the Soviet invasion of Czechoslovakia in August 1968, in the Slovak case we can also speak about domestic sources of legitimacy. Certain elements of domestic political tradition were employed in the implementation of the Slovak version of Normalisation. As well as economic and social factors, the illiberal and anti-Western version of Slovak nationalism also played an important role. The 'national dimension'—the nationalisation of the communist regimes in Central and Eastern Europe—started in the 1960s, though in conditions where Soviet dominance was strictly respected. It was precisely in the 1960s when the majority of the

[19] *Referendum on Accession of the Slovak Republic to the European Union 2003. Participation of the Eligible Citizens in Referendum by Districts*, Bratislava, Statistical Office of the Slovak Republic, available at: http://www.statistics.sk/ref_2003/webdata/en/graf/kart1_a.htm, accessed 7 August 2008.

[20] *Sme*, 8 April 2008.

representatives of the Normalisation era launched their careers at the highest levels of communist politics, and when the main representative of the regime—Gustáv Husák, achieved his political comeback after his release from prison. Thus the Slovak version of Normalisation had many features in common with Poland and the regime of Władysław Gomułka in the 1960s. Gomułka had also been imprisoned in the purges of the 1950s and after his political comeback he decided to build a Polish version of 'domestic' or 'national communism' in the conditions of Soviet domination (Davies 2003, pp. 33–38).

The Slovak version of the Normalisation regime was more successful than the Czech one because in Slovakia larger segments of society were incorporated into official structures, and Slovak society, including any potential opposition, remained fragmented. Even after the political changes in 1989 members of the previous communist establishment continued to play an important role in Slovak political and economic life. Therefore programmes of 'lustration' and 'de-communisation' or 'de-bolshevisation' could not succeed in Slovak conditions—at least not in the 1990s.

The main legacy of the Normalisation era in Slovak politics after 1989 was the weak role of ideology and political programmes in the agenda of political actors and the high level of the intertwining of the state with the ruling political parties and particular group interests. The main political conflicts within Slovak society that took place before 1989 (the future of Czechoslovakia, relations between the Hungarian minority and the majority population, conflicts between democracy and authoritarianism, conflicts about the geopolitical orientation of Slovakia), generally continued after the 'Velvet Revolution' as well, and they acquired a crucial importance in Slovak political processes in the 1990s. The element of continuity is the weakness of civil society in Slovakia, especially at the beginning of the 1990s, and the low level of political activity among citizens is confirmed by the failure of the referenda in Slovak politics.

Due to the ambivalent perceptions of communism and the Normalisation regime in particular, which are a mixture of positive attitudes and critical remarks, anti-communism is still the ideology of the minority in Slovak society. At the same time, communism is for many people—and particularly for members of the political elite—an important part of their personal history. This is the reason for the ambivalent attitude towards coming to terms with the past. The high degree of personal continuity among the political elites from the communist era caused the negative attitudes to the process of lustration, first launched in 1990. Immediately after 1992 the 'lustration law' ceased to be implemented in Slovakia. Later, the establishment of the Institute for National Memory (Ústav pamäti národa) in 2002, whose role is to document the crimes of the communist and fascist regimes in Slovakia during the years 1939–1989 and to publish the personal files of the Communist State Security (ŠtB), was accompanied by a lack of interest among the majority of the political elites. Two attempts to disband the institute, in 2007 and 2008, show just how painful discussion of the communist past is in contemporary Slovakia.

The Slovak version of '*Ostalgie*' (the German word play for nostalgia for the East) can be seen in the positive attitude of the overwhelming majority of Slovaks towards Dubček as the symbol of democratic traditions together with the positive perceptions of the anonymous Normalisation era. It is a symbol for the reality of contemporary Slovak politics, torn between democratic modernisation and authoritarian traditions.

Slovak Academy of Sciences

References

Auer, S. (2004) *Liberal Nationalism in Central Europe* (London and New York, Routledge).

Bárta, M. & Mencl, V. (eds) (1993) *Československo roku 1968, 2. díl: počátky normalizace* (Prague, Ústav mezinár vztahu—Parta).

Bell, D. (1990) *Kulturowe sprzeczności kapitalizmu* (Warsaw, PWN).

Blažek, P. & Pažout, J. (2008) *Nejcitlivější místo režimu. Výbor na obranu nespravědlivě stíhaných (VONS) pohledem svých členů* (Prague, Pulchra).

Blehová, B. (2006) *Der Fall des Kommunismus in der Tschechoslowakei* (Vienna, Lit Verlag).

Bugajski, J. (1994) *Ethnic Politics in Eastern Europe: A Guide to Nationality Policies, Organizations, and Parties* (New York and London, M.E. Sharpe).

Císařovská, B. & Prečan, V. (eds) (2007) *Charta 77: Dokumenty 1977–1989* (Prague, Ústav pro soudobé dějiny AV ČR).

Cohen, S. (1999) *Politics Without Past* (Durham and London, Duke University Press).

Davies, N. (2003) *Polsko. Dějiny národa ve středu Evropy* (Prague, Prostor).

Doskočil, Z. (2006) *Duben 1969: Anatomie jednoho mocenského zvratu* (Brno, Doplněk).

Eyal, G. (2003) *The Origins of Postcommunist Elites: From Prague Spring to the Breakup of Czechoslovakia* (London and Minneapolis, University of Minnesota Press).

Fisher, S. (2002) 'The Troubled Evolution of Slovakia's Ex-Communists', in Bozóki, A. & Ishiyama, J. T. (eds) (2002) *The Communist Successor Parties of Central and Eastern Europe* (London and New York, M. E. Sharpe).

Gyárfášová, O. & Velšic, M. (2000) 'Dynamika verejnej mienky', in Pešek, J. & Szomolányi, S (eds) (2000).

Kalinová, A. (1991) 'Ladislav Ján Kalina', *Romboid*, 26, 5.

Kalinová, L. (1999) *K sociálním dějinám Československa v letech 1968–1989* (Prague, Vysoká škola ekonomická).

Kaplan, K. (1993) *Sociální souvislosti krizí komunistického režimu 1953–1957 a 1968–1975* (Prague, Ústav pro soudobé dějiny AV ČR).

Kaplan, K. (1997) *'Všechno jste prohráli!' (Co prozrazují archivy o IV. Sjezdu Svazu československých spisovatelů 1967)* (Prague, Ivo Železný).

Kmet', N. (2000) *Postavenie cirkví na Slovensku 1948–1951* (Bratislava, Veda).

Kmet', N. & Marušiak, J. (eds) (2003) *Slovensko a režim normalizácie* (Prešov, Vydavatel'stvo Michala Vaška).

Kopeček, L. (2002) 'The Slovak Party of the Democratic Left: A Successful Post-Communist Party?', *German Policy Studies*, II, 2.

Kopeček, L. (2006) *Demokracie, diktatury a politické stranictví na Slovensku* (Brno, Centrum pro studium demokracie a kultury).

Kotian, R. & Matejčíková, D. (1999) 'Občan si nedá stranami nadirigovat', koho má volit', tvrdí koaličný prezidentský kandidát R. Schuster', *Sme*, 15 February.

Krivý, V. (1999) 'Volebné výsledky', in Bútora, M., Mesežnikov, G. & Bútorová, Z. (eds) (1999) *Kto? Prečo? Ako? Slovenské vol'by '98* (Bratislava, IVO).

Kurlansky, M. (2004) *1968: The Year That Rocked the World* (New York, Ballantine Books).

Kusin, V. (1978) *From Dubček to Charter 77. A Study of 'Normalisation' in Czechoslovakia 1968–1978* (New York, St. Martin Press).

Lesňák, R. (1998) *Listy z podzemia. Kresťanské samizdaty 1945–1989* (Bratislava, USPO).

Maňák, J. (1997) *Čistky v Komunistické straně Československa 1969–1970* (Prague, Ústav pro soudobé dějiny AV ČR).

Mikloško, F. (1996) *Čas stretnutí* (Bratislava, Kalligram).

Mináč, V. (1970) *Dúchanie do pahrieb* (Bratislava, Smena).

Mlynář, Z. (1987) *Problémy politického systému. Texty o roce 1968, normalizaci a současné reformě v SSSR* (Köln, Index).

Mlynář, Z. (1990) *Mráz přichází z Kremlu* (Prague, Mladá fronta).

Musil, J. (1995) *The End of Czechoslovakia* (Budapest, Central European University Press).

Pekník, M. (ed.) (2002) *Česká a slovenská společnost v období normalizace: Slovenská a česká spoločnosť v čase normalizácie. Liberecký seminar 2001* (Bratislava, Veda).

Pekník, M. (ed.) (2006) *Verejná mienka a politika. Historické vedomie slovenskej spoločnosti* (Bratislava, Veda).
Pešek, J. (ed.) (2003) *Aktéri jednej éry na Slovensku 1948: 1989* (Prešov, Vydavatel'stvo Michala Vaška).
Pešek, J. (2006) *Centrum moci. Aparát Ústredného výboru Komunistickej strany Slovenska 1948–1989* (Bratislava, AEPress).
Pešek, J. & Barnovský, M. (2004) *V zovretí normalizácie* (Bratislava, Veda).
Pešek, J. & Letz, R. (2004) *Štruktúry moci na Slovensku 1948: 1989* (Prešov, Vydavatel'stvo Michala Vaška).
Pešek, J. & Szomolányi, S. (2000) *November 1989 na Slovensku. Súvislosti, predpoklad a dôsledky* (Bratislava, Nadácia Milana Šimečku).
Piekalkiewicz, J. (1972) *Public Opinion Polling in Czechoslovakia 1968–69. Results and Analysis of Surveys Conducted during the Dubcek Era* (New York, Ardent Media).
Pithart, P. (1990) *Osmašedesátý* (Prague, Rozmluvy).
Ramet, S. (1995) *Social Currents in Eastern Europe: The Sources and Consequences of the Great Transformation* (Durham, NC and London, Duke University Press).
Renner, H. (1989) *A History of Czechoslovakia since 1945* (London and New York, Routledge).
Rychlík, J. (1998) *Češi a Slováci ve 20. století. Česko-slovenské vztahy 1945–1992* (Bratislava, Academic Electronic Press).
Rychlík, J. (2002) *Rozpad Československa* (Bratislava, Academic Electronic Press).
Sikora, S. (1997) 'Sociálne a politické zdroje pokusu o reformu socializmu v Československu a jeho ohraničenost'', in Štefanský, M. & Zágoršeková, M. (eds) *Krízy režimov sovietskeho bloku v rokoch 1948–1989* (1997) (Banská Bystrica, Pedagogická spoločnost' J. A. Komenského).
Šimulčík, J. (1999) *Katolícka cirkev a nežná revolúcia 1989* (Prešov, Vydavatel'stvo Michala Vaška).
Šimulčík, J. (2003) *Čas svitania* (Prešov, Vydavatel'stvo Michala Vaška).
Sivoš, J. (ed.) (2008) *XII. správa ZNB. Dokumenty k činnosti Správy kontrarozviedky v Bratislave v rokoch 1974–1989* (Bratislava, Ústav pamäti národa).
Škaloud, J. (2003) 'Rozdiely v priebehu normalizácie v Českej a Slovenskej republike a dopady po jej skončení na samostatné štáty', in Kmet', N. & Marušiak, J. (eds) (2003).
Skilling, H. G. (1976) *Czechoslovakia's Interrupted Revolution* (Princeton, Princeton University Press).
Skilling, H. G. (1981) *Charter 77 and Human Rights in Czechoslovakia* (London, G. Allen & Unwin).
Słownik (2007) *Słownik dysydentów. Czołowe postacie ruchów opozycyjnych w krajach komunistycznych w latach 1956–1989, T. 1; T. 2* (Warsaw, Karta).
Štefanský, M. (1992a) 'Invázia, okupácia a jej dôsledky', in *Slovenská spoločnost' v krízových rokoch, III* (Bratislava, Komisia vlády SR pre analýzu historických udalosti z rokov 1967–1970—Politologický kabinet SAV).
Štefanský, M. (1992b) 'Niektoré aspekty ekonomicko-sociálneho vývoja na Slovensku', in *Slovenská spoločnost' v krízových rokoch 1967–1970. I* (Bratislava, Komisia vlády pre analýzu historických udalostí z rokov 1967–1970—Politologický kabinet SAV).
Štefanský, M. (ed.) (1992c) *Slovensko v rokoch 1967–1970. Výber dokumentov* (Bratislava, Komisia vlády S. R. pre analýzu historických udalostí z rokov 1967–1970).
Szomolányi, S. (1999) *Kl'ukatá cesta Slovenska k demokracii* (Bratislava, Stimul).
Výskum (2004) *Výskum historického vedomia slovenskej verejnosti (november 2003)* (Bratislava, Odbor mediálneho výskumu Slovenského rozhlasu–Ústav politických vied SAV).
Weiss, P. (2005) 'K problematike postkomunistickej identity', in Marušiak, J. & Ferencová, M. (eds) (2005) *Teoretické prístupy k identitám a ich praktické aplikácie: Zborník zo seminára* (Bratislava, Veda).
Williams, K. (1997) *The Prague Spring and its Aftermath: Czechoslovak Politics 1968–1970* (Cambridge, Cambridge University Press).
Wódz, J. (ed.) (2004) 'Jak wyjść z lasu. Inicjatywa prezydenta daje szansę na unowocześnienie polskiej lewicy', *Rzeczpospolita*, 1 September, available at: http://new-arch.rp.pl/artykul/503421_Jak_wyjsc_z_lasu.html, accessed 22 August 2008.
Žáček, P. (ed.) (2002) *ŠtB na Slovensku za 'normalizácie'. Agónia komunistickej moci v zvodkách tajnej polície* (Bratislava, Ministerstvo spravodlivosti SR).
Zala, B. (1993) *Cesty k demokracii* (Bratislava, Print-servis).
Žatkuliak, J. (ed.) (1999a) *Národná rada v kontexte slovenských dejín. 150. výročie vzniku prvej Slovenskej národnej rady* (Bratislava, Národná rada SR–Slovenská historická spoločnost' pri SAV).
Žatkuliak, J. (1999b) 'SNR a Slovensko v rokoch 1969–1989. Zhrnutie', in Žatkuliak, J. (ed.) (1999a).
Žatkuliak, J. (ed.) (1999c) *November 1989 a Slovensko. Chronológia a dokumenty 1985–1990* (Bratislava, Nadácia Milana Šimečku–Historický ústav SAV).
Žatkuliak, J. (2008) 'Spor o novú ústavu československej federácie v druhej polovici 80. rokov XX. storočia', *Historický časopis*, 56, 1, pp. 161–90.

Criticism and Destiny: Kundera and Havel on the Legacy of 1968

CHARLES SABATOS

THE REFORM MOVEMENT THAT BECAME KNOWN AS THE 'Prague Spring', the most radical social experiment in the communist Eastern Bloc during the turbulent events of 1968, brought Czechoslovakia to the centre of world attention. This attempt at 'socialism with a human face' evoked different reactions among the Czechs themselves, as did the Soviet-led invasion that ended it that August. The novelist Milan Kundera and the playwright Václav Havel, both of whom had played important roles in the liberalisation of culture during the 1960s that had paved the way for the events of the Prague Spring, took contrasting positions in the period immediately following the invasion. Their personal and artistic backgrounds also differed considerably: Kundera had first gained recognition as a lyric poet with orthodox communist themes, only later gaining prominence for his innovative fiction, while Havel, who was of a slightly younger generation and from a wealthy Prague family, had never joined the Communist Party. Both of them took what they defined as 'critical' positions toward the reform movement, but Kundera's concept of 'critical thinking' idealised what he called the Czech national 'destiny', while Havel called for the 'courage' to look at the difficult issues of the present. At the time, this polemic was seen as representing two camps: reform communists, such as Kundera, and those non-communists more sceptical of the possibility of true reform, including Havel. Over the following two decades, their disagreement over the legacy of the Prague Spring took on greater significance outside Czechoslovakia, as Kundera and Havel became the two best-known Czech writers in the West. Kundera, living in exile in France, became a major figure in contemporary world fiction, while Havel, who remained in Prague and was imprisoned several times for his role in the dissident movement, became a leading voice for human rights.

In 1984, the publication of Kundera's essay 'The Tragedy of Central Europe' became a turning point in Western perceptions of the communist bloc at the height of the Cold War. Kundera's concept of Central European culture (which he saw as inherently Western and alien to Soviet-style communism) emerged from his earlier claims of a unique 'Czech destiny' and expanded to include the other 'small nations' of

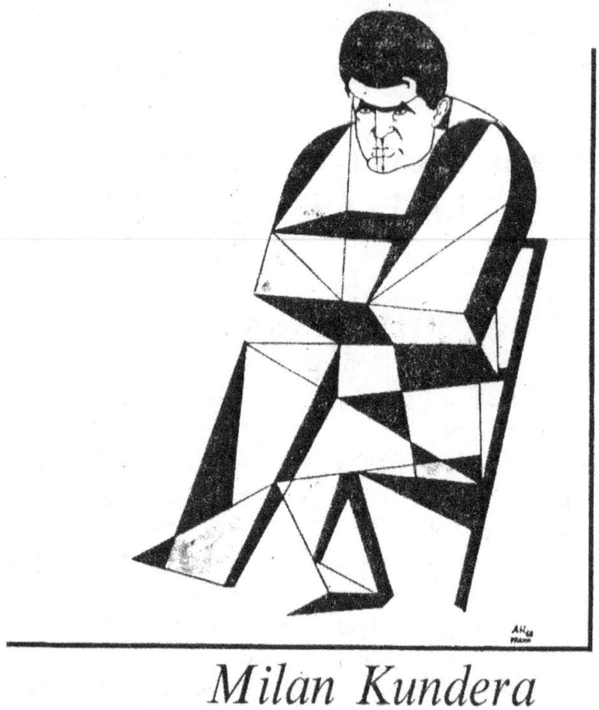

FIGURE 1. MILAN KUNDERA BY ADOLF HOFFMEISTER. COPYRIGHT PERMISSION MARTIN AND ADAM HOFFMEISTER

the region. At the same time, Kundera's novel *The Unbearable Lightness of Being* (partly set during the events of 1968) became an international bestseller, reviving interest in the Prague Spring. However, Havel took a more sceptical view towards the uniqueness of 'Central Europe' as a cultural identity, as he had towards Kundera's concept of 'destiny' in 1968. Following the so-called Velvet Revolution and the fall of the communist regime in 1989, the paths of Kundera and Havel diverged even more sharply, as Havel became the first post-communist Czechoslovak President and Kundera remained in exile. Yet they remain the two most authoritative and influential figures of Czech culture in the West, and their differing perspectives continue to define the international image of the Czech Republic 40 years after the Prague Spring.

National existence and critical thinking

The decade following the communist seizure of power in February 1948 was a politically and culturally bleak one for Czechoslovakia. Following a very tentative thaw in the late 1950s, the 1960s were a period of gradually increasing openness in film, drama and literature. By 1967, this movement toward greater freedom in Czech culture took on greater momentum.

FIGURE 2. VÁCLAV HAVEL BY ADOLF HOFFMEISTER. COPYRIGHT PERMISSION MARTIN AND ADAM HOFFMEISTER

The Fourth Congress of the Czechoslovak Writers' Union in June 1967, particularly the speeches by Milan Kundera and his fellow novelist Ludvík Vaculík, was a major turning point. Josef Korbel has described the speeches of this congress as

> fascinating ... The [Czech] language, which had been mutilated by russisms during the Stalinist years, shines in all its richness and beauty; the themes, formulated up to then only in journals in scholarly terms, are expressed in a scintillating variety of literary styles. (Korbel 1977, p. 277)

In contrast to the usual socialist platitudes expressed at such official events, Kundera's address to the Congress turned the question of 'national existence' into something almost metaphysical. In this speech, he suggested that the effort needed to maintain an independent existence gave the Czechs a broader perspective than that of other nations that have played a larger role in European history. Unlike larger nations which consider their existence as 'beyond all question', the 'somewhat cheerless and intermittent history of the Czech nation, which has passed through the very antechamber of death, gives us the strength to resist any such illusion' (Kundera 1971, p. 169). Kundera traced Czech doubts over their independent existence back to the writer Hubert Gordon Schauer, who challenged the National Revival by asking whether Czech culture was worthy of existence in an independent nation. Such doubts,

Kundera claimed, set the Czechs apart from their larger European neighbours: 'For those European nations who partook in the mainstream of history the European context comes quite naturally ... For the Czechs nothing was ever a self-evident possession: not even their language nor their European status' (Kundera 1971, p. 171). This, he argues, is where the 'greatness' of Czech culture lies:

> The whole course of our nation's history, torn between democracy, fascist enslavement, Stalinism and socialism, and further complicated by its unique nationality problem, features every important issue that has made our twentieth century what it is ... Our nation then has experienced, I daresay, more than many others have in this century and, if its genius has been alert, it will now know more than the others. (Kundera 1971, p. 176)

Kundera's speech was followed by one from his fellow Moravian, Ludvík Vaculík, who was even more radical in calling for reforms. The controversy over the Congress was one of the first signs of the increasing openness in Czech culture that led to the fully-fledged reform movement in the spring of 1968.

After the Slovak Alexander Dubček was appointed first secretary of the Czechoslovak Communist Party (*Komunistická strana Československa*, KSČ), censorship was essentially removed and open criticism of the regime was possible in the mass media for the first time in 20 years. The journal of the Union of Czechoslovak Writers, *Literární noviny*, which had been nearly shut down following the June 1967 Congress, was renamed *Literární listy* and 'became an arts periodical with a circulation of 300,000, the largest in Europe' (Holý 2008, p. 119). In the 4 April 1968 issue of *Literární listy*, Václav Havel published the essay 'On the Theme of an Opposition', which called for a genuine opposition party to the all-powerful Communist Party. Havel who, unlike many of the leading proponents of reform, had never belonged to the Communist Party, evoked 'the strong and specific Czechoslovak democratic and humanistic tradition', and suggested that the new opposition party 'could be a democratic party drawing on this tradition of democracy and humanism'. Even in this bold proposal, however, he urged caution:

> Of course, this does not mean that the party would arrogate to itself the right to be the only legitimate representative of democracy, just as the Communist Party cannot arrogate to itself the claim to be the only genuine force of socialism. (Reprinted in Havel 1992, pp. 30–31)

In calling for a genuine choice in politics, Havel not only challenged the 20-year communist dominance of Czechoslovak politics, but insisted that the communists take responsibility for their past mistakes (and crimes): 'the fact that many non-communists saw communist error for what it was at a time when communists did not have the slightest idea they were wrong, needs to be acknowledged in retrospect, however unpleasant this may be' (Havel 1992, p. 33).

By pushing the meaning of the Prague Spring beyond an internal affair between reformist and more orthodox communists to include the large, mostly silent non-communist segment of society, Havel was advocating the same 'power of the powerless' that would later become the main theme of his well-known essay of that title. In contrast with Kundera's abstract concepts of history and national existence,

Havel called for simple (but radical) political action, simply by criticising the existing state of affairs. 'Self-criticism', in which Party members who were seen to have deviated from orthodox ideology were forced to apologise for their 'mistakes', was a common method of social control under the communists. Havel took this concept further, suggesting that the Communist Party needed to undertake the process of self-criticism as a whole. [In fact, Kundera's first novel *The Joke* (*Žert*) which had been published in 1967, was one of the earliest attempts to subject the Party to self-criticism from within, by ruthlessly exposing the ideological excesses of the brutally humourless Stalinist years.]

In August 1968, the sweeping social changes in Czechoslovakia were halted by the invasion of Soviet and other Warsaw Pact troops. Dubček and other Czechoslovak leaders were forcibly taken to Moscow, and upon their return, all hopes of continuing reform were shattered. However, a feeling of popular resistance persisted among the Czechs and Slovaks well into the following year and reached its pinnacle in the self-immolation of Jan Palach in January 1969. In the uncertain period following the invasion, before full press censorship had been reimposed, *Literární listy* reappeared for a brief time under the shortened title *Listy*, and in December 1968, Milan Kundera published an essay in *Listy* under the title '*Český úděl*' ('The Czech Destiny').[1] Returning to his ideas from the congress of the previous year, he argued that in contrast to 'great nations' whose sheer size guarantees their existence, small nations must constantly 'create values' that give them the right to exist. Again he rhetorically cited Schauer's scepticism: 'Was it really worth it to set our small nation back up in the middle of Europe? What values does it bring or intend to bring to humanity?' He suggested that with the Prague Spring, the Czechs and Slovaks 'had directed their challenge at the world'. However, 'this challenge was not based on the Czechoslovaks wanting to replace the present socialist model with another one, just as authoritarian and suitable for export'. (Kundera makes a notable shift here from 'Czechs and Slovaks' to the more unified 'Czechoslovaks' within the space of two sentences.)

> The meaning of the Czechoslovak challenge was something else: to show what limitless democratic possibilities had been lying fallow till then in the socialist social project, and to show that these possibilities can only develop when an individual nation's political identity is fully set free. (Kundera 1968, p. 3)

Counting on unified public support for the goals of the Prague Spring, he also attested to his 'enormous hope for the future' (Kundera 1968, p. 3). In his conclusion, Kundera praised Czech patriotism for being based not on 'fanaticism' but on 'critical thinking'.[2] He warned, however, against the 'critical stance of the weak' that becomes pessimistic

[1]The translations of Kundera's 'Czech Destiny' essay and Havel's response are those of the present author (the title has been translated elsewhere as 'The Czech Fate' and 'The Czech Lot'). The full debate was recently published in English for the first time; see Baer (2006, pp. 140–63). The original Czech texts were reprinted in *Literární noviny*, 52, 2007, pp. 18–20, and are available on the journal's web archive at www.literarky.cz, accessed July 2008.

[2]In Czech, he used the rather theoretical term *kriticismus* rather than the more common 'criticism' or *kritika*.

and 'creates the ideal climate for defeat' (Kundera 1968, p. 5). For him, there was a second, positive form of:

> critical thinking ... which is capable of unmasking illusions and presumed certainties, but is itself full of self-confidence ... This critical thinking, which caused the whole Czechoslovak Spring and held out against the attacks of lies and irrationality in the autumn, does not belong just to some elite, but as we have seen, it is the greatest virtue of the entire nation. (Kundera 1968, p. 5)

Kundera's assertion that Czech culture's unique 'genius' allowed it to 'resist illusion', from the 1967 Fourth Congress speech, was echoed in his claims for a uniquely Czech form of critical thinking that could preserve the spirit of reform even in the face of a military occupation.

The same term 'critical thinking' played an important part in Václav Havel's response to Kundera's essay, published in the journal *Tvář* in January 1969. Havel's scepticism was apparent from his title, which simply added a question mark to Kundera's 'The Czech Destiny?' As Kieran Williams has explained, Havel 'mourned [Kundera's] article as an example of typical Czech myopia (celebrating past glories rather than addressing present needs) and passive patriotism (rationalising a disaster as a moral victory)' (Williams 1997, p. 183). Just as Kundera used the term of 'Czech patriot' to indirectly praise his own critical stance, Havel (1968/1969, p. 5) used it to indirectly criticise Kundera: 'Whenever the Czech patriot does not have enough courage (without which, of course, real criticism is unthinkable) to look the cruel but *open* present in the face, he turns to the better but *closed* past when everyone was united'. This position, Havel charges, was 'dangerous' because it drew one's attention away from 'the tense questions of today ... Let it flaunt the words "traditional Czech critical thinking" (*tradičním českým kriticismem*) a hundred times, this attitude is not critical in the least: it flees from *criticism* (*kritika*) into *illusion*' (Havel 1968/1969, p. 5). Havel made a subtle but key semantic shift here from Kundera's term 'critical thinking' (with an intellectual, even literary connotation) to the more general *kritika* or 'criticism', a highly politicised term in the socialist context. The gap between these two terms illustrates the difference between these two key figures of 1968: for Kundera, literature and culture lay at the heart of Czech survival, while for Havel, true criticism called for concrete acts of resistance.

The end of Central Europe: a new beginning

Kundera's early optimism about the lasting effects of the Prague Spring soon proved to be unrealistic. The 'Czech Destiny' polemic was among the last writing that either Kundera or Havel were permitted to publish in Czechoslovakia until the fall of communism 20 years later.[3] By late 1969, Dubček had been forced entirely from power, and thousands of writers, intellectuals and academics who had publicly supported the reforms were gradually removed from their jobs and pushed into

[3]See Matějka (1990) for an overview of this polemic and its repercussions in the Czech intellectual community.

manual labour; a widespread cultural purge that was officially known as Normalisation. During this period, Havel followed his earlier commitment to political engagement, which brought him continuous difficulties with the regime. In his open letter of April 1975 to President Gustav Husák, Havel returned to the importance of culture for a nation's existence:

> It is culture that enables a society to enlarge its liberty and to discover truth—so what appeal can it have for the authorities who are basically concerned with suppressing such values? There is only one kind of truth they recognize: the kind they need at the given moment. (Havel 1986, p. 16)

Jan Vladislav has described this letter as 'an undoubted milestone in the history of the Czech spiritual resistance of the seventies' (Havel 1986, p. xv). Havel further developed the question of truth in his famous call for 'living in truth' in his 1978 essay, 'The Power of the Powerless'. A decade after the Prague Spring, he reflected on its legacy for the current struggle between the regime and the small but growing opposition:

> The Prague Spring is usually understood as a clash between two groups on the level of real power: those who wanted to maintain the system as it was and those who wanted to reform it. It is frequently forgotten, however, that this encounter was merely the final act and the inevitable consequence of a long drama originally played out chiefly in the theatre of the spirit and the conscience of society. And that somewhere in the beginning of this drama, there were individuals who were willing to live within the truth, even when things were at their worst ... One thing, however, seems clear: the attempt at political reform was not the cause of society's reawakening, but rather the final outcome of that reawakening. (Havel 1986, p. 60)

This essay was widely reprinted in English and became Havel's most influential piece among Western readers. He became even better known, however, due to his role as a leading spokesperson for Charter 77, an attempt by a small group of 'dissidents' (although Havel himself distanced himself from that term) to 'live in truth' under a regime that had attempted to crush all forms of independent thought.

Kundera emigrated to France in 1975, and four years later his first novel to be written in exile, *The Book of Laughter and Forgetting* (*Kniha smíchu a zapomnění*), was published in French translation.[4] This novel begins with one of the most famous images in his work:

> In February 1948, Communist leader Klement Gottwald stepped onto the balcony of a Baroque palace in Prague to address the hundreds of thousands of his fellow citizens packed into Old Town Square. It was a crucial moment in Czech history—a fateful moment of the kind that occurs once or twice in a millennium. (Kundera 1980, p. 3)

[4]The Czech original appeared two years later, published by the exile press 68 Publishers in Toronto.

This description of the communist takeover of Czechoslovakia focuses on the Slovak communist Vlado Clementis, who was later executed in the infamous show trials of 1953. According to the narrator, Clementis was standing next to Gottwald and gave him his fur cap, but after his execution, he was airbrushed out of all the photographs of this famous event, leaving only his cap behind. Thus he becomes a symbol for one of Kundera's central themes: 'the struggle of man against power is the struggle of memory against forgetting'. The passage is notable for its reference to the 'fateful moment' that turned Czech history from its millennium of Western orientation toward the East, which alludes both to the 'Czech destiny', and the sense of tragedy that he would develop in his subsequent essays. However, this description, which seems to a Western reader to bear the authority of historical truth, is an example of the unreliability of Kundera's narrative voice. Petr Bílek, for example, points out that the 'Baroque palace' in Old Town Prague is actually Rococo (Bílek 2000, p. 42); Kundera was surely aware of this, but presumably changed it because the latter architectural style has less literary resonance. Such changes, whether minor or major, show the liberties that Kundera was willing to take with historical facts in his novels. Cut off by censorship from the Czech reading public, he was now writing almost entirely for Western readers, leading him to simplify some details of the Czech cultural and historical context for a version of 'truth' that he saw as more aesthetically and philosophically effective outside of that context.

At roughly the same time, Kundera also began to write a series of cultural and political essays in French that increased his prominence as a leading figure of Central European culture—a term he himself reclaimed from disuse after four decades. Philip Roth (1980) published an interview with him in *The New York Times Book Review* in November 1980, which was reprinted as an afterword in early English-language editions of *The Book of Laughter and Forgetting*.[5] In response to Roth's suggestion that the 'fates of Eastern Europe and Western Europe' were 'radically different matters', Kundera (1980, p. 10) explicitly compared the Czech destiny to the similar fates of other 'small nations' of the region: 'Bohemia, Poland, Hungary, just like Austria, have never been part of Eastern Europe ... It was here, in Central Europe, that modern culture found its greatest impulse'. He continued with his insistence on 'Russian civilization' as entirely opposed to 'Western culture', and with the insinuation (highly provocative at that time of high tension between the two superpowers) that what happened to much of Central Europe could happen to Western Europe as well:

> The post-war annexation of Central Europe (or at least its major part) by Russian civilization caused Western culture to lose its vital centre of gravity. It is the most significant event in the history of the West in our country, and we cannot dismiss the possibility that the end of Central Europe marked the beginning of the end for Europe as a whole. (Kundera 1980, p. 10)

Compared to his writings in 1967–1968, he made two important shifts in his argument, turning his focus from 'Czech destiny' to the broader fate of Europe, and suggesting

[5]Roth had visited Prague several times in the 1970s and was one of Kundera's earliest and strongest supporters in American literary circles.

that the post-1968 'tragedy' in Prague foreshadowed the future fall of Western culture itself.

'The Tragedy of Central Europe', published in 1984, challenged the Western reader's assumptions about the immutable division of Europe into East and West. 'There are no longer any illusions about the regimes of Russia's satellite countries', he argued. 'But what we forget is their essential tragedy: these countries have vanished from the map of the West' (Kundera 1984a, p. 103). Although the boundaries of his Central Europe are roughly those of the former Austro–Hungarian Empire, he insisted, 'Central Europe is not a state: it's a culture or a fate. Its borders are imaginary and must be drawn and redrawn with each new historical situation' (Kundera 1984a, p. 106). He described this fate as the 'great *common situations* that reassemble peoples, regroup them in ever new ways along the imaginary and ever-changing boundaries that mark a realm inhabited by the same memories, the same problems and conflicts, the same common tradition' (Kundera 1984a, p. 107, emphasis in original). Kundera accused the Soviet Union of suppressing the national aspirations of its subject states, but Western Europe was also to blame for forgetting its common history; and he warned that this might be a fatal mistake: 'in our modern world where power has a tendency to become more and more concentrated in the hands of a few big countries, *all* European nations run the risk of becoming small nations and of sharing their fate' (Kundera 1984a, p. 109, emphasis in original). One of the essay's notable claims referred to the Jews not only as 'the principal cosmopolitan, integrating element in Central Europe' but also as the 'small nation par excellence', moving Kundera's 'realm' further away from existing political borders and toward a cultural identity (Kundera 1984a, pp. 107–08).

While this passionate attack on the Russian domination of the Eastern bloc moved away from Kundera's earlier emphasis on Czech culture, it borrowed elements from his previous essays. Drawing on the issue of 'national existence' from his 1967 speech, Kundera defined a small nation as 'one whose very existence may be put in question at any moment; a small nation can disappear and it knows it' (Kundera 1984a, p. 108). In his attack on the Russian domination of the 'small nations' of Central Europe, Kundera suggested that this 'family of small nations has its own vision of the world, a vision based on a deep distrust of History ... The people of Central Europe ... represent the wrong side of this History: its victims and outsiders' (Kundera 1984a, p. 108). From 'The Czech Destiny', Kundera recycled the idea of 'fate', simply applying it to the region as a whole. His prediction of 'the beginning of the end for Europe' in the Roth interview was echoed in his statement in the later essay: 'Thus it was in this region of small nations who have "not yet perished" that Europe's vulnerability, all of Europe's vulnerability, was more clearly visible before anywhere else' (Kundera 1984a, p. 109). Kundera's message that much of the communist bloc was inherently and immutably West European in its traditions was welcomed by its Western readers at the height of Cold War tensions between the Soviet Union and the United States, and his essay became widely cited in political contexts far removed from the circles of literary scholarship.

Efforts to develop a critique of the East–West division of Europe (and to break down Western indifference to the fate of Eastern Europe) date back to the earliest years of the Cold War, most notably in Czesław Miłosz's book *The Captive Mind* (1955). However, the use of the term 'Central Europe' to imply that part of Europe's

Western culture had been lost to communist rule only became widely accepted after Kundera's 'Tragedy of Central Europe', which became a starting point for an international discussion that focused on the connections between the Central European cultures. This debate, which included the Hungarian writer György (Georg) Konrád and the Yugoslav novelist Danilo Kiš, promoted the concept of a transnational and multicultural 'Central European' identity. Seen from the perspective of the 1980s, the relatively benign autocracy of the Austro–Hungarian Empire seemed to be a lost golden age. According to Vladimír Macura, Kundera used the theme of Central Europe as a 'theoretical expansion of the [themes] he had discussed earlier, without realising that he had not left the language of the National Revival myth' (Macura 1999, p. 74). At the same time, as Macura points out, Czech writers such as Kundera did not draw on the concepts of Central Europe from the early twentieth century by such Austrian and German writers as Friedrich Naumann. Rather, it was as if the theme had been 'born anew' as a 'personal reaction to the trauma of the defeat of the Prague Spring in 1968' (Macura 1999, p. 71). Thus the chief aim of the debate over 'Central Europe' was not pure nostalgia, but an attempt to surmount the existing clash between political ideologies by forming a new sense of interconnected cultural identity. It drew on the humanistic traditions of German and Jewish culture lost during the Nazi and communist periods, and created a new image for the region even before the revolutions of 1989.[6]

Václav Havel's 1985 essay 'An Anatomy of Reticence' implicitly disagrees with Kundera's privileging of Central Europe as a prophetic region, much as he rejected the idea of a uniquely critical Czech spirit in 1968:

> I believe that a distinctly central European skepticism is inescapably a part of the spiritual, cultural, and intellectual phenomenon that is central Europe as it has been formed and is being formed by certain specific historical experiences ... [It is] occasionally somewhat incomprehensible in its ... ability to turn a provincial phenomenon into a global anticipation of things to come. At times it gives the impression that people here are endowed with some inner radar capable of recognizing an approaching danger long before it becomes visible and recognizable as a danger. (Havel 1986, p. 175)

Havel himself seemed sceptical of this 'impression', but Kundera remained a key point of reference for his essay. Later in the essay, Havel suggested,

> one of the traditions of the central European climate of which I have been speaking is ... an intense fear of exaggerating our own dignity unintentionally to a comic degree, a fear of pathos and sentimentality, of overstatement and what Kundera calls the lyric relation to the world. (Havel 1986, p. 180)

[6]One useful overview of the 'Central European' question as it stood on the verge of the 1989 changes can be found in the edited collection by George Schöpflin and Nancy Wood, *In Search of Central Europe* (1989). The editors note that Kundera refused to allow 'The Tragedy of Central Europe' to be reprinted in this volume, although the majority of the articles are direct reactions to his argument.

He contrasted the self-deprecating irony of the Czech dissidents with the 'earnest, perhaps even somewhat pathetic' outlook of Western peace activists, who do not face serious punishment for their political engagement: 'Since we pay a somewhat higher price for our interest in the destiny of the world, we may also have a stronger need to make light of ourselves, to desecrate the altar, as so aptly described by [Mikhail] Bakhtin' (Havel 1986, p. 183). Havel's ironic sympathy toward these Western activists gives way to sharp criticism: how can they ignore 'the fact that one important European country attacked a small neutral neighbour five years ago, and since that time has been conducting on its territory a war of extermination which has already claimed a million dead and three million refugees?' This indifference toward the 1980 Soviet occupation of Afghanistan fills him with 'total disgust and a sense of limitless hopelessness', heightened by the fact that in 1968 he had shared the Afghans' 'specific historical experience' of Soviet tanks rolling into his homeland (Havel 1986, p. 184). Like Kundera, Havel draws on national and regional history, but he emphasises the common experiences of small, vulnerable nations around the world rather than laying claim to a unique destiny (whether Czech or Central European).

The lightness of history in Kundera's fiction

The same questions of history and nation that underlie Kundera's definition of Czech identity emerged in his best-known novel, *The Unbearable Lightness of Being* (*Nesnesitelná lehkost bytí*) (2006a). Its plot follows the interwoven destiny of two couples over a period of nearly 20 years, from the early 1960s to the early 1980s. Tomáš is a surgeon whose years of womanising come to a temporary end when he meets and marries Tereza. After a brief attempt at exile in Switzerland following the Prague Spring, they return to Czechoslovakia, where Tomáš is forced to leave his job and becomes a window-washer. Nonetheless, this gives him the opportunity to resume his sexual conquests, which provokes Tereza's helpless jealousy.

Kundera described the Czech 'euphoria' after the Soviet invasion as a 'drunken carnival of hate', which ended with the return of Alexander Dubček from Moscow, and his speech over the radio, gasping for breath, that made the situation clear to the Czechs: 'the country would have to bow to the conqueror. For ever and ever, it will stutter, stammer, gasp for air like Alexander Dubček' (Kundera 1984c, p. 26). In his essay collection *The Art of the Novel*, Kundera interpreted this passage for his readers: 'Not only must historical circumstance create a new existential situation for a character in a novel, but History *itself* must be understood and analyzed as an existential situation'. He then connected the 'public domain' of the Czech destiny with the private one of Tereza's sexual insecurity: 'in the face of Tomaš's infidelities, she is like Dubček faced with Brezhnev: defenseless and weak' (Kundera 1988, p. 38, emphasis in original). As Helena Kosková has suggested, 'the tragic fate of Tomáš and Tereza has its parallel in the fate of the whole nation, which is itself only a reminder of the mortal danger facing all of European culture' (Kosková 1996, p. 107). While he does not directly refer to the Central European question in this interpretation, Kundera's definition in 'The Tragedy of Central Europe' of the Central Europeans as the 'victims and outsiders' of history seems to have an echo here in Tomáš's 'victimisation' of the faithful but defenceless Tereza.

The narrative voice of Kundera's novels often reflected some of the observations that he made in his politically oriented writings from the same time period. However, a distinction must be made between the point of view in Kundera's essays, which could be taken as a relatively close approximation of the author's views, and the narrative voice in the novels, which often seems deceptively 'essayistic', but should be approached with more caution. Kundera's novels do reflect some of the same concerns as his essays, but as Jan Čulík has explained, 'the narrator's emphatic pronouncements are to be taken as only one of many polyphonic voices and as an invitation to critical thinking' (Čulík 1999, p. 220).

In Part Five of *The Unbearable Lightness of Being,* Kundera introduced his most extensive 'essayistic' observations in the novel:

> Anyone who thinks that the Communist regimes of Central Europe are exclusively the work of criminals is overlooking a basic truth: the criminal regimes were made not by criminals but by enthusiasts convinced they had discovered the only road to paradise. (Kundera 1984c, p. 176)

The question of whether the communists were responsible for their party's murderous activity reminds Tomáš of the tale of Oedipus, who put out his own eyes when he realised his acts, even though he had committed them unintentionally. When he hears communists 'shouting in defence of their inner purity' Tomáš thinks, 'as a result of your "not knowing", this country has lost its freedom, lost it for centuries, perhaps, and you shout that you feel no guilt?' (Kundera 1984c, p. 177).

He read the same question of guilt discussed in 'a weekly newspaper published in three hundred thousand copies by the Union of Czech Writers. It was a paper that had achieved considerable autonomy within the regime and dealt with issues forbidden to others' (Kundera 1984c, p. 178). Dissatisfied with the paper's coverage of the issue, Tomáš writes his own essay on the subject, which is printed in this widely circulated newspaper; his refusal to repudiate it after the invasion costs him his job. This weekly is obviously *Literární noviny,* which Kundera described in similar terms, but by name, in 'The Tragedy of Central Europe'. In the essay, Kundera has the following footnote:

> The weekly publication, *Literární noviny* (*Literary Journal*), which published 300,000 copies (in a land of ten million people) was produced by the Czech Writers' Union. It was this publication that over the years led the way to the Prague Spring and was afterwards a platform for it . . . The articles devoted to history, sociology and politics were not written by journalists but by writers, historians and philosophers . . . I don't know of a single European weekly in our century that has played as important a historical role nor played it so well. (Kundera 1984b, p. 117)

With its strikingly similar phrasing, this is perhaps the most direct textual link between Kundera's two most influential works; the 'important historical role' that *Literární noviny* played in the Prague Spring was also tied to one of the central moral struggles of the novel.

Later in *The Unbearable Lightness of Being*, the narrator connects Tomáš's personal dilemma of whether to sign a petition supporting political prisoners to the larger question of Czech history, comparing the courage of the Czechs in 1618 (which led to their destruction after the Thirty Years War) and their caution in 1938, when

> their capitulation led to the Second World War, which in turn led to the forfeit of their nation's freedom for many decades or even centuries ... If Czech history could be repeated, we should of course find it desirable to test the other possibility each time and compare the results. (Kundera 1984c, p. 223)

This, of course, is impossible:

> The history of the Czechs will not be repeated, nor will the history of Europe ... History is as light as individual human life, unbearably light, light as a feather, as dust swirling into the air, as whatever will no longer exist tomorrow. (Kundera 1984c, p. 223)

Within the space of a few pages, Kundera moves from the active role carried out by *Literární noviny*, a key case of the importance of culture in 'The Tragedy of Central Europe', to a more fatalistic viewpoint echoing his reflections on national 'destiny' from 1968.

The Unbearable Lightness of Being has probably defined the 'Prague Spring' for international readers more than any other novel (and even inspired a film that dramatised the invasion). However, some Czech critics felt that it distorted aspects of their experience. For example, Milan Jungmann (the former Editor-in-Chief of *Literární noviny*) judged Kundera's work in terms of historical accuracy, rather than acknowledging his inaccurate representations as reflecting the limitations of any fictional narrator. Jungmann pointed out how Kundera had erased his own communist past by dismissing his writings from the period before the Prague Spring as 'kitsch' that should be forgotten:

> Kundera rejects everything that made him a collaborator in the creation of socialist culture ... He wants to push into oblivion everything he wrote in its context, everything that indicates his attempt through criticism to find the buried paths leading out of the mess made of Marx's original ideas.

Jungmann (who himself worked as a window-cleaner in the 1970s) took issue with such details as Tomáš being forced to leave his skilled job for menial labour: 'During normalization people from many professions became window-cleaners—journalists, lawyers, priests, historians, diplomats, technicians, etc., but not a single doctor ... In reality [the police] would have forced him to return [to the hospital]. Here the facts of life are turned upside down' (Jungmann 1988, p. 243).[7] As Hana Pichová has pointed out, 'Jungmann openly reproaches Western criticism for lack of rigor, scepticism, and questioning in regards to Kundera. All of these qualities, one is led to assume by Jungmann, are inherently and evidently present in the readership behind the iron curtain' (Pichová 2002, p. 106). Twenty years later, when *The Unbearable Lightness of Being* was finally published in the Czech Republic for the first time, Jungmann

[7]For a translation into English, see Goetz-Stankiewicz (1992).

defended his earlier essay from the 'negative response' it had received and accused his critics of not admitting 'any attempt at critical thinking' (Jungmann 2006, p. 11). While Jungmann represents one extreme in the Czech reception of Kundera's work, his scepticism toward Kundera's reinterpretation of the Prague Spring was shared by other Czech writers, including Václav Havel.

In an interview with Karel Hvížd'ala in 1986, Havel returned to the debate over the Czech destiny, placing some of the fictional events of *The Unbearable Lightness of Being* in perspective. In response to Hvížd'ala's comparison of Kundera's international success with the 'harsh criticism' his work faced in Prague, Havel asked: 'isn't this continuing fear of being out of step with the rest of the world a clear sign of provincialism?' (Havel 1990, p. 171). Regarding the issues that had emerged in his polemic with Kundera in 1969, he stated: 'I am quite familiar with Kundera's *a priori* scepticism regarding civic actions that have no immediate hope of being effective ... and I do not share that scepticism'. Discussing the actual writers' petition circulated soon after the beginning of Normalisation, Havel described it as deeply significant, not only from his own experience as a political prisoner drawing support from the solidarity of others, but because 'after fifteen years of antlike work that often seemed Don Quixote-ish', the Czechoslovak government could no longer expect 'that no one will dare criticize it' (Havel 1990, p. 175). Then he turned to Kundera's concept of Central Europe, towards which he was as sceptical as he was toward the idea of 'Czech destiny':

> I can't avoid feeling that his notion of a Europe pillaged by Asia, his image of the spiritual graveyard, his idea that amnesia rules history and that history is an inexhaustible source of cruel jokes, all this lends support to the notion that nothing has changed in Czechoslovakia since the beginning of the 1970s, that all those petitions are as hopeless and absurd as they ever were, that they are even more clearly the desperate acts of lost souls who are trying to draw attention to themselves in a way that is tragically empty of meaning. (Havel 1990, p. 176)

Havel suggested that Kundera 'may be something of a prisoner of his own scepticism' because his 'terror of appearing ridiculous ... prevents him from perceiving the mysterious ambiguity of human behaviour in totalitarian conditions' (Havel 1990, p. 177). This comment reflected (although in more generous terms) Jungmann's accusations of Kundera's simplistic portrayal of events. Finally, alluding specifically to the 'Czech destiny' debate, Hvížd'ala asked Havel about the issue of national identity, as reflected in Gordon Hubert Schauer's question on the need for a Czech nation. Once again, Havel suggested that 'if our national fate depends on anything, then it depends chiefly on how we acquit ourselves in our human tasks' (Havel 1990, p. 180). He explains that he was 'bothered' by Kundera's attempt to explain the Soviet invasion as a fulfilment of 'the ancient Czech destiny ... What was really a consequence of these events—Czech destiny or fate—was presented as their cause'. Tracing the 'historical alibi' in Kundera's writings (from the 'Czech Destiny' to *The Unbearable Lightness of Being*), Havel found his 'dehumanization of history' as 'an excessive extrapolation of his own disillusionment'. History is not 'elsewhere', he concluded in an apparent allusion to Kundera's novel *Life is Elsewhere*; 'we all contribute to making it . . . Life does not take place outside history, and history is not outside of life' (Havel 1990, p. 180). In this return to his polemic of nearly 20 years earlier, Havel related Kundera's influential essay 'Tragedy of Central Europe' to his bestselling novel *The Unbearable Lightness of Being* more directly than have most Western critics. The weakness of the small nations before history, like Dubček before Brezhnev, was not merely the absurd tragedy that Kundera claimed it to be; Havel pointed out once again that resistance to political forces is largely a matter of perspective.

Although Kundera had attempted to move away from the constraints of national identity over the course of the 1980s, by first broadening his concept of 'Czech destiny' to other nations and then turning away from it altogether, his popular appeal, critical success, and moral authority in the West remained closely tied to his Czech background. In a 1989 essay, 'The Rediscovery of Central Europe', Tony Judt alluded to Kundera's 'peculiarly Czech vision', which he described as 'gloomy, sceptical, suspicious, self-critical, and insecure', and continued with the more general observations:

> [It] is the Czechs, more than most, who have opened up for debate the original wisdom of destroying the multinational [Habsburg] state, and their sense certainly is that it is Czechoslovakia, as the most western of the lost lands of Europe, that has suffered the most from events since 1918. Between this and the often-noted analogy with the Jewish experience (the Czechs frequently detecting an affinity in the situation and a precariousness about the two peoples), it is not surprising that the Czech understanding of what is at stake in Central Europe, and what has been lost, has been most influential in forming Western opinion. (Judt 1991, pp. 32, 47)

By the end of that year, much of Eastern Europe had been freed from communist rule, but it was the dramatic yet relatively peaceful 'Velvet Revolution' in Czechoslovakia that became (perhaps only second to the opening of the Berlin Wall) a symbol of hope for a better future in the region. While Kundera did not participate in the revolution itself, his writings from the 1980s had laid the foundation for its appropriation by the West as a 'rediscovery' of a forgotten land. However, the events of 1989, which brought Havel to power as the first post-communist (and ultimately last) President of Czechoslovakia, seemed to validate his views over Kundera's on the true legacy of 1968: as a call to civic resistance.

Conclusion

Since the end of communism the differing perspectives of these two key figures have continued to shape the way the Czech nation is perceived in the West. However both Kundera and Havel had a mixed connection with the Czech nation following the end of communism. After Havel's first year or two in power, the reality of politics soured his relationship with the Czechoslovak public, particularly the Slovaks. He was unable to prevent the split of Czechoslovakia into two separate republics, and in 1993, he became the first President of the new Czech Republic. In November of that year, Kundera and Havel were both planning to attend the Prague premiere of the former's play *Jacques and His Master,* which according to Louis Charbonneau (1993, p. 3B) in a contemporary report, 'would have represented the reconciliation of Czech literature's prodigal son with the father of Czech dissidence under Communism'. In the end, however, Kundera chose not to come. As Charbonneau speculated (reflecting Czech opinions at the time), 'perhaps Kundera's refusal to appear at this event demonstrated not only his notorious contempt for journalists and the media in general, but also that he is still unable to swallow the fact that history proved Havel right and him wrong' (Charbonneau 1993, p. 3B).

Havel remained in power for another decade before finally retiring from politics in 2003. In a speech at Columbia University in 2002, on his last official visit to the United States as Czech President, he observed: 'I am just beginning to understand how everything has, in fact, been a diabolical trap set for me by destiny'. He gently mocked his own reputation in the West as a 'fairy tale hero' insisting, 'there is no more relying on the accidents of history that lift poets into places where empires and military alliances are brought down'. While there was no direct reference to the legacy of the Prague Spring in this speech, Havel referred to his 'opportunity to take part in truly world-changing historical events' which 'has been worth all the traps that lay hidden within it'. He concluded with three 'old certainties', one of which is, 'evil must be confronted in its womb and, if there is no other way to do it, then it has to be dealt with by the use of force' (Havel 2002, p. 4). When he retired from office, he was still revered worldwide as a spokesman for human rights, but some Czechs criticised one of his final decisions as president: adding his official support (now as leader of a NATO member state) to the US-led invasion of Iraq.[8] In his recent return to his earlier career as a playwright, however, he has met with critical success; his new play *Odcházení* (*Leaving*), that premiered in May 2008 (exactly four decades after the peak of the Prague Spring), was praised by Czech and Slovak critics.[9]

Kundera, by contrast, did not return to Czechoslovakia except for brief visits, and moved away from his native language by beginning to write his novels entirely in French. He did not translate these new books into Czech, yet refused to allow them to be translated by anyone else, thus cutting Czech readers off from most of his work since 1989. While some of these novels are set in France and may be seen as aimed largely at Western readers, even his last novel *Ignorance*,[10] which treats the theme of exiles returning to post-communist Prague, is still not available in Czech. He has republished some of his earlier Czech-language books in the Czech Republic, but has declined to republish others. Oddly, this self-censorship of his own past work parallels the way that his work was cut off from Czech readers by the Czechoslovak regime. In 1991, Kundera's first novel *The Joke* was republished in Czechoslovakia. In the afterword to this edition, he rejects his 'politico-cultural writings from the sixties' as well as 'all those essays meant to explain to the foreign public the essence of the Czech situation' with the exception of the essays

[8]Steiner (2005) examines the moral ambiguity of Havel's initial support for the invasion.
[9]See, for example Uličianska (2008).
[10]This was published in French in 2000 and in English translation in 2002.

he included in *The Art of the Novel.*[11] He explained that he had written these essays

> more to serve my countrymen's cause than to discover and say anything new; with those essays, I did not wish to join in the Czech literary debate and therefore I do not intend to translate them into Czech or republish them. (Misurella 1993, pp. 163–64)[12]

Thus the original edition of *The Unbearable Lightness of Being* could scarcely be obtained by Czech readers for over 20 years. Its first publication in the Czech Republic, in 2006, generated intense interest from critics and the reading public, showing his continued importance for Czech culture despite the distance he has maintained from post-communist Czech society (Trávníček 2007).

In his latest collection of essays, *The Curtain,*[13] Milan Kundera revisited some of the literary and political themes that had preoccupied him 20 years earlier. Despite the vast political changes since that time, he insisted that the cultural distinction between 'large' and 'small nations' has remained the same, and thus his ideal of Europe as 'maximum diversity in minimum space ... is even more imperilled now' (Kundera 2006b, p. 31). The only way to fully understand literary works, Kundera suggested, is to see them not only in terms of their 'small' national context, and the 'large' world context, but most importantly, in the 'median' regional context. For Czech literature, of course, the 'median' context is Central Europe, and Kundera even mentions his most famous essay on the theme, 'A Kidnapped West, or The Tragedy of Central Europe' (Kundera 2006b, p. 45). Once again he returns to the idea of destiny: 'Is it true that the borders of Central Europe are impossible to trace in any exact, lasting way? It is indeed! Those nations have never been masters of either their own destinies or their borders ... Their unity was *unintentional*' (Kundera 2006b, p. 46, emphasis in original). Most importantly, however, he makes two different observations, first that his use of 'Central Europe' was inspired by the Prague Spring, the Soviet occupation, and Normalisation, and secondly, that he later used the term for non-political purposes. 'In fact' he asks rhetorically, 'would I myself ever have made use of [the] notion [of Central Europe] if I had not been rocked by the political drama of my native land? ... There are words drowsing in the mist that, at the right moment, rush to our aid' (Kundera 2006b, p. 46). In the final section of *The Curtain,* Kundera reflected upon 'the Czech writers and artists of the nineteenth century who, within a miraculously brief span of time, had awakened a dormant nation' (Kundera 2006b, p. 155).

During the period following the invasion of Czechoslovakia in 1968, when the very existence of Czech culture seemed to be under threat, he thought of the National Revival: 'A unique situation: the Czechs, all of them bilingual, thus had the chance to choose: to be born or not to be born; to be or not to be'. In this context, Kundera returned to Hubert Gordon Schauer, whose speculations on 'national existence' had

[11]Even 'The Tragedy of Central Europe' was left out.

[12]The online archive of *The New York Review of Books* lists 'The Tragedy of Central Europe' and other essays by Kundera, but 'at the author's request' these texts are no longer available (accessed May 2008). The *New York Review of Books* online archive is available at: http://www.nybooks.com/archives/.

[13]The French original was published in 2005, and an English translation in 2006.

strongly influenced his own thoughts on Czech destiny during this period. He evoked the 'courage' of Schauer, who asked: 'Would we not be more useful to humanity if we joined our spiritual energy to the culture of a larger nation that is already at a far higher level than the nascent Czech culture?' In the end, Kundera was 'unable to put myself in my ancestors' skin' and understand their motivations; why did they decide 'to create not merely a poem, a theatre, a political party, but a whole nation, even with its half-lost language?' (2006b, p. 156). In the final pages of what may be his last work, he concludes not with the accomplishments of Czech literature, but its shortcomings:

> Perhaps a novel, a great novel, could have made me understand how the Czechs of that time had experienced their decision. Well, such a novel has not been written. There are cases where nothing can make up for the absence of a great novel. (Kundera 2006b, p. 157)

Kundera's outlook here is surprisingly pessimistic, dwelling on the historic weakness of Czech culture, rather than the unique 'vision of history' of the small nations—perhaps because his nation's destiny, after the fall of communism, no longer seems in doubt.

The fall of communism and the eastward expansion of the European Union to the shores of the Black Sea has left Kundera's 'Tragedy of Central Europe' so dated that today its lament for Western civilisation appears almost quaint. And yet many of Kundera's and Havel's concerns regarding the historical role of 'small nations' are still as valid as they were in 1984 or even 1968. Tom Stoppard's play *Rock 'n' Roll* presents a cross-cultural dialogue between British and Czech intellectuals on the meaning of the Prague Spring.[14] The main character Jan (a Czech student at Cambridge who returns to Prague after the Soviet occupation) argues with his friend Ferdinand over the question of national destiny and resistance. In his introduction to the play, Stoppard credits the essays by Kundera and Havel for inspiring this section (Stoppard 2006, p. 4). Forty years after the Prague Spring, its legacy continues to be defined in the West by their debate over the Czech destiny and the need for 'criticism' in situations of political crisis.

Yeditepe University, Istanbul

References

Baer, J. (ed.) (2006) *Preparing Liberty in Central Europe: Political Texts from the Spring of Nations 1848 to the Spring of Prague 1968* (Stuttgart, Ibidem-Verlag).
Bílek, P. (2000) 'Pojem "exilu" jako koncept neustálého zprostředkovávání a míjení', *Host*, 16, 5.
Charbonneau, L. (1993) 'Czech Culture and its Masters', *Prognosis*, 26 November.
Čulík, J. (1999) 'Milan Kundera', in Serafin, S. (ed.) (1999) *Dictionary of Literary Biography*, Vol. 232, (Detroit, Gale).
Goetz-Stankiewicz, M. (1992) *Good-bye, Samizdat: Twenty Years of Czechoslovak Underground Writing* (Evanston, Northwestern University Press).
Havel, V. (1968/1969) 'Cesky úděl?', *Host do domu*, 15.
Havel, V. (1986) *Living in Truth* (London, Faber and Faber).
Havel, V. (1990) *Disturbing the Peace*, translated by Paul Wilson (New York, Knopf).

[14]The play premiered in London in 2006, and was also performed on Broadway and at the Czech National Theatre in 2007.

Havel, V. (1992) *Open Letters*, edited by Paul Wilson (New York, Vintage).
Havel, V. (2002) 'A Farewell to Politics', *New York Review of Books*, 19, 16, 24 October.
Holý, J. (2008) *Writers Under Siege: Czech Literature Since 1945* (Brighton and Portland, OR, Sussex Academic Press).
Judt, T. (1991) 'The Rediscovery of Central Europe', in Graubard, S. (ed.) (1991) *Eastern Europe ... Central Europe ... Europe* (Boulder, Westview Press).
Jungmann, M (1988) *Cesty a rozcesty* (London, Rozmluvy).
Jungmann, M. (2006) 'Kunderovi obránci v ofsajdu', *Literární noviny*, 48.
Korbel, J. (1977) *Twentieth-Century Czechoslovakia: The Meanings of its History* (New York, Columbia University Press).
Kosková, H. (1996) *Hledání ztracené generace* (Jihočany, H & H).
Kundera, M. (1968) 'Ceský úděl', *Listy*, 1, 19 December.
Kundera, M. (1971) 'Speech at the Fourth Congress of the Czechoslovak Writers' Union', in Hamšík, D. (ed.) (1971) *Writers Against Rulers* (New York, Random House).
Kundera, M. (1980) *The Book of Laughter and Forgetting*, translated by Michael Heim (New York, Knopf).
Kundera, M. (1984a) 'A Kidnapped West or Culture Bows Out', *Granta*, 10.
Kundera, M. (1984b) 'The Tragedy of Central Europe', *New York Review of Books*, 31, 7, 26 April.
Kundera, M. (1984c) *The Unbearable Lightness of Being*, translated by Michael Heim (New York, Harper & Row).
Kundera, M. (1988) *The Art of the Novel*, translated by Linda Asher (New York, Harper & Row).
Kundera, M. (1991) *Žert* (Brno, Atlantis).
Kundera, M. (2006a) *Nesnesitelná lehkost bytí* (Brno, Atlantis).
Kundera, M. (2006b) *The Curtain*, translated by Linda Asher (New York, Harper Collins).
Macura, V. (1999) *Český sen* (Prague, Lidové noviny).
Matějka, L. (1990) 'Milan Kundera's Central Europe', *Cross Currents*, 9.
Misurella, F. (1993) *Understanding Milan Kundera: Public Events, Private Affairs* (Columbia, SC, University of South Carolina Press).
Mitosz, C. (1953) *The Captive Mind*, translated by Jane Zielonko (New York, Vintage).
Pichová, H. (2002) 'Milan Kundera and the Identity of Central Europe', in Tötösy de Zepetnek, S. (ed.) (2002) *Comparative Central European Culture* (West Lafayette, Purdue University Press).
Roth, P. (1980) 'An Interview with Milan Kundera', *New York Times Book Review*, 30 November.
Schöpflin, G. & Wood, N. (1989) *In Search of Central Europe* (London, Polity Press).
Steiner, P. (2005) 'Václav Havel and the Invasion of Iraq (with Constant References to the Soviet-led Occupation of Czechoslovakia in 1968)', 20 August, available at: http://vulgo.net, accessed July 2008.
Stoppard, T. (2006) *Rock 'n' Roll* (London, Faber).
Trávníček, J. (2007) 'Jednadvacet let poté: druhé čtení', *Host*, 1.
Uličianska, Z. (2008) 'Havlovo neodchádzanie', *SME*, 24 May.
Williams, K. (1997) *The Prague Spring and Its Aftermath: Czechoslovak Politics, 1968–1970* (Cambridge, Cambridge University Press).

Index

Page numbers in **Bold** represent figures.